Uphill Against Water

Volume 11 in the Series
Our Sustainable Future

SERIES EDITORS

Cornelia Flora
Iowa State University

Charles A. Francis
University of Nebraska–Lincoln

Paul Olson
University of Nebraska–Lincoln

.

Peter Carrels

Uphill Against Water

The Great Dakota Water War

University of Nebraska Press

Lincoln • London

⊗ The paper in this book
meets the minimum requirements of
American National Standard for
Information Sciences—Permanence of Paper for
Printed Library Materials,
ANSI Z39.48-1984.

Library of Congress Cataloging-in-Publication Data
Carrels, Peter
Uphill against water:
the great Dakota water war / Peter Carrels.
p.   cm.—(Our sustainable future)
Includes bibliographical references (p.   ) and index.
ISBN 0-8032-1496-0 (cloth: alk. paper)
ISBN 0-8032-6397-X (pbk: alk. paper)
1. Water resources development—South Dakota—History.
2. Water resources development—South Dakota—
Citizen participation—History.
3. Missouri River Basin Project (U.S.)
Oahe Unit.   I. Title.   II. Series.
TC424.S8C37   1999
333.91′15′09783—dc21   98-24291   CIP

Contents

Illustrations

Photographs

Map

Acknowledgments

Financial support for this book came from several key sources. The South Dakota Committee on the Humanities (now called the South Dakota Humanities Council) provided generous funding that enabled me to conduct many of the interviews I used to write this book. For obvious reasons, United Family Farmers was very interested in this project, and the organization provided financial assistance to cover expenses related to my research. There were also many individuals who provided me with monetary assistance to cover expenses related to research. Their checks of $50 or $100 added up to more than $3,000.

Thanks to Harriet Montgomery, a resident of Aberdeen, South Dakota. Harriet's interest in preserving history and protecting water resources was the reason she founded the Montgomery Collection. Located on the campus of Northern State University, in Aberdeen, the Montomgery Collection was an invaluable resource for me as I researched and wrote this book.

Northern State University supplied the audiocassette tapes I used when recording interviews and for several years provided me with an office on campus to make access to the Montgomery Collection more convenient.

Librarians at Alexander Mitchell Public Library in Aberdeen and at the Beulah Williams Library at Northern State University generously helped me to conduct research. The staff at the Bureau of Reclamation's archival facility in Billings, Montana, was also very cooperative and helpful.

Thanks to those who took time to share their feelings with me about the Oahe project. Their interviews shaped this book and provided me with some fond memories. Jim Abourezk cooked me lunch. Dave Weiman bought me lunch. Bill Janklow took me to the store so he could buy cigarettes. Bob Hipple showed me Oahe dam. Roy Runge showed me his beautiful ranch. On a crisp winter day, Rich Madson guided me to his favorite spot on the James River. We cleared snow and grilled steaks.

Finally, thanks to Tom Carrels, Michael Melius, Richard Opper, John Davidson, Jay Davis, and Harriet Montgomery for reviewing various chapters of my manuscript.

Preface

I set out to write a book about a gritty group of farmers who battled South Dakota's political, business, and water development establishment from 1973 to 1982. The subject of the dispute was a large Bureau of Reclamation irrigation project called the Oahe (pronounced *a-WA-he*) Unit. Bureau planners and engineers believed they could move water from the Missouri River's Oahe reservoir a hundred miles east to the James River valley and irrigate 750,000 acres there. Their ambitious dream was contagious, and the Oahe Unit, named after the Oahe dam and reservoir, gained widespread popularity in South Dakota and became synonymous with progress. But not everyone saw the project as progress.

The dissident farmers warranted a story, I thought, not only because of the shrewd, intense grassroots war they waged against the irrigation project, but also because their struggle to stop the project coincided with, and to some extent impacted, the reshaping of water development policy in the West.

Conversations with Art and Helen Metzinger prompted me to rethink the scope of the book. The Metzingers had fought a bitter but futile battle with the U.S. Army Corps of Engineers that ended in 1956 when the government acquired their beloved farm along the Missouri River in central South Dakota. Five years later the farm was drowned behind Oahe dam. In 1976, after resettling on a new farm, the Metzingers received a visit from another water agency. This time they learned from the Bureau of Reclamation that their new farm lay in the path of a canal that would convey Oahe reservoir water to irrigators. The Metzingers were informed that if they didn't sell their land willingly to the federal government, it would be condemned and taken from them anyway. Art and Helen couldn't believe it. The same water that covered their first farm would flow in the canal that necessitated condemnation of part of their second farm.

It became clear that telling the Oahe story meant more than simply describing a political fight over irrigation. I realized that the lineage of the Oahe Irrigation Project extended back to before the federal government built the Oahe dam—to even before they'd dreamed up the Oahe dam. The sequence of events that led to the possibility of Missouri River water traveling in a canal by the Metzingers' doorstep stretched deep into the history of the West.

Introduction

Perhaps no single issue in the area of water development has created as much interest and has so divided South Dakotans as has the Oahe Irrigation Project.

Senator George McGovern, D-SD, 1977

I wrote this book while living in my hometown, Aberdeen, South Dakota, a community located on prairie that was once the floor of a lake filled with runoff from a great glacier. This is fine wheat-growing country, level as a pan and hardly a rock to trip over. But rainfall is another matter.

Aberdeen lies on the western edge—the driest edge—of midwestern agriculture, where dairy and grain farming shift to cattle and sheep ranching. Most years are good for grain growers, but bad years come just often enough to cause irritating anxiety. Although dry spells of destructive duration are infrequent, it is inevitable they will occur. The problem is that one never knows when.

East of the anxiety belt, in Iowa, Minnesota, or eastern Nebraska, there is far less worry about precipitation. Folks in those places expect it, and most of the time they get it. Further west, in the western Dakotas and Nebraska, and on the sagebrush plains of Montana and Wyoming, there is also little uncertainty. Folks in those places don't expect much moisture, and most of the time they don't get much. It was here, in Aberdeen's trade area, all of it within the anxiety belt, where the Great Dakota Water War was waged.

Since white people first settled the American plains they have had an uncomfortable relationship with the natural forces that shape the region. Frontier-era cartographers dismissed the plains as barren, but the first wave of corporate entrepreneurs with an interest in the region sought to dispel that characterization.

Although the plains weren't as bleak or unpromising as first described, the region's earliest promoters resorted to denial and deceit to lure settlers there. Later, after communities and a rural culture had been established in the region, a new generation of promoters sought to bolster the economy of the plains. The Oahe Irrigation Project was part of that effort.

George McGovern, whose words open this introduction, was right. The controversy over the Oahe Irrigation Project escalated into one of the most bitter political fights in the history of South Dakota. Coming at the same time as the nation's emerging environmental movement, Oahe also became the first hotly debated environmental issue in the state's history.

Reaching its stormy height in the 1970s and early 1980s, the Oahe controversy split the state's social and political landscape so severely that not until the mid-1990s did emotions cool. The discord was particularly bitter in the areas where irrigation was proposed.

The controversy also had national repercussions. In 1977, President Jimmy Carter launched a campaign to reform federal water-development programs— and the fate of a South Dakota water project became linked to this man from Georgia.

Residing where I did helped me write this book, but personal experience that preceded the start of this project was an added asset. In January 1981, I began working as a landowner organizer for the Oahe Conservancy Sub-district. Now defunct, the sub-district had been formed in 1960 to serve as local sponsor and promoter of water development, particularly the Oahe Irrigation Project.

My position at the sub-district had little to do with the irrigation project; the emphasis in my own job was on formulating and carrying out a grassroots plan to clean up the James River. But as a member of the staff team, I had a special vantage point: not only was the staff small, but most members of the sub-district's locally elected board were very active, and their phone calls and visits to our Aberdeen office frequent.

This version of the history of the Oahe project remembers those who championed the Oahe project and those who fought it. This book documents a movement of people living outside the normal sphere of political decision making who labored against formidable obstacles in their effort to influence governments.

American water policy, as permitted and promoted by our federal government, has provided many benefits for this nation, but it has also caused tremendous environmental destruction, wasted billions of dollars, and left countless victims in its wake. Although the impacts of federal planning and construction agencies were extraordinarily profound, their foresight was often extraordinarily shallow and myopic.

During my research I was repeatedly reminded of a quote attributed to H. L. Mencken, the brash journalist. Mencken wrote: "Men become civilized not in proportion to their willingness to believe, but in proportion to their readiness to doubt."

It seems to me that the leading disciples of dams, diversions, and irrigation projects often failed to analyze, critically, the projects they supported. Though their advocacy was always vigorous, their understanding was often limited. They were as willing to believe as they were unwilling to doubt.

1

The Deceivers

Reason is the first casualty in a drought.
Marc Reisner, *Cadillac Desert*

From a downtown rooftop in a promising new city, the so-called rainmaker
summoned precipitation from the heavens. In the dirt streets below, residents of
Aberdeen, South Dakota, watched eagerly, hopefully, their eyes searching the
overcast sky for rain clouds. It was the last day of June 1893, and young wheat
and corn plants sagged in the dry heat. No rain would fall that day.

Rainmaker Morris had come up from Kansas not long before, selling his
rainmaking services to communities along the way. Aberdeen's leaders agreed
to a standard contract, one that stipulated a generous remuneration of five hundred dollars if Morris could deliver at least one decent shower during the five
days he would conduct his operation.

Morris was reputable and highly recommended. The rainmaking business he
represented was based in Goodland, Kansas, and was owned by bankers, lawyers, judges, druggists, and other prominent people there. So confident were
Aberdonians of the rainmaker's ability, they bought out the local stock of um-
brellas as he commenced his calling.

Like flimflam men selling patent medicines, rainmakers roamed the North
American plains in the early 1890s looking for customers. At the time, there
was a sense of legitimacy to their enterprise. Railroads funded experiments and
sent rainmakers on extensive tours through the countryside. Franchise companies sold their rainmaking methods to cities and towns, and their agents were
vigilant for news about parched localities, preferably those near towns filled
with anxious merchants. One lucky rainmaker was offered a deal to produce
rainfall by a consortium of forty western Kansas counties: for every acre of cul-

tivated cropland that received precipitation, the rainmaker would receive ten cents—a deal that might earn him as much as $20,000. It is unclear to what extent, if at all, the rainmaker cashed in on this offer. In Aberdeen and many other communities, rival rainmakers, competing for contracts, debated the benefits of their respective approaches to the art before large crowds.

While Aberdonians listened to such debates, twenty miles away a farmer was breaking conventional farming rules and learning lessons that would land him a place in agricultural history. Hardy Webster Campbell had moved from Vermont to Dakota Territory in 1879. He had suffered several crop failures between 1880 and 1885, when it occurred to him that his biggest problem wasn't the land or the climate, it was his style of farming. Campbell began experimenting with what he called "soil culture," or the practice of conserving moisture in the soil. He recognized that farming in Dakota required farming methods different from those in eastern states.

"Don't try to change nature's laws to fit your own methods and habits," Campbell declared, "but change your notions and habits to conform with nature's ways and thereby utilize both."[1] To take advantage of the region's fertile soils and compensate for its uncertain precipitation, he invented implements and devised surface mulches to retain moisture in the soil. His yields multiplied and began, regularly and dramatically, to exceed those of his neighbors.

By 1895, Campbell's success attracted the attention of a railroad executive who offered him the chance to manage a string of experimental farms in Nebraska. Campbell accepted the challenge. Soon, Campbell was publishing his own magazine, *Campbell's Soil Culture Magazine*, and he later authored a series of highly popular farming manuals. These were published almost yearly between 1901 and 1916.

To thousands of plains farmers, Campbell became an exalted figure, and he was later labeled by plains historian Walter Prescott Webb as the "greatest evangelist of dry farming."[2] But in 1893, the citizens of Aberdeen and Brown County did not turn to the ideas of their neighbor when dry weather threatened their crops. They wanted instant relief, so they hired a rainmaker.

Rainmaking enjoyed a brief run of popularity, especially on the plains. In 1891, the U.S. Congress appropriated at least $9,000 for rainmaking experiments. Though patents had been issued regarding artificial rain-producing techniques, there was nothing absolute about the practice. When the 1891 North Dakota legislature offered a reward to the inventor of a foolproof rainmaking system, no one stepped forward to collect.

In 1892, the federal government authorized another $10,000 for rainmaking tests. In one research trial, federal scientists lofted balloons filled with explosive gas. High above the land, the balloons were detonated. The theory behind such concussion rainmaking was based on an observation that heavy rainstorms often followed large military battles. Rainmaker Morris adhered to another popular approach—reliance on the emission of certain gases into the atmosphere.

On the final day of Morris's contract, 4 July 1893, while citizens frolicked outdoors celebrating Independence Day, a heavy downpour occurred. A local newspaper likened Morris to a second Moses, and the community had a new hero. After two more days of intermittent showers, a group of citizens begged Morris to call off his influence before the area was flooded.

As Aberdeen celebrated the rainmaker, it rejected the value of irrigation. The same feeling about irrigation was found across South Dakota. Although irrigation supporters managed to establish a state agency in 1890 to promote and investigate irrigation, the agency encountered determined resistance and in 1896 was discontinued. The first report of the new office, issued in 1890 by State Irrigation Engineer Fred Coffin, described the widespread misgivings about artificial watering of farmland. Some irrigation opponents, he wrote, worried that irrigation wasn't cost-effective, or that the land wasn't irrigable, or that water supplies were insufficient. Quite a large number of people, reported Coffin, "strenuously opposed even the discussion of irrigation."[3]

Leading the opposition were business promoters and land speculators, who worried that potential settlers might be scared off by the implication that, if irrigation was necessary, the state's climate was unsuitable for agriculture. These people were concerned, Coffin said, because "if the word got out that it was necessary to irrigate in Dakota, in order to insure good crops, immigration would shun us."[4] South Dakota's feelings about irrigation were faithfully represented in the nation's capital by Senator Gideon Moody, a Republican lawyer from Deadwood. Moody helped lead the fight against John Wesley Powell, the nation's most prominent irrigation advocate.

Powell, best known for his daring expedition by wooden boat down the uncharted, ferocious Colorado River in 1869, was also a land-use visionary and one of the most recognized scientists of his day. His extensive travels in the West rewarded him with insights few could match. He challenged the nation's leaders to accept the environmental realities of the plains and the West and to adopt more appropriate policies for settling the region. "I think it would be almost a criminal act to go on as we are doing now," Powell told a congressional committee, "and allow thousands and thousands of people to establish homes where they cannot maintain themselves."[5]

Powell ridiculed the myths and misconceptions used by greedy railroads and economic boosters to lure settlers to the West. One spectacularly unsupportable allegation, concocted by Charles Dana Wilber, a real-estate speculator and town builder, and given credibility by a Nebraska climatologist named Cyrus Thomas, was that the mere act of farming brought on precipitation—a notion anointed with the catchy words, "rain follows the plow." Business promoters used the phrase like an advertising jingle. Unsuspecting new farmers tilled and planted the region's arid lands in the same manner as was done in the older regions of the country. It later became evident that in many instances dust and ruin, not rain and prosperity, followed the plow.[6]

There were other empty assurances used to tempt prospective settlers: pitchmen for the railroads proclaimed that Wyoming was as fertile as Illinois; a state agency in Kansas advertised their state as having the most agreeable climate in the world; Kansas officials spread false rainfall averages to encourage settlers to make Kansas their new home; and Nebraska's Bureau of Immigration suggested that their state's climate was naturally invigorating and would produce muscular, intelligent, and heroic people. In the weeks before recommending the city hire Rainmaker Morris, a newspaper in Aberdeen authoritatively assessed the weather of South Dakota: "It has been well demonstrated that drouth is as foreign to South Dakota as to any other section and that this state is no more subject to extremely dry seasons than any other state in the Union."[7]

To support agriculture in the West, including the plains, Powell proposed using impounded water from dammed rivers to irrigate strategic parcels of land. He also believed that the private sector and the region's young states lacked the means to build big dams and develop sizeable irrigation projects; the development of an irrigation empire, he declared, necessitated federal participation.

These ideas were described by a Powell representative at South Dakota's first constitutional convention. Powell himself took that message to constitutional conventions in North Dakota and Montana. In Washington, Powell sought funds for a study of potential dam sites and irrigation areas. But his dreams collided with the fears of Senator Moody and others. Moody accused Powell of being an outsider to the West who did not adequately understand South Dakota. The South Dakotan and his colleagues from other western states stripped Powell's request to near nothing.

But the time was ripe for a new solution to drought. By 1895, the public's interest in rainmaking had subsided. Despite the promises of the railroads, the fears of Gideon Moody, and the denial by economic boosters about drought, it was inevitable that destructive dry spells would strike areas of the plains. Irrigation offered a more reasoned approach to combating drought than did slogans, rainmakers, or denial. William Smythe, an editorial writer for an Omaha, Nebraska, newspaper, emerged as a leading spokesman for irrigation. Smythe had encouraged Nebraska farmers to irrigate and had helped organize a state irrigation convention. Later, he was selected to direct a group that established the National Irrigation Congress. In 1892, that group convened in Salt Lake City for its first annual meeting.

Though westerners had gradually come to realize the value of irrigation, they were still reluctant to accept federal help. Their tradition of self-sufficiency contrasted with the notion of participating in a federal program. But by 1889, westerners on their own had brought water to only 3.6 million acres of land. This was the equivalent of just three midsized counties in South Dakota. Resistance to federal help softened when many of the privately developed irrigation projects floundered, and in 1896 the National Irrigation Congress passed a resolution calling for strong federal support for irrigation. Four years later, both the Republican and Democratic Parties advocated federal assistance for irrigation.

The presidency of Theodore Roosevelt brought a greater interest in western issues and natural resource management to the White House. Roosevelt and top government officials, among them Gifford Pinchot, Frederick Newell, and W. J. McGee, believed it was time the nation inventory its natural resources and abandon the haphazard exploitation that had characterized the traditional attitude toward wildlife, water, minerals, and timber. These men believed that careful planning was essential in order to utilize and properly conserve natural resources. This was the beginning of the conservation movement.

In June 1902, thanks to Roosevelt, Congress passed the Newlands Reclamation Act. The legislation was named after Francis Newlands, a congressman from Nevada who was a fervid believer in irrigation and an admirer of John Wesley Powell. The act established an irrigation agency called the Reclamation Service that would be staffed with engineers and scientists. This fulfilled the administration's goal of using "experts" to manage resources.

John Wesley Powell must have felt great personal satisfaction with the recognition that federal help was needed to develop irrigation. However, he died only three months after the government enacted the landmark legislation. Had he lived, he would likely have been disappointed with the behavior of the new agency. Conservation leaders may have insisted on the guidance of experts to plan the use of resources, but Congress had a different agenda. Encouraged by local boosters, Congress promoted projects for political purposes, and the Reclamation Service obliged. Irrigation development was pursued at a furious pace, often without adequate study.

Previously, entrepreneurs and businessmen in the West resorted to irresponsible promotions to entice settlers. Now, boosters of the region's economic possibilities embraced the irrigation program with fervor equal to that with which they formerly supported the rain-and-plow fraud and denied that serious drought existed at all. In 1903, a three-day conference of Minneapolis, St. Paul, and Duluth business interests was held to support irrigation development on the northern plains. The region's farmers, however, remained apprehensive. A 1904 plan to irrigate twenty thousand acres in western North Dakota was promoted by bankers, commercial clubs, and area newspapers, and two years later, a large proportion of landowners had been persuaded to sign irrigation contracts—but when the project was built, the delivered water was so expensive that farmers refused to use it.

South Dakota's first reclamation project was developed on the dry plains north of the Black Hills. Between 1905 and 1911, Orman dam was built across Owl Creek, a tributary to the Belle Fourche River in Butte County. In its early days, Orman ranked as one of the largest earthen dams in the world. South Dakota boosters were giddy with the looming impact of this grand proposal. But Orman's dimensions—impressive, at 6,500 feet long and 115 feet high—and some related engineering complications helped bankrupt the project's original contractors. To fill Orman's reservoir, water from behind a diversion dam on the adjacent Belle Fourche River would be transported via a canal, six and one-half miles long. A distribution system containing five hundred miles of ditches would irrigate up to ninety thousand acres in the valley of the Belle Fourche River. The irrigation project, known as the Belle Fourche Project, had its headquarters in Newell, a town named after Frederick Newell, the Reclamation Service's first director. So taken with irrigation were the citizens of Newell that sports teams at the local high school were nicknamed the Irrigators. Orman dam was later renamed Belle Fourche dam.

As one of the first projects of the new reclamation effort, the Belle Fourche Project was important. But the project was continually hamstrung by mistakes, among them serious errors regarding soil classifications. It was discovered that almost half the project area contained heavy gumbo soils not suitable for sustained irrigation. Project planners also failed to recognize the limited flows in the Belle Fourche River. When the land was dry and needed water most, the river, too, was dry.

Reclamation's program was struggling throughout the West. After just two decades, from 1902 to 1922, only 10 percent of the money loaned to irrigators to build and maintain projects had been repaid; 60 percent of the irrigators were defaulting on their repayment contracts, despite the absence of interest on their loans. By 1927, as many as one-third of all reclamation farmers had sold their irrigated property. Wealthy absentee landowners and agribusinesses were buying the land and becoming the new irrigation farmers. The federal government's goal of helping install small farms in the nation's newest region was not working. To fix the mess, reform measures were initiated by the Reclamation Service. New funding sources for the Reclamation Fund were found, including royalties from oil drilling. Hydropower revenues were also brought into the funding picture and the period of a project's repayment to the federal treasury was extended to fifty years.

The Reclamation Service entered the 1930s with a new name, the U.S. Bureau of Reclamation. The agency received a boost when Franklin Roosevelt became president in 1932. Motivated by Roosevelt's desire to create jobs and help local economies survive the Great Depression and the dust bowl, the bureau built dam and diversion projects in a mad rush. Thus began the golden age for water engineers. In 1936 alone, the four largest concrete dams ever built, Hoover, Shasta, Bonneville, and Grand Coulee, were being erected in the West. Hoover dam, arguably the most ambitious engineering undertaking in history, rose from the deep floor of the wild Colorado River canyon in just three years. In remote Montana, on the Missouri River, construction of a monumental earthen dam called Fort Peck was also under way. These projects and others fortified the confidence of those who desired dominion over nature. Mighty rivers could be harnessed by dams, and drought-threatened regions could be rescued by irrigation.

Soon there was a new breed of rainmaker confidently roaming the West, and opportunities were plentiful.

2

The Big Dry

It was during the dirty thirties when South Dakota was bare. There was
nothing green growing in the state.

Bob Hipple, interview, August 1988

There was no one in South Dakota more determined to use irrigation to defeat
drought than Robert Hipple. The baking aridity and economic depression of the
1930s etched vivid, lasting memories for Hipple and others who lived through
those gloomy years. Theirs was a generation whose lives would be shadowed
forever by the big dry.

Robert Hipple observed parched, suffering South Dakota through the eyes of
a journalist. He had entered newspapering in 1905 at age five when his father
purchased Pierre's *Capital Journal* and young Bob began peddling papers on
the streets of the state capital. Following a stint in the army and graduation from
Yale University, Hipple returned to his hometown at age twenty-three to become editor of the newspaper.

Few states were as adversely affected by the brutal weather of the 1930s as
South Dakota. Above-average precipitation during the 1920s teased farmers and
ranchers into cultivating previously unfarmed land. But in 1933, when the first major dust blizzards roared through the region, the significance of that miscalculation
became apparent. Much of the newly plowed topsoil rose into the sky like smoke
and billowed away. Tough times forced good and bad farmers alike off the land,
and by 1934 a massive exodus of South Dakotans was under way.

Between 1930 and 1940, 85 percent of South Dakota's counties lost population. Farming counties in the center of the state were particularly hard hit. Overall, the state's population dropped from 693,000 to 643,000. No plains state
lost a greater percentage of its residents during the same period. Many of the

folks who stayed, struggled. By December 1934, 39 percent of the people in South Dakota needed government help to survive. That was the highest percentage of any state in the nation. Nearly half of South Dakota's farmers were on relief rolls.[1]

As water holes shriveled and hordes of grasshoppers consumed the surviving vegetation, the state's cattle industry faltered. In 1934 alone, the government bought more than 915,000 head of cattle from distressed farmers and ranchers unable to feed their herds. This was 40 percent of the state's total. The government's going price for the starving cattle was ten dollars a head. The purchased livestock were slaughtered and processed at canneries set up in at least five locations in the state. This canned raw meat was distributed to needy families across the nation.

Bob Hipple's printing business contracted with the government to print labels for the cans of raw beef. "We'd print a million labels at a time . . . to go on those cans," recalled Hipple.[2] It was not, Hipple emphasized, the type of printing he wanted to do. Sitting erect at his rolltop desk, Hipple wrote or edited countless stories about drought. One hot day he penned an editorial describing the despair he saw around him. According to Hipple, it was in that editorial that the expression "dirty thirties" originated. Stepping outside, through the front door of his newspaper office, Bob Hipple often gazed at the nearby Missouri River. Hipple had come to believe that the Missouri was useless in its natural state. He noted that even during the dust bowl's blast-furnace days, the Missouri flowed past Pierre. It had been reduced to a shallow, sluggish trickle, a wisp of its former self, but it was wet nonetheless, and those waters, Hipple believed, were being wasted. In all directions, Hipple saw farmland burning beneath a hot sun. There was a better place for that water, he dreamed, than in the shifting, muddy channel.

Hipple was transformed from dreamer to activist when he was visited by a man who was resolved to bring irrigation to the Dakotas. W. Glenn Sloan, an engineer and the assistant chief with the Bureau of Reclamation's regional office in Billings, Montana, was assigned to explore the upper Missouri River basin for irrigation development sites. A minister's son, Sloan embraced irrigation as his own personal ministry. His fantasy was to use irrigation to save millions of acres in the region. Not content merely to scan maps and examine bulletins, Sloan did a good bit of legwork, traveling throughout the vast Missouri basin. The intent of those tours was as much to make friends with local officials and opinion makers as to observe terrain, rivers, and reservoir sites. While making the rounds in Pierre, Sloan discovered a kindred spirit in Robert Hipple.

9

Glenn Sloan faced a daunting challenge as he tried to promote irrigation in the Missouri basin. The Great Plains Commission, convened in 1936, concluded that most of the large irrigation projects in the Missouri basin were of dubious feasibility.[3] Not only had irrigation ruined land, the commission reported, but irrigators in the region's nine original reclamation projects weren't paying the government for the water delivered to them. It had become obvious that despite the absence of interest charges, none of the nine would pay for themselves within the forty-year repayment period required by Congress. Two hundred years was a more likely expectation.[4] The Bureau of Reclamation began to realize that federal irrigation projects in the Missouri basin could not be self-supporting.

A new financing arrangement came to Sloan's rescue. It was decided that all the revenues generated by water projects within a single river basin would be lumped together into the same account. No longer did it matter, for example, if an irrigation project was a financial loser. Under the new plan, hydropower revenues generated within a river basin could be used to offset irrigation's financial shortcomings in that same basin. Dams producing electricity became cash registers, and the till was opened to develop irrigation. This was reclamation pork barrel at its ingenious best.

Adjusting policy and promoting passage of legislation creating a friendly atmosphere for reclamation were just the first obstacles that had to be overcome by the Bureau of Reclamation. The biggest hurdle facing the agency as it eyed irrigation development in the Missouri basin was the need to build dams to store water.

For centuries, otherwise smart people have foolishly settled on flood plains. That was true for those white Americans who put down roots in the Missouri River valley. The bottomlands beside the river offered shady cottonwood groves, shelter from the wind, and convenience to water and transportation.

Between 1937 and 1943, the city of Omaha, Nebraska, proudly spent more than $4 million to improve Eppley Field, the city's municipal airport. It seems a fair question to ask: Why did Omaha decide to build and then improve its airport on land immediately adjacent to the Missouri River? Why did the city pour millions into an airport situated on the flood plain of one of the most flood-prone rivers on the continent? It wasn't as if there were not other useable expanses of land available in the Omaha vicinity. Such sites were, in fact, abundant. The Missouri River did in 1943 what it had been doing frequently for thousands of years. But the difference between the flood of 1943 and most other previous floods was the enormous volume of water that powered its way down the river valley.

During the winter of 1942–43, snow had fallen frequently and prodigiously throughout the entire Missouri River basin. A huge blizzard in March added more moisture to a watershed whose river channels and streambeds were already bursting. Old-timers along the Missouri predicted a massive flood, rivaling the great 1881 event, and they were right. Through the Dakotas, the river swarmed outside its channel, covering farms, forcing livestock and families to the blufftops. At Pierre, the river gauge showed a depth of 19.65 feet on 6 April. That was about 4.5 feet above flood stage. Some 278,000 cubic feet of water per second surged past Pierre that day, or the unfathomable equivalent of about 180 trillion gallons. It was perhaps the largest daily volume of water that had ever flowed in that stretch of the river. Dozens of families abandoned their threatened homes, while a hastily thrown up dike saved part of the city's business district. Bob Hipple and others looked on, annoyed and awed at the river's raw, unchecked power. Hipple was chagrined that so much valuable water was departing the region without being saved for future use.

On 9 April, as the river rose past nineteen feet in Omaha, residents were evacuated from low-lying northern and eastern neighborhoods. Hundreds of workers toiled in rainy, dreary weather to raise and reinforce existing levees. Across the river, in Council Bluffs, Iowa, a barricade about two miles long was shored up with rock and sandbags to protect the northern part of that city. By the time the flood of 1943 reached its crest of 22.45 feet, Eppley Field was covered by seven feet of water. For six weeks, water obscured the recently refinished runways. Commercial traffic was rerouted to Des Moines, Iowa, and Lincoln or Kearney, Nebraska.

April's flood in the Dakotas, Iowa, and Nebraska turned out to be only the first of three major floods on the river that year. During May, heavy spring rains in Iowa and Missouri added to the high water, and the southernmost two hundred miles of the river overflowed. When a third flood came in June, causing waterlogged levees to crumble, residents along the river had seen enough. At least six lives had been lost. About 1.8 million acres of land were inundated, and the downtown districts in Kansas City, Omaha, and Sioux City had been navigable by boat. In Omaha alone, some thirteen hundred families lost their homes. Sioux City's opulent municipal auditorium, still under construction, stood in several feet of water. Damages from throughout the basin exceeded $50 million. The flood-plain culture was in shambles.[5]

Colonel Lewis Pick, chief of the Corps of Engineers' office for the Missouri basin, located in Omaha, had personally witnessed the river overwhelm the city. He had watched helplessly as levees were overtopped and weary volunteers hurried to high ground. It must have seemed to Pick that the corps had been badly beaten, even humiliated, by the cold, dark waters of the Missouri. But instead of questioning the wisdom of building homes, businesses, and airports along the river, Pick and others blamed the river for their troubles.

At a flood-control conference held in Omaha that summer, Colonel Pick stressed that rebuilding dikes along the river was not a complete answer to the flooding problem. The best solution, he contended, was to build dams to store flood flows. He noted that dams could also provide water for irrigation projects, for hydropower generation, and to provide stable flows for navigation. "To do all this," he told the audience, "we [the corps] need two things—a project and money. The Engineers can get the project. It is up to you to get the money."[6]

By 1943, the Corps of Engineers had already developed a long relationship with the Missouri River. In the early days of Missouri navigation, the corps maintained a three-foot depth in the river channel to assist commercial shippers, and the agency built and maintained levees in various sections of the lower river to ease flooding. Later, the national navigation standard dropped to six feet, and the corps complied as far north as Sioux City, Iowa. When the national standard dropped another three feet, the corps faced a dilemma. If it did not develop a nine-foot channel, the Missouri would not be able to handle the boats and barges preferred by the shipping industry. The agency also had to determine how to reliably provide enough water for the deepened cargo lane.

Though Colonel Pick had little experience in flood-control engineering, he did possess an extraordinary energy and a rigid devotion to the Corps of Engineers. His initial assignment to Omaha included orders to speed up World War II installations in the Omaha area. To that end, he ordered his employees to work a seven-day week. On the Sunday following that command, he phoned his key personnel. Those who had not come to the office were immediately transferred out of the Missouri River division.[7]

The militaristic Pick viewed the Missouri as an enemy: his approach to the river was like that of a field marshal preparing for war. Within ninety days, the colonel had his bold strategy in finished form. To conquer the uncooperative river, Pick wanted bank stabilization and channelization measures, including fifteen hundred miles of levees lining each side of the river's lower eight hundred miles. He also called for the construction of twenty-three new dams. Eighteen of the proposed dams would be constructed on tributaries, but the remaining five dams would serve as the linchpins in the grand plan. All five would be earthen structures built on the river's wide main channel in the Dakotas. This engineering challenge would employ the knowledge gained during construction of the Fort Peck dam.

The corps was proud of its efforts at Fort Peck, despite the fact that sprawling Fort Peck reservoir drowned four Indian irrigation projects. Completed in 1940, Fort Peck was an earthen dam that measured four miles long and 250 feet high. At the time, it was the world's biggest dam. Decades later, when viewing Earth from the Moon, it was claimed that only two examples of human engineering were visible: China's Great Wall and the Fort Peck dam. As a flood-control dam, Fort Peck had not accomplished much, despite its extraordinary dimensions. President Roosevelt pressed for dam construction to provide jobs to a nation needing work. At the height of construction, nearly eleven thousand people were employed to build the dam. Perhaps double that many moved to the new and temporary communities that suddenly appeared near the dam site.

Pick's plan was aimed primarily at assisting navigation and preventing flooding, the corps's favorite water-development objectives. The mainstem dams would be particularly useful in that double duty. Not only would they block and impound high flows on the river, they would allow the corps to manipulate flow levels for the benefit of towboats and barges plying the waters of the soon-to-be expanded shipping channel downstream of Sioux City.

Nearly as remarkable as the scope of Pick's plan was the length of his report. In only twelve pages, he laid out his far-reaching proposal. Some of that brevity can be attributed to the fact that Pick performed little analysis of his plan's conflicts with other river proposals. For example, Pick did not describe how his plan related to the nine-foot navigation channel that was being simultaneously promoted in Congress. Hardly any mention was made regarding irrigation or hydropower. Apparently, it did not concern Pick that one of the dams—the Garrison dam proposed for North Dakota—would submerge twenty-one thousand acres of land that the Bureau of Reclamation had recently begun irrigating at a cost of more than $1 million. Pick projected the cost of his enormous plan at $660 million.

The appearance of Pick's report and his public-relations tour touting the plan caused much anxiety in the Bureau of Reclamation. Not only did the content of Pick's plan bother the bureau, the agency worried it might lose out on many irrigation and hydropower possibilities if the corps plan was adopted by Congress. In 1944, the Missouri was a major river without a single dam between Fort Peck and the river's confluence with the Mississippi near St. Louis, some eighteen hundred miles downriver. To dam builders and water developers, that unplugged stretch of water was sweet temptation, and both the corps and the bureau desperately wanted control. The two rival agencies had previously waged war elsewhere, vying for water development opportunities in other river basins, but their conflict over the Missouri would rank as their most egregious confrontation. This political struggle had the flood-control and navigation establishment of the East facing the reclamation establishment of the West in a mostly undeveloped crossroads region.

The odds favored the corps. Though both agencies loved to build dams and subdue rivers, maturity and clout distinguished them. The corps, founded during the Revolutionary War and organized in 1794 and more than a century older than the Bureau of Reclamation, had cultivated broader, stronger political support.

By May 1944, Glenn Sloan and the bureau had completed and delivered their own Missouri River plan to Congress. As expected, Sloan's plan differed from that of the corps. For starters, Sloan estimated the plan outlined in his 211-page report would cost $1.3 billion. The bureau targeted irrigation development and hydroelectric generation as its primary goals. Some ninety dams and reservoirs were proposed, and diversions from the impoundments would be built to irrigate several hundred irrigation projects containing 4.7 million irrigation acres, doubling the basin's existing irrigation. Sloan rejected Garrison dam and placed less emphasis on mainstem storage, preferring to build on tributaries nearer potential irrigation tracts. For example, dams and irrigation projects were proposed for every sizeable river in western South Dakota.

Sloan's proposal for a massive dam north of Pierre, South Dakota, contrasted with the corps's plan to construct a smaller dam near that location. The bureau wanted a high dam to facilitate the diversion of water out of the reservoir and east by gravity flow toward potential irrigation tracts totaling some 750,000 acres in the James River valley, about one hundred miles away.

The bureau's plan to irrigate lands in eastern South Dakota marked a significant shift for the agency. Never before had federal irrigation development been proposed so close to the Midwest's farm belt. The proposed irrigation project would not open new lands to farming, as did many other bureau projects; in fact, the land to be irrigated was already farmed. But the bureau defended its proposal, explaining that irrigation would stabilize existing agriculture. It was, said the agency, a great new frontier for irrigation development.

The central issue separating the corps and the bureau as they tussled over the Missouri was whether or not irrigation and navigation could coexist at the levels each agency proposed. Three states in the river's upper basin, Wyoming, Montana, and North Dakota, were fearful the water needed to float commercial cargo would preclude development of large irrigation projects. Those states allied themselves with the Bureau of Reclamation. Conversely, those states in the lower basin, Iowa, Nebraska, Kansas, and Missouri, worried that massive diversions of water for irrigation in the upper basin would threaten navigation. These states favored the corps.

Working on behalf of Pick's plan was South Dakota's governor, M. Q. Sharpe. Sharpe believed there was plenty of water in the Missouri River to provide for both irrigation and navigation. He liked the corps's plan calling for several large dams to be built on the Missouri in his state. Those dams, Sharpe knew, translated into lots of jobs and economic activity. He hoped that locks could one day be installed on the dams and that his state would develop river ports. Governor Sharpe carried considerable political clout: he was a founder and leader of the Missouri River States Committee, a group made up of the governors and state engineers of states in the Missouri River basin.

Bob Hipple does not recall the exact date, but sometime in 1943, Governor Sharpe requested that Hipple meet with South Dakota Congressman Francis Case, Glenn Sloan, and Lewis Pick in Pierre. Hipple would serve as host for the first part of the meeting, Sharpe having other obligations. Hipple went to the Saint Charles Hotel where he met Lew Pick for the first time. Glenn Sloan arrived several minutes later, and Hipple handled the introductions. It was the first time the rivals had met. When Congressman Case arrived, the four men went to the dining room for lunch.

According to Hipple, conversation during the meal was dominated by Case and Sloan, and the topic was irrigation. Pick listened attentively as irrigation's merits were discussed. At the conclusion of lunch, and immediately before the group left to meet Governor Sharpe, Pick surprised Sloan by telling him he was very interested in irrigation and wanted to talk with him about it. He invited Sloan to accompany him by car to Omaha, and Sloan quickly said yes. Hipple speculates that it was as a result of the conversation during the drive that Pick agreed that irrigation should be an integral aspect of Missouri River reservoir benefits.[8]

No matter what part the friendly auto trip together played, reconciliation of the two plans occurred because both agencies realized that if their bickering continued neither agency might be able to develop anything new in the Missouri basin. President Franklin Roosevelt had grown impatient at the inability of the corps and the bureau to reach an agreement. The dispute between the rival agencies had become so intense that the *Saturday Evening Post* described it as one of the great political fights in the history of the nation. "There has been nothing quite like this since the great issues of prohibition and woman's suffrage were hammered out," said a *Post* article.[9] To solve the impasse, President Roosevelt advised formation of a new agency—one to be called the Missouri Valley Authority (MVA)—to rule the Missouri River. The concept alarmed the corps and the bureau. Enactment of an MVA would divert many opportunities in the ripe, immense Missouri basin to the new organization.

Like Roosevelt, leaders from Missouri River states had grown weary of the conflict, and they requested the president and Congress to force the corps and the bureau to resolve their differences. With pressure building from outside and inside the Missouri basin, and with the MVA threat hanging over their heads, the two agencies met on 17 October 1944 in Omaha. Among those representing the bureau was Glenn Sloan. Lew Pick was absent, having been assigned to Burma to build the Ledo Road. After two days, an agreement was reached and spelled out on a one-page document. And the Pick-Sloan compromise was born.

Before the joint plan would become law as part of the 1944 Flood Control Act, some fine tuning remained. Skeptical upper-basin interests continued to doubt that adequate water was available for all Pick-Sloan objectives. Senators Joseph O'Mahoney of Wyoming and Eugene Milliken of Colorado maneuvered an amendment onto the flood-control bill that permitted Missouri River shippers to operate only if there was no conflict with the needs of the upper basin for irrigation, stock water, and water for domestic, municipal, industrial, and mining uses. With acceptance of the amendment, upper-basin interests relaxed and supported the legislation. The measure was approved by Congress, and on 22 December 1944 President Roosevelt signed the Flood Control Act into law.

But the controversy was not ended. Critics lashed out at the two water agencies, calling the Pick-Sloan Plan a "shameless shotgun marriage."[10] The criticism was justified. When the bureau and the corps reconciled their separate plans, they did nothing more than accept the other's ideas and marry the two plans in one monumental blueprint. Nearly all original features of the once-separate plans survived the reconciliation.

In his book *The Water and the Power*, Albert Williams echoed Pick-Sloan's critics: "The Army Engineers and the Bureau had not . . . stopped fighting for any reason of a final reconciliation of aims," he wrote. "They had stopped fighting only because they had lately learned that the clenched fist is not the best instrument with which to dip into the public trough."[11]

Passage of the Pick-Sloan Plan started one of the most ambitious, comprehensive, costly, and controversial river-breaking plans ever devised. The package included proposals for more than three hundred separate projects and more than one hundred dams on the Missouri's main channel and tributaries. Though none of the mainstem dams would be as large as Fort Peck, they would be substantial. Garrison, the only mainstem dam planned for North Dakota, would be 2.5 miles long and 210 feet high. Oahe, though not as long as Garrison, would top out at 242 feet. Fort Randall would be the first of the mainstem dams to be built. Gavins Point and Big Bend would follow. All would be earthen structures.

The new mainstem dams would create as much as ninety million acre-feet of water storage, enough to cover 98 percent of South Dakota with one foot of water. Drowned beneath the dam's enormous reservoirs would be eight hundred miles of natural river channel and more than 1.5 million acres of land. Conservative estimates put Pick-Sloan's total cost at close to $2 billion. This figure has since proved to be a dramatic underestimation. Billions have been spent, and only a portion of the overall plan has been developed.

In one of the most consequential agreements of the Pick-Sloan reconciliation, the Corps of Engineers was given the authority to build and control the large dams and reservoirs planned for the river's mainstem, while some of the dams to be constructed on tributaries—those whose uses were primarily hydropower generation and to provide storage for irrigation projects—became Bureau of Reclamation responsibilities. The bureau would also divert water from the mainstem impoundments for irrigation development.

The bureau was enthused about its assignment. Nearly 5 million acres in the upper Missouri River basin would be irrigated by the Pick-Sloan Plan. In North Dakota, 1.3 million acres would receive water. South Dakota, Montana, and Nebraska would each receive about 1 million irrigated acres. All told, there were a whopping 137 separate irrigation projects. But the biggest projects were what really excited the bureau, among them an ambitious undertaking in South Dakota named the Oahe Unit.

Suddenly, South Dakota was in line to receive huge federal appropriations for dams and diversions. All the state's politicians applauded the opportunities ahead, and the public eagerly awaited the start of the program. Clerks, barbers, bankers, bartenders, lawyers, teachers, farmers, laborers—it seemed that everyone wanted water. Everyone, that is, except those whose lands would be covered by a dam, drowned by a reservoir, or crossed by a canal.

3

The Big Dam

The site of an Indian Mission along the Missouri River in Hughes County was called Oahe, and there are two versions for the Dakota name. The first is that "Oahe" comes from Titankaahe, "place of the big house," and was named after the large Mission building that was erected in 1874. The second version is that the name comes from Oahede, "foundation." . . . The Oahe Dam and Reservoir, built near the town of Pierre in 1958 by the U.S. Army Corps of Engineers and the Department of the Interior, was named after the Mission. The U.S. Army Corps of Engineers says the name came from Oahede.

Virginia Driving Hawk Sneve, *The Dakota's Heritage*

Dam builders must have liked the word *Oahe* and its translation, for the word implied heft, strength, reliability. It seemed an appropriate name for the world's largest rolled-earth dam. Promoters of the Oahe Irrigation Project, too, must have liked the name. It implied that this irrigation project would be the basis for an enhanced, more reliable agricultural economy in South Dakota—the foundation for a future of great economic growth.

It happened on a soggy April day in 1947. Traveling on horseback in a driving rainstorm, Ted Albright was rounding up cattle on his ranch in South Dakota's Hughes County when he came on a peculiar sight. Mired down in the middle of a muddy field, wheel hubs barely exposed in a couple of feet of standing water, was a dark, oversized van. Some damn fool without permission to be on my land, cursed Albright. Leaning forward in the saddle, peering through the shower, he thought the vehicle was a military personnel carrier. It looked to be loaded with people and gear.

Albright steered his mount to the strange truck. Strapped to the roof was equipment that appeared to be related to surveying. Inside, he could see, were seven or eight men. Wiping his face and eyes, Albright looked down from atop his horse, introduced himself, and asked if he could help. Over a partially rolled-down window, the driver slowly eyeballed Albright and then remarked that the men worked for the federal government. He said Albright's help would be appreciated.

Later, after his hay horses extricated the truck, Albright indulged his curiosity. "So, what are you fellas doing out here?" he asked, looking through the driver's open window as he tended to the animals.

"We're surveying," the driver declared.

Albright nodded, but pushed further. "Yeah, but what are you surveying for?"

The man hesitated, and then one of the others spoke. He told Albright they were surveying a route for a large canal. Now it was Albright's turn to pause. "A canal?" he finally uttered. "What kind of canal?"

"An irrigation canal," came the response.

Standing in water and mud, rain dripping from his hat and coat, Albright puzzled for a moment. At the time, irrigation did not seem like a priority. He looked beyond the driver at the other faces inside the truck. They were all looking at him. "What are you talking about?" the rancher queried.

"Well," replied the man at the steering wheel, "we're going to build a dam across the Missouri River north of Pierre, take water from behind the dam and run it in the canal over to the James River country north of Redfield."

Albright stepped back and drew in his breath. Trying to organize his racing thoughts, he looked west toward the distant and not visible Missouri River, thought about its deep, wide valley, and then he took a long look east through the mist. It was at least another hundred miles cross-country to Redfield. "You guys are crazy as hell," was all the startled Albright could manage to blurt back.[1]

When Albright repeated the story to his neighbors, they dismissed the dam and canal as just another grand government scheme for the river, one of the many that had surfaced through the years but had never come to fruition. Albright was not so sure. Never before had he heard of surveyors working so far from the river. He had sensed a confidence, a sureness of purpose, in the men he'd helped out.

There had been dreams of dams on the Missouri in the Dakotas at least since John Wesley Powell proposed one for "the big bend" in 1871.[2] The idea got serious when, early in the twentieth century, Doane Robinson proposed several modest structures on the river in South Dakota. Robinson, the state's historian, wanted to develop irrigation and navigation and produce state-owned hydropower for rural residents, towns, and schools. He circulated a petition to demonstrate the plan's popularity, and the state legislature sanctioned a statewide vote on the idea. Regional jealousies doomed the proposal, however, and the public soundly rejected the measure in 1922. Other than a few random newspaper editorials lamenting the lack of Missouri River development and periodic teams of engineers examining the river, little had happened since the lopsided election.[3]

Unbeknown to Ted Albright and his neighbors, Glenn Sloan was busy networking with South Dakota's business and political leaders. Sloan and the U.S. Bureau of Reclamation realized that passage of the Pick-Sloan Plan meant nothing unless the agency could secure appropriations from Congress. Sloan knew that without a big dam on the Missouri north of Pierre, an irrigation project serving the James River valley was not feasible. He also realized that convincing South Dakota leaders about the prospect of large-scale irrigation was essential to gain their support for a high dam at Oahe and other mainstem dams.

The first stop for Sloan in any new town was the chamber of commerce. That was followed by a visit to the community's newspaper. The strategy was simple: arouse business leaders and they would contact their congressman. Sloan's persuasiveness was evident by his influence on Huron, South Dakota, a small city of about twelve thousand people along the James River. Huron newspaperman Bob Lusk said Glenn Sloan forever changed his community. "We never dreamed of irrigation until Glenn Sloan came to town and called a meeting," remembered Lusk. "Sloan said that we had seven hundred and fifty thousand acres of the best irrigation land in the United States."[4] As the years passed, Lusk used his newspaper to promote Oahe, and Huron became a center of irrigation enthusiasts.

In early 1948, South Dakota Governor M. Q. Sharpe was asked by the state's delegation to visit Washington to help convince the House Appropriations Committee to fund Oahe dam construction. At the time, Congress was not favorably disposed toward the proposal. The dam was viewed as a jobs project for South Dakota, and that was considered too narrow an objective since South Dakota was a lightly populated state and Oahe was an expensive project.

Governor Sharpe was reluctant to leave Pierre because the state legislature was in session and at a critical juncture, so he asked Bob Hipple to testify in his place. Hipple eagerly accepted the assignment. Before Hipple left for Washington, he and the governor composed a statement. Hipple also prepared a brochure for members of the appropriations committee.

When he arrived at the hearing, Hipple was told he would have only ten minutes before the committee. After distributing the brochures, Hipple began to read his prepared remarks. Soon there were many questions about the dam and the Missouri River. Hipple's knowledge served him well on that fateful day. Instead of delivering a canned and hurried message, Hipple spent forty-five minutes answering questions and expressing his feelings about Missouri River development. Following Hipple's appearance, the committee voted to authorize money to begin Oahe dam. Later that year, at a location 6 miles north of Pierre and 1,072 miles upstream from the Missouri's confluence with the Mississippi, the dam called Oahe began to rise from the broad floodplain.

The dam was fitted between two burly bluffs facing each other across two miles of river bottom. In the river's main channel, far below the bluff tops, was a scenic and sizeable island often used by local sportsmen. Wood Island would be smothered by the dam. At the dam's groundbreaking, on 16 September 1948, Lew Pick told four thousand cheering spectators that the occasion was "the happiest day of my life."[5] After Pick's speech, a group of dignitaries, including Pick, Glenn Sloan, various politicians, and Bob Hipple, sank spades and turned earth to commemorate the start of construction. Though the start of Oahe dam may have been the happiest day of Pick's life, for thousands of others it marked the beginning of an unhappy, traumatic time. It also marked the beginning of the end of the wild Missouri River in central South Dakota. The dam's impact on wildlife would be staggering, but the implications for the river valley's human inhabitants were just as devastating. And though there were few complaints about the environmental destruction, there were many protests from those who owned land and lived along the river.

Perhaps the first serious opposition to Oahe dam preceded Bob Hipple's trip to Washington. The community of Mobridge, located on the river about a hundred miles north of the proposed dam, knew that Oahe reservoir would require new bridges for the highway and railroad that spanned the Missouri and served the community. The town worried that the new bridges would be relocated away from existing locations. There was also concern about the town's water supply and sewage system. Both would be affected by the reservoir. The loss of valuable lands to the reservoir meant a diminished tax base and a damaged agricultural economy. Community leaders were aware that the dam was associated with the proposed irrigation project, and they ridiculed watering land in the already productive James River valley.

Congressman Karl Mundt took Lew Pick and Glenn Sloan to Mobridge on 30 November 1946 to calm the locals. Mundt told a large crowd that the Oahe dam would transform Mobridge into the most important industrial center in South Dakota. Inexpensive electrical power from Oahe dam and the availability of abundant water were among Mundt's reasons for making such a prediction. Pick, who had risen in rank from colonel to general, warned that if the community did not join the effort to develop the river, the entire Missouri River program was endangered. It was a typical military perspective: fall into line, Mobridge, or face the wrath of your fellows. Sloan's presentation proved especially appealing. He outlined a plan to irrigate land in the Mobridge area. This was big news, as the federal agencies had not before mentioned irrigation around Mobridge.

The Mobridge newspaper headlined its front-page coverage by declaring the community had been converted to support the big dam and the Missouri River plan. "Mobridge Drops Opposition to High Dam at Oahe in Interest of Program," read the headline. The subheading revealed the primary reason community leaders had switched their position: "33,000 Acres of This Area to Get Irrigation, Say Pick and Sloan."[6]

The luxury of hindsight allows a revealing sidebar to the events in Mobridge. It is worth noting what was not mentioned, either at the meeting or in the newspaper article: There was no forecast regarding the economic boom that recreation on Oahe reservoir would one day bring to Mobridge. Neither Pick nor Sloan nor Mundt nor Mobridge's leaders anticipated it. That oversight reflected the mentality of the times. Recreation was an afterthought in the development of the Oahe dam. The focus was on downstream flood control, navigation, hydropower, industrial uses of water, and irrigation. No one imagined that fishing Oahe's stocked waters would one day draw anglers from across the country, and that recreation would become a vital industry in Mobridge and in other communities along the reservoir.

After Mobridge was converted, the next notable opposition to Oahe dam came from Frank Ferguson and L. R. (Roy) Houck. Both were Republican state senators. Ferguson, a farmer from the James River valley area in Sanborn County, downstream from Huron, challenged the value of the dam by refuting the feasibility of the irrigation project for which it was being built. "Those of us who have worked the land in the James River valley," stated Ferguson, "know that a very small percentage of it will continue to successfully produce through an extended period of above normal rainfall. . . . We know that if excessive water is applied, nature's balance will be upset. The top soil will become charged with salts from the subsoil. . . . The landscape would change from one of grassy, well managed units to one lacerated with canals and ditches which would have a damaging effect on the soil and streams."[7] Ferguson led a large, feisty contingent of Sanborn County farmers opposed to the government's irrigation idea. In 1952, a legislative hearing about irrigation was held in Woonsocket, the Sanborn County seat. Although 1952 was drier in the James River valley than any year in the 1930s, some five hundred Sanborn County farmers crowded into the county courthouse and cheered as Ferguson announced that irrigation was not welcome in Sanborn County.

Roy Houck's emphasis was the Missouri River valley, where his ranch along the river in Potter and Walworth Counties contained some eight thousand acres. If a high dam were built, Houck and his family would be forced to relocate. Houck and at least seventy-eight other landowners along the Missouri River formed the Oahe Reservoir Landowners Association and circulated a petition asking that the planned 242-foot-high Oahe dam be downsized. Instead of a reservoir impounding more than 23 million acre-feet of water, they advocated one to hold 6 million acre-feet.[8]

Houck and Ferguson accused the Bureau of Reclamation of ignoring the opinions of farmers and ranchers. "There is a clear lack of support from the people," stated Ferguson. "It is clear that the proponents . . . are largely spokesmen for promotional groups who hope to benefit from such funds that will be spent in the area during the period of construction. It is to this group that the Bureau of Reclamation is endeavoring to sell the project. . . . It appears that this project is being offered as an excuse for inundating hundreds of thousands of acres of good, productive agricultural land."[9]

Former South Dakota Governor M. Q. Sharpe noted the plan to irrigate lands along the James River had drawn more criticism than any other aspect of the Pick-Sloan Plan. To counter anti-irrigation forces, Sharpe suggested that water-development advocates focus on getting the dam built. Once the dam is up, Sharpe advised, start work on the irrigation plan.[10]

Roy Houck and Frank Ferguson correctly predicted that landowners in the future Oahe reservoir site would resist Corps of Engineers offers to buy land. Of the more than twenty-one hundred nonfederal and privately held parcels of land that changed hands to accommodate Oahe reservoir, at least half were reluctantly sold, often under circumstances of considerable duress.[11] Some of this land was acquired by the corps through forced taking, using the powers of con-

23

demnation. Landowners who refused to sell their land willingly to the corps ended up in a courtroom fighting for a larger land payment. Condemnation was an unpleasant proceeding for those who chose such action, but the results showed how the government undervalued the property it condemned. The courts almost always awarded more money than the corps originally offered. But the increase was mostly negated by court costs and attorney fees.

Roy Houck eventually lost his ranch, and though he was paid half a million dollars, he felt the amount was inadequate. Houck was told by a local appraiser who worked for the corps that appraisers desiring future work with the agency kept appraisals within a low range that was set by the agency.[12]

Art and Helen Metzinger owned a farm that is now beneath more than one hundred feet of reservoir water. Helen described the setting, located in an area called Peoria Bottoms, six miles upriver from the present site of Oahe dam. "It was the most wonderful place in South Dakota," sighed Metzinger, as she recalled their farm along the river. "It was subirrigated. . . . We had lots of trees, sandy soil, natural shelter. It was a wonderful place for livestock. The valley and the timber provided shelter for livestock during tough weather. The bottomlands were fertile, and the corn grew as high as your head and higher. Standing on your tractor seat you couldn't see over it. We both grew up on the treeless, windswept prairie. It was like dying and going to heaven down there."[13]

Nothing had come easy for the Metzingers. They had married in 1938, a tough time for nearly anyone trying to scratch a living from the land. Helen had just graduated from high school. There were no family gifts of land or generous inheritances. All Helen wanted was the opportunity to work hard and make something for herself and her family. Born in a two-room shanty on the prairie of eastern South Dakota, she shared with her husband Art the same modest dream: to someday own a small family farm. The couple leased the place along the river in 1946 after the owner's wife died. Rent was reasonable. That was because the lonely owner was eager to move off the place; it was also because the government was investigating the vicinity for a dam site.

Both Metzingers remember their early doubts about the dam. "It was too big to be a reality," was Helen's memory of her initial reaction to the plan. "It was beyond comprehension."[14] Not only did the possibility of such a massive dam seem remote, the couple was preoccupied with farming and the excitement and satisfaction of establishing their own place. "You have your daily chores, the daily worries," explained Helen. "You're young, you're building a family, trying to provide for them. You're trying to establish yourself. We didn't think about it [the dam]. It all crept up on us gradually."[15]

After a couple of years, the Metzingers bought their first land, a section that was further away from the river than their leased land. Their new property ranged up the sides of the river valley and contained a vein of gravel. It was the gravel that drew the corps to the Metzingers. "We were one of the first [farms] to be approached [by the corps] . . . and it was because of the gravel," Helen explained. "We were offered thirty dollars an acre. It wasn't a fair price." Though that crumbled rock was used to build access roads for construction and the facing of the dam, its value was not included in the government's appraisal of the Metzingers' property.[16] The Metzingers felt their land was worth closer to a hundred dollars an acre, not considering the gravel. But money, both Metzingers agreed, was not the main issue. For them their farm was priceless. Not only did they love their home, but the fertile land along the river consistently grew forage crops for their cow herd.

The corps accused the couple of buying the land as a speculative venture. They charged the couple with wanting to increase their investment at the expense of the government. The Metzingers denied that, saying what they really wanted was to be left alone. But that was not to be. The corps pressured them relentlessly. "They contacted us many times," said Helen, referring to a diary she kept of the corps's visits. "Each time they left with a threat. They said if we didn't take their offer they would condemn us. We were very afraid."[17] Finally, reluctantly, the Metzingers agreed to thirty dollars per acre. The deal was consummated in March 1956.

During testimony she delivered in 1960 to a Senate committee investigating corps land-acquisition complaints, Helen Metzinger offered a scathing indictment of the agency and posed a fundamental question about federal projects requiring condemnation: "We were . . . treated as obstacles. . . . We are displaced people in our own country. . . . Anyone who calls this a free country as our ancestors meant it to be should hang his head in shame and despair for such alienation of rights of citizens. . . . Thousands of people have profited and benefited from these projects. . . . Why then—for a project so supposedly worthy—should it be necessary for the landowners who have donated their homes to make the supreme sacrifice? Pushed out and forgotten. This is the despair we live with every day. I have seen it eat into our lives and I feel for the well-being of our family because of it."[18]

For years, the Metzingers struggled to recover from their setback. It was impossible to duplicate what they had had, especially with the paltry payment they'd received. They eventually found a house to rent in Fort Pierre and leased some pasture for their cattle. Art commuted daily to the new land, and Helen found a job in county government to make ends meet. All the while they patiently rebuilt their finances, hoping to find another farm.

In 1966, the Metzingers finally discovered a place to buy. Their new house needed lots of work, but it was in the country. The bitter wounds of their experience with the federal government still stung, but they were happy to be settling down again. After being uprooted from the river bottom by an insensitive bureaucracy a decade earlier, the last thing they imagined was another land dispute with the federal government. Who would have guessed that their new farm lay in the path of what one day would be the route of the Oahe Irrigation Project's main canal? The water that covered their first farm would flow in a canal that would ruin their second farm.[19]

Many non-Indians have no idea of the extent of sacrifice and injustice endured by Indian tribes at the hands of the Army Corps of Engineers during the construction of the Missouri River mainstem dams. The federal government's treatment of Missouri River tribes during the development of Pick-Sloan is an embarrassing and shameful legacy. The Corps of Engineers trampled on Indian rights to secure the bottomlands it needed for reservoirs. Condemnation proceedings were used liberally, despite a 1920 U.S. Supreme Court ruling that mandated congressional approval before such actions could be taken against Native Americans. In the Missouri River project, the corps never received such approval.[20] The takings also violated earlier treaties that guaranteed the perpetual integrity of Indian reservation land. All told, more than 350,000 acres, or about 550 square miles, were purchased from reluctant Indian tribes for the mainstem dams in the Dakotas. No public works project in the history of the United States destroyed so much Indian land as did the Pick-Sloan Plan.[21]

Three of the four mainstem dams in South Dakota flooded approximately 202,000 acres of Sioux land. North Dakota's Three Affiliated Tribes (Mandan, Hidatsa, and Arikara) lost 155,000 acres of their Fort Berthold Reservation to Garrison dam's Lake Sakakawea. Before there was a Garrison dam, unemployment on the Fort Berthold reservation had been near zero; the Native American people living there enjoyed a prosperous economy. After the dam flooded 94 percent of the Three Tribes' crop and grazing land, unemployment soared to more than 70 percent, and 349 families, comprising 1,544 people, were forced to abandon their homes. The dam and reservoir severed the Fort Berthold tribes, isolating half of the reservation from the other, and creating communication and transportation hardships. The social ills that befall a group of uprooted, jobless people spread quickly. Alcoholism, broken families, and broken spirits

26

swept through the reservation like a plague.[22] For their sacrifice to Pick-Sloan, the Three Tribes were paid thirty-three dollars an acre. Tribal members reluctantly accepted the meager offer as Garrison dam backed water over their lands. The corps was so confident it would evict the Indians, it closed the dam before concluding negotiations with them.

According to the legislation creating Garrison dam, Native Americans at Fort Berthold would not be allowed to fish or to graze and water their cattle along the reservoir. Indian mineral rights and hunting and trapping rights were also denied. The Indians would not be allowed to share in any oil or gas royalties on the taken lands. An Indian request for low-cost power from the dam was ignored. The Indians were denied the opportunity to use the irrigation facilities associated with the dam and reservoir and were prohibited from cutting down the great groves of trees soon to be drowned. Obviously, the uprooted Indian people needed lumber to build new homes. Apparently, the government preferred that the timber go to waste.[23]

The corps's coldhearted behavior toward the Fort Berthold tribes was no different than its dealings with other Missouri River Indians. The agency seemed just as confident that the Sioux could be evicted from along the river with minimal considerations. Construction of Fort Randall, Big Bend, and Oahe dams, all of which threatened Sioux landholdings, was started before Sioux leaders had been formally approached about compensation for their land.

The immense size and location of Oahe reservoir translated into disaster for the Sioux living on the Cheyenne River and Standing Rock reservations in South and North Dakota. The name Oahe was not the only thing the federal government took from the Sioux. Among Pick-Sloan projects, Oahe reservoir destroyed more Indian land—160,000 acres of Sioux reservation—than any other. Not only did the two reservations lose their best grazing land, they lost most of their cultivated farm tracts and gardens and nearly all of their timber and wildlife resources. The Cheyenne River agency had to relocate its largest community and headquarters from a pleasant spot near the river to the desolate plain west of the reservoir.

Thirty percent of the people living on the Cheyenne River Reservation—180 families—were forced to leave their homes. More than 100,000 acres were drowned. At the Standing Rock Reservation, Oahe's waters covered 56,000 acres, and 25 percent of the reservation's residents were driven to new homes. Both reservations struggled valiantly but futilely with the corps to gain acceptable monetary settlements. In the end, the Cheyenne River Sioux were paid $2 million for their land, or about $19 per acre. The total financial settlement amounted to $10.6 million, which included property payment and relocation and rehabilitation provisions. Standing Rock, by observing what transpired between their Cheyenne River neighbors and the corps, fared better in negotiations. Even though Standing Rock lost less land, a settlement totaling $12.3 million was negotiated.

Not only did the corps bully and shortchange the Sioux, they were heartless in other ways. The Indians at Standing Rock received notice of eviction in January 1960. The affected residents had until the end of February to vacate their land and homes. The corps could have waited until warmer weather to impose relocation on the Indian people. A more reasonable eviction schedule would not have altered the progress of Oahe dam construction.[24]

As they had done with the Three Tribes, the government refused Indian requests for convenient access to the reservoir and for cheap hydropower. When the Sioux arranged to harvest woodlands doomed by Oahe reservoir to build homes, barns, and fences, the corps intervened through litigation. Though the corps eventually lost their case, the delay prevented the trees from being salvaged.[25]

The manner in which the federal government dealt with Indian and non-Indian landowners in the path of Oahe and other Missouri River reservoirs contradicted the purposes of the Pick-Sloan Plan. Although it was the stated intent of the government to use Missouri River basin water projects to assist and further the economic prosperity of those living in the Missouri basin, those residents negatively impacted by the projects were excluded from the government's purported generosity and the noble spirit of the plan. In order to help one group of citizens, the government turned its back on others. The economic fortunes of many people were reversed as the program to help others was unleashed. Although dam building certainly requires some disruption of citizens and communities, the treatment endured by the unfortunate ones in the basin was tragic. Better ways, more reasonable ways of dealing with the victims of Pick-Sloan should have been an integral part of the overall plan. The federal government's cruel, authoritarian behavior flawed the foundation of Missouri River development, and as time passed it continued to haunt other aspects of Pick-Sloan.

While work progressed on erecting Oahe dam and ousting residents from along the river, the South Dakota legislature was laying the groundwork for state involvement in federal water-development projects. To develop and maintain the so-called Oahe-James irrigation project, it was necessary to create conservancy districts within the state. These special districts exist as regional governmental entities with taxing powers. Often containing multiple counties and numerous municipalities, they are a necessary contractual link between the federal government and the localities containing a federal water project.

Introduced late in the 1957 legislative session, a bill to create an Oahe Conservancy District outlined a district including Marshall, Brown, Spink, and Sully Counties. It was felt that because these counties would benefit from irrigation, that was where local taxes should be collected for the project. The cities of Mitchell and Huron were also included in the proposed district.

Joe Grimes, who had left the Bureau of Reclamation to become executive director of the South Dakota Water Resources Commission, lobbied for the measure, explaining that federal interest in the Oahe-James project had cooled because South Dakota had not aggressively pursued irrigation. The bill, said Grimes, would provide hard evidence of the state's interest. Unless South Dakota claimed its share of Missouri River flows, warned Grimes, downriver states would secure rights to the water first.[26]

City officials and chambers of commerce echoed Grimes, while farmers opposed the measure, suggesting the district's board of directors was not accountable to citizens. The legislature chose a compromise approach, asking the legislative research council to study the idea until the 1959 session. Water-development supporters, worried that the delay conveyed the wrong message to Washington, obtained passage of a resolution urging Congress to continue funding irrigation studies in the state.

A clamoring for irrigation had intensified by the time the 1959 legislative session began. The Greater South Dakota Association, an organization promoting industry and commerce, tantalized its members with incredible forecasts. "The proposed [Oahe-James] irrigation," stated the group's newsletter, "will result in 3,477 new farm units . . . a total population increase in the project area of 46,000 . . . [and] a rise of $103,000,000 in the annual volume of business over the present total."[27]

During the previous summer, an event was held that so inspired those present that even the glowing economic predictions were forgotten for an hour or so. On a boiling August afternoon, with temperatures exceeding 100°F, more than sixteen thousand wide-eyed onlookers gathered to celebrate the dramatic construction closure of Oahe dam. Though ultimate completion of the dam would not occur until 1962, the river had finally been plugged. Water from the growing reservoir reached the dam's intake and flowed from the outlet over the weir of the stilling basin.

The structure that was visible in August 1958 was awesome indeed. Oahe would be the largest rolled-earth dam on the planet, measuring 9,300 feet long, soaring 242 feet from its mile-wide base, and requiring some 92 million cubic yards of dirt. How much earth is that? Consider this: the 60-mile-long Panama canal, completed in 1914, required the excavation of 211 million cubic yards of earth; the materials used to erect Oahe could fill in 25 miles of the great canal's length. Oahe dam was big in other ways. With a price tag of $345 million, it was by $54 million the most costly of the Pick-Sloan mainstem dams.

As imposing as the dam was, the dimensions of the reservoir it would create commanded special attention. Peering northward to where the bright sky met the faintest edges of rolling land, the people gathered that August day had difficulty imagining that Lake Oahe would one day link the capital cities of the two Dakotas. But it was true. The reservoir behind the massive dam would reach beyond the horizon to Bismarck, North Dakota.

For residents of a state that not too many years earlier had suffered from a horrible shortage of water, the reservoir's capacity, its scale, was breathtaking, almost unimaginable. Lake Oahe would stretch northward 250 miles and its shoreline would exceed 2,200 miles. The mammoth reservoir would hold more than 23.5 million acre-feet of water—enough to cover all of South Dakota with five inches of water.

At the dam's final dedication, held 17 August 1962, President John Kennedy praised the construction effort and connected the conquest of the Missouri River to the initiative and opportunity that results from a democratic form of government. "This dam provides a striking illustration of how a free society can make the most of its God-given resources," the president told the crowd. "Too often we take for granted these miracles of engineering and milestones in river development. Too often we see no connection between this dam and our nation's prosperity, our national security and our leadership of those nations who cherish their freedom. But the facts of the matter are that this dam, and many more like it, are as essential to the expansion and growth of the American economy as any measure the Congress is considering on taxes or unemployment—and this dam and the others like it are as essential to our national strength and security as any military alliance or missile complex."[28]

Oahe dam was constructed in the days before the United States recognized the value of preserving river environments. The Missouri's natural attributes were obscured by the needs of commerce and convenience. One *Time* magazine correspondent referred to the Missouri as "the most useless river there is."[29] The impressed onlookers at the 1958 and 1962 celebrations overlooked the fact that to be drowned beneath Oahe's waters would be one of the nation's unique and irreplaceable areas, including some of the finest wetlands in the hemisphere. The riparian corridor bordering the river through all of South Dakota had been designated a state wildlife refuge. In North Dakota, the river's islands had been granted refuge status.

Also ignored was the historical significance of the Missouri. A great remnant of Lewis and Clark's route would be flooded over. A long stretch of the river that hosted one of the nation's great explorations would disappear. Oahe dam itself may have covered a campsite used by the Corps of Discovery.

To now stand on the enormous dam and gaze northward at the reservoir and at fishing boats skittering about, it is difficult to imagine what once existed there. The river's main channel, the artery that fed and fueled the most diverse ecological community on the northern plains, has been swallowed whole. Gone is Wood Island and dozens of other islands. Gone, too, are the river's dune beaches, its gravel and sandbars, and the highwater chutes and backwater marshes where many species of wildlife flourished. Wooded coulees and verdant draws are also gone. Great groves of cottonwood trees still stand in the old floodplain, their roots anchored to the reservoir's muddy floor and their sun-bleached, naked limbs poking through the water's surface like carcasses picked clean. They are reminders of the forests that once thrived in the valley.

The overall extent of the dam's natural casualties was and is impossible to calculate. But the federal government did measure the land types that were flooded. It was determined that about 62,000 acres of woodlands perished beneath Oahe reservoir. So did 100,000 acres of grasslands, 44,000 acres of wetlands and main river channel, and 17,000 acres of hay and croplands.[30] Years later, as wildlife species that formerly relied on the Missouri's natural habitat plummeted toward extinction, wildlife scientists began to understand the magnitude of this ecological disruption. The scientists realized that a vast region reaching far beyond the river valley onto the adjacent rolling plains was also impacted by the destruction of the natural river.

Along with building Oahe and the four other mainstem dams, the Corps of Engineers proceeded with its plans for the undammed stretches in the lower reaches of the river. Between Sioux City and the Missouri's mouth near St. Louis, where the corps channelized the river to curb flooding and facilitate navigation, the natural destruction rivaled that of the dammed stretches. In the three decades following passage of Pick-Sloan, the corps erected a system of levees and revetments and dredged and straightened the channel. The project reduced the river's length in the lower states from 859 miles to 732 miles.

Dammed and shackled, the Missouri's ecosystem rapidly deteriorated. Before Pick-Sloan, spring flooding had triggered certain behaviors in fish and delivered nutrients to feed aquatic creatures. Because of flooding cycles, bottomland forests had prospered; riverine wetlands and backwaters were regularly freshened; thick blankets of gravel and sand were rolled onto river bends during floods, creating large dune formations; and sandbars and islands punctuated the meandering main channel. All these habitat types disappeared as the river was channelized and intensive farming began to encroach on the floodplain.

In the absence of periodic flooding, the lower river's wildlife populations tumbled. Between Sioux City and St. Louis, half a million acres of wetlands disappeared. Forests once inhabited 76 percent of the floodplain in the lower reaches; the corps's river-modification project reduced that to less than 15 percent. In the place of the natural river was a dredged trench, providing a shipping lane, three hundred feet wide and nine feet deep, for barges and towboats. Fish habitat was nearly gone. The shoreline was steep and uninviting to wildlife and humans. The river had become a lane of commerce and an open ditch to deliver water to power plants, industry, and municipalities, and to carry away sewage and waste.

The message of water developers was clear: If a dam the size of Oahe could be built across the Missouri, the construction of an irrigation project should pose no problems. Riding this euphoric momentum, irrigation promoters brought an expanded version of the conservancy-district vision into the 1959 session of the South Dakota legislature. Instead of isolating one specific region of the state to form a single district, as was the case in 1957, it was proposed that the entire state would become a conservancy district. Under provisions in the law, local interests would be allowed to organize into regional conservancy sub-districts, with each sub-district possessing its own locally elected board of directors.

"We don't anticipate as much opposition as last session," declared South Dakota's Governor Ralph Herseth.[31] Herseth and other supporters of the conservancy district did not have to contend with Frank Ferguson in the legislature: Ferguson's final term as a legislator ended in 1956 when he served as president pro tempore in the senate. Roy Houck had last served in the senate in 1954, though he was the state's lieutenant governor from 1955 to 1959. As the session opened, it was obvious that support for the concept was widespread. But the bill's length and complex language bothered some lawmakers. Soon the measure was stuck in partisan power plays, with most Democrats supporting the measure and most Republicans opposing it.

The bill's cheerleaders steered clear of technical matters, preferring to in-

voke images of prosperity and economic growth that would accompany formation of the conservancy district. Ed Downs, a Democratic senator from Aberdeen, epitomized this mindset when he linked passage of the bill with irrigation. "We want to keep South Dakota green, and gentlemen, I tell you if we
pass this bill, we keep South Dakota green," he proclaimed.[32] Other irrigation
promoters emphasized the need for the state to demonstrate to the rest of the nation that it wanted water-resource development and was prepared to defend its
right to use Missouri River flows. With most of the state's newspapers chanting
similar themes, the opposition softened and the senate passed the measure by a
vote of twenty-eight to seven. All seven members voting no were Republicans.

When the house took up the matter, only Ralph Hillgren, a Republican from
Sioux Falls, aggressively attacked it. Hillgren charged that irrigation would
cost so much per acre that it would not be economically feasible. But Hillgren
found few allies. The house approved the measure on 5 March 1959, and Governor Herseth quickly signed the measure into law.

Bob Hipple and others pounced on the opportunity to establish a sub-district
to use Oahe reservoir water. Led by a Potter County banker named Cecil Stil-
gebauer, they set up a meeting with water-development promoters from northeastern South Dakota. Individuals representing only four counties attended that
first meeting. Hipple and his colleagues realized that a substantial project like
the one they hoped for required a sizeable sub-district, encompassing more than
four counties. Representatives from fourteen north-central and northeastern
South Dakota counties showed up at the next meeting. Two counties that promoters hoped to attract into the new sub-district, Marshall and Clark Counties,
were not represented.[33] Sanborn County, another county eyed at one time by irrigation promoters, was omitted.

Although there were few, if any, official county representatives on hand,
those who were present at the 1 June 1959 meeting in Pierre participated in decision making that had important ramifications. The group discussed boundaries
and how to divide the sub-district into areas to be represented by a board of directors. It was determined that fifteen counties plus half of another one would
comprise the sub-district. It was also suggested that the sub-district be divided
into nine rural areas, with one director elected by the voters of each of these
areas. It was proposed that two at-large directors would serve those living in the
sub-district's municipalities.

The concept calling for nine rural directors was quickly approved by those at
the meeting. But the matter of determining how municipalities would be represented was sent to the conservancy district for further study. Eventually, it was

decided that both municipal directors would be at-large representatives, voted into office by residents of all sub-district municipalities. At conservancy or water districts across the West, it was more common for local judges to select the board's directors than to have local citizens elect them. Preferring the democratic process to determine sub-district directors was a generous and populist gesture by sub-district organizers. The rationale for the rural emphasis on the sub-district's board of directors was based on the source of the district's tax revenues. The monies to fund sub-district activities and obligations would come from property taxes, and most property taxes were paid by rural landowners. Another reason rural areas were given a more potent voice on the board was that rural residents would be more directly impacted by the development of the irrigation diversion project.[34] The decision to emphasize rural interests and empower them with voting privileges would have tremendous consequences on the future politics of the sub-district. Participants at the 1 June meeting also agreed that there should be a petition drive to place the formation of a sub-district on the general ballot. They were confident that support for the proposal would be strong.

Bob Hipple served as chairman of the committee that circulated petitions in each county included in the proposed sub-district. The question would land before the voters in November 1960. Hipple's newspaper and others across the proposed sub-district ardently promoted formation of the water district. A typical headline in the *Aberdeen American News* offered voters a choice: "Keep Water or Give It Away?" Beneath the headline the article stated: "Would you give it away. . . . Or would you vote to keep it around awhile to see if you could find some use for it—like irrigation, manufacturing, sanitation or creation of new lakes and putting more water in the creek?"[35]

An intensive informational effort was pursued by county extension agents and other state agriculture officials. Their position, of course, strongly supported formation, and they used three themes to justify irrigation: fear of drought; fear of losing what they called the state's rightful share of Missouri River water; and the importance of Missouri River water for economic prosperity. Their campaign literature compared water to gold: "It [water] belongs to those who stake a claim to it." And for South Dakotans to stake their claim, the extension service advised, "they must organize and approve, through elections, the formation of conservancy sub-districts."[36] South Dakotans were advised to pursue water development to guarantee a prosperous future for their children: "The future of South Dakota—which is so closely tied to the development and use of Missouri River water—is in the hands of the citizens of South

Dakota," said proponents. "Whether you—as a citizen of South Dakota—want to take advantage for yourself and your children will decide the future of this state."[37]

On Tuesday, 8 November 1960, voters in the yet unnamed but so-called Missouri River Conservancy Sub-district voted overwhelmingly to organize a sub-district. While state law required that at least 60 percent of the voters in the proposed district must approve the new government entity, more than 85 percent of those who cast ballots approved sub-district formation. Only one town—tiny Wetonka in McPherson County—out of ninety-four municipalities within the sub-district's boundaries came short of supporting formation by the required 60 percent. Wetonka's citizens favored the sub-district, but only by a narrow ten to seven margin. The final tally throughout the sub-district was 50,503 voting yes and only 8,712 voting no. Even the most optimistic sub-district supporters were surprised at the margin of victory.

Voters in the sub-district area also chose their first board of directors. Bob Hipple, who had run unopposed, was elected as one of two directors representing sub-district municipalities. Of the ten other Oahe advocates elected, nine of them representing rural areas, only three had faced competition to win seats.

On the same 1960 election day, Ralph Herseth, a Brown County farmer-rancher and an enthusiastic supporter of irrigation development, lost his bid for a second term as governor. But under the state's next governor, Republican Archie Gubbrud, irrigation development would remain a top priority. "Missouri River development," he declared, as he hailed creation of the sub-district, "is one of the biggest hopes for South Dakota and should be pushed as fast as possible."[38]

4

The Big Dream

Residents of South Dakota have . . . counted on new irrigation to justify the large sacrifice in agricultural land which the [Missouri] reservoirs required.

U.S. Bureau of Reclamation, "Report on Oahe Unit"

In the summer of 1960, the the U.S. Bureau of Reclamation released its first report containing a comprehensive, though purely prospective, blueprint of the Oahe Irrigation Project. That report contradicted Glenn Sloan's glowing pronouncement that the James River valley contained 750,000 acres of the finest irrigation land in the United States. Unceremoniously, and without apology, the bureau had reduced Sloan's grand plan by more than one-third. Oahe's new design proposed watering 482,000 acres. Oahe supporters in South Dakota were not happy about the shrinkage, but that wasn't the only unpleasant surprise in the report. The bureau also announced it was planning to construct the project in stages. The first phase, yet to be authorized by Congress, would irrigate only 298,000 acres. Even with the modifications, Oahe was one of the largest projects the bureau hoped to build. Based on 1959 prices, the estimated cost of Oahe's ultimate plan would be a hefty $514 million. It would be the most expensive federal project ever developed in South Dakota.

The bureau's 1960 report made it sound routine to annually remove water from Oahe reservoir and deliver it more than one hundred miles to the James River valley.[1] Approximately two hundred feet below the surface of Oahe reservoir, at elevation 1,410 feet above sea level, Missouri River water enters seven large intake tunnels that feed Oahe dam's hydropower generating system. Each tunnel measures twenty-four feet in diameter. At maximum load, with all seven intakes operating fully open, more than four million gallons of water per second power the system's turbines to produce electricity. Under the plan, water for the Oahe Irrigation Project would be diverted from tunnel number seven through four intake tubes leading to a pump house to be built on the reservoir shoreline. Although not as massive as the power plant tunnels, the seven-foot-wide tubes would be big enough for an elephant to walk through. The Oahe project's pump house and its four giant electric motors and pumps could power 8,900 gallons of water per second through four fat pipes to the crest of a nearby river bluff. There, at elevation 1,716 feet, the water would be discharged into the head-works of the Pierre canal. For the remainder of its journey to the James River valley, the water would travel downhill, assisted by gravity. The bureau hoped to move 800,000 acre-feet of water through this system each year.

No depths were specified for any reach of the Pierre canal's thirty-seven miles, but it was obvious this would be a sizeable gash across the prairie. Water conveyed through the canal would flow to the Blunt reservoir, located a short distance northeast from the town of Blunt. En route to Blunt reservoir, Oahe water would cross the wide valley at Medicine Knoll Creek in a single-barrel concrete siphon, or tube, four thousand feet long and twenty-one feet wide. Inside the siphon, water would build up speed as it plunged downhill, passing beneath the creek and a rail line in a tunnel before rushing up to the crest on the eastern side of the creek's valley. Following this dramatic crossing, the water would resume its journey in an open ditch.

The Blunt reservoir would be another substantial feature. Backed up behind a dam that would be 89 feet high and 7,300 feet long, the reservoir could impound up to 631,000 acre-feet of water. Probable operating storage would be less, about 185,000 acre-feet, covering 21,000 acres under up to 72 feet of water. The reservoir would regulate water destined for irrigation tracts in the proposed Missouri Slope Irrigation District, in nearby Potter and Sully Counties, and also the larger irrigation areas along the James River. From the east end of Blunt reservoir, at an elevation of about 1,690 feet, water would move east in the Highmore canal, 38 miles long. This canal would be routed through Highmore pass, an almost imperceptible breach in the breaks and bluffs bordering the Missouri River that led to the broad, flat James River lowlands. After miles of gradual descent through the Missouri River coteau, the canal's elevation would be quickly lowered several hundred feet using a series of engineered drops that ended near the junction of two separate canals. Here the water would either be directed toward irrigation tracts on the west side of the James River or toward tracts on the east side of the river. East of the Highmore canal, the project consisted of 150 miles of large, main ditches and two regulatory reservoirs,

Cresbard reservoir, in Faulk and Edmunds Counties, and the Byron reservoir, an expansion of an existing lake in Beadle County.

When Missouri River water finally arrived at irrigation tracts along the James River, it would be at elevations as low as 1,295 feet. On the nearly level lake plain, a maze of smaller ditches, called laterals, would distribute the flows to individual irrigators. As the water circulated through these laterals, it would be aided by relift pumps—necessary because of the flat terrain. In the Missouri Slope area, about 258 miles of small canals and laterals, as well as 15 relift pumps, would distribute the water to farm units. Irrigation areas in the James River valley would be served by 1,800 miles of laterals and some 280 relift pumps.

An even more complex aspect of the design was the project's drainage system. The Bureau of Reclamation recognized that soils in the James River valley were not sufficiently permeable to survive continual watering. To protect soils from waterlogging and alkaline buildup, tile drains would be installed beneath irrigated lands. Irrigation water passing through the soil would enter these perforated tile tubes and be diverted away from the root zone. A gridwork of some 14,000 miles of tile drains would be buried beneath the irrigation area. The tile drains would carry water into a system of larger, open drains called collector drains. More than 2,200 miles of these surface drains would convey water to the main drain system. The main drains, 503 miles of them, would be created by straightening and enlarging existing streams and draws. Within the irrigation areas in Brown and Spink Counties, the destination for drained irrigation water was the James River. The bureau was already aware of the water-quality problems its project would create. Laden with farm chemicals, the runoff and return flows from thousands of irrigated acres would easily overflow the James River's small, winding channel. To accommodate the new flows without causing flooding, the bureau endorsed a Corps of Engineers proposal to straighten and deepen the river as it flowed through the irrigation areas.

The focus of the project was on supplying irrigation water, and the bureau lavished praise on the contributions Oahe would make to irrigation farmers. Agriculture in the Oahe Unit, the bureau declared, would come to resemble the prosperous Midwest corn belt. "The Oahe Unit," stated the agency, "will bring about a livestock production and fattening economy similar to that in the major corn-producing areas."[2] Corn, said the bureau, would be the major row crop to benefit from irrigation. James River valley farmers, accustomed to worrying about rainfall and enticed by the references to Iowa and Illinois, were not surprised at the mention of corn; what did surprise them was the bureau's prediction that sugar beets would be one of the most profitable crops on the project.

Irrigation was not the only facet to Oahe. The report identified twenty-two cities and towns that could receive municipal and industrial water. The water would be removed from a project canal and transported, at a cost to be borne by the community, to suitable water storage and treatment facilities. Oahe planners also described the project's beneficial effects on fish and wildlife resources, as well as on recreation opportunities. It was estimated that twenty-eight fish and wildlife areas would be developed under the overall plan. The bureau asserted that wildlife in the Oahe area would be better off as a result of the project. Recreational development, aimed mainly at anglers and boaters, would be primarily associated with the three new reservoirs and the James diversion dam, located on the James River north of Huron.

The document concluded with a description of the project's economic benefits. After explaining that the stabilization and expansion of agricultural production and income were key benefits of the project, the bureau launched into a series of dramatic predictions that were certain to arouse local chambers of commerce and statewide business organizations. "Many new processing plants will spring up in the area and existing ones will be expanded [because of Oahe]," the agency claimed, specifying that thirty such new plants would be needed to handle the increased farm production made possible by Oahe. These new plants, according to the report, would employ three thousand people who annually would be paid nearly $4.5 million. More people and a larger tax base, the agency said, translates into "a more abundant life for both rural and urban people."[3] The bureau forecast that the wave of new processing plants, the growing population, and the new agricultural prosperity created by Oahe would spark a phenomenal yearly increase of some $284 million in commercial activity through the Oahe area.

The report explained that the drastic reduction in irrigation acreage was necessary because lands originally considered irrigable did not satisfy the agency's more recent investigations. The main factor had to do with soil drainage. It was concluded that not all lands in the James River valley could be drained adequately, even with artificial methods. According to the bureau, the best irrigation soils in the valley were found in an area bisected by the James River in Brown and Spink Counties and known to geologists as the Lake Dakota plain.

The city of Aberdeen occupied an intermittently spongy spot on prairie that once had been the center of this glacial lake, and the prime irrigation grounds were just east and south of the city. The landscape here is distinct from the rest of South Dakota. It is the flattest part of a state noted for its flatness. During the Pleistocene, or Ice Age, beginning two to three million years ago, at least four major ice sheets descended into South Dakota. Thousands of years separated each advance, with glacial retreat and thaw occurring during the long intervals. Today, more is known about the final period of glaciation than about the first three. About eighteen thousand years ago, an ice sheet now named for the state of Wisconsin began receding northward as temperatures rose, exposing land that had long been covered by the massive bulk of ice. Deglaciation was a slow process, involving the melting of ice six million square miles in area and two miles thick at the center.

The final phases of glacial melt in eastern South Dakota took place nine or ten thousand years ago. As the glacier melted, large amounts of runoff resulted, and rivers and streams were born. Some of the runoff pooled in glaciated valleys, creating lakes. In what is now northeastern South Dakota, a broad, shallow valley, one hundred miles by twenty-five miles, filled with meltwater—a formation geologists named Lake Dakota. Although it existed for only several thousand years before emptying via the earliest version of the James River, Lake Dakota had a profound effect on the land it covered. During the lake's life span, fine-grained, glacial sediment, carried by winds and water, settled to the floor of the lake, filling irregularities and dramatically reducing relief. By the time the lake drained, its bottom was blanketed by a smooth mat of these sediments. Snaking southward across the level land was the shallow main channel of the James River. With its modest capacity and slight gradient, the James is a watercourse that overflows at the slightest provocation.

The flat terrain of the old lake bed appeared to the bureau to be an ideal place for irrigation. But the most vital aspect of any irrigation proposal is the capability of the soils to remain fertile after years of being watered. In this regard, the bureau's rationale was less compelling. Lands in the lake plain were made up of silts, clay, and smaller admixtures of sand. Anyone who farmed the valley knew how impermeable some land could be. *Gumbo* is the word locals use to describe such soils after a hard rain. Water sits on the surface, creating a shallow, slippery, pudding-like layer. The necessity of installing tile drains at varying depths was an admission by the government that the irrigation of soils on the lake plain was not a simple proposition, and that there were environmental dangers involved. Even if the drains functioned well, they would eventually wear out. The issue of drain replacement was not addressed. Who would pay for such an enormous undertaking? How long would it take? How would nonirrigated lands adjacent to irrigation lands be impacted?

Another reason the bureau reduced the number of acres it proposed to irrigate was the loss of Missouri River hydropower that would result if the full 750,000 acres were watered. More water for irrigation meant less water would be available to pass through the turbines at Oahe dam. Hydropower users guarded their resource and were a powerful adversary to the removal of water from the Missouri system above generating facilities.

A fundamental reason for building the project in stages was practical economics. The bureau believed that funding from Congress for a phased approach would be more likely to succeed than would funding for the entire project. Excluded from the first phase were tracts of land east of the James River, in Brown County. This area would be included in a second phase. This was also the area where the most vocal opposition to irrigation existed.

George Schuller, a successful, soft-spoken farmer from east of the James River in Brown County, was a leader of a protest group called, simply, Anti Oahe. The impetus for forming the group was none other than Frank Ferguson, Oahe's ubiquitous opponent. Ferguson made many trips to Brown County during the 1950s and 1960s to encourage and assist opposition there. Farmers in eastern Brown County opposed Oahe because they were already doing well without the project. There was no reason, said Schuller, to switch from successful dryland farming to expensive and doubtful irrigated agriculture.

Born in 1914 to a farm couple who planted the first crops in the Claremont area of northeastern Brown County, Schuller said that in the seventy-seven years since his parents had planted their first crop, "only seven years were bad."[4] Like many of his neighbors, Schuller pursued a patient, conservative brand of farming. His operation was a diversified one, with corn and wheat as the main crops. Feeding calves to be sold as fat cattle served as the backbone of the farm. George Schuller lived modestly, worked hard, saved his money, and bought land. His efforts and frugal lifestyle paid dividends. Schuller's holdings multiplied, he became a wealthy man, and he later purchased a rural bank.

One of the things the Anti Oahe group did was circulate petitions protesting the project in their immediate area. "I circulated the petition in my township and all but one fellow signed it," recalled Schuller, "so I knew we had the support of the local people."[5] When the group sent a representative to Washington with the petitions, they expected an attentive reaction from elected officials. "We were ignored," shrugged Schuller, "and it seemed hopeless, but we were convinced we were right."[6]

No one familiar with the history of the Bureau of Reclamation would have been surprised at the substantial reduction in irrigation acreage proposed in the 1960 report. The agency had a history of exaggerating the potential of its projects while building a foundation of local supporters. Glenn Sloan's figure of

750,000 acre had never been anything but a very rough estimate, the result of a superficial irrigation survey. Bureau insiders referred to such estimations as windshield surveys. Glenn Sloan had presented the figure as if it were an official agency statistic, and South Dakotans believed him.

The 750,000-acre figure was also an integral part of the 1-million-acre irrigation proposal the bureau had pitched to South Dakota when the federal government first peddled its Pick-Sloan Plan. For decades, politicians and irrigation supporters in South Dakota pointed to the valuable bottomlands inundated behind Pick-Sloan's mainstem dams and cited the 1-million-acre irrigation goal as appropriate compensation for the lost land. The bureau continually reminded South Dakotans of the so-called debt owed their state by the federal government, and identified that debt as a rationale for building Oahe. Even though the 1-million-acre figure had never been anything but theoretical, and was more symbolic than scientific, South Dakotans clung to it as gospel.

With thousands of engineers and planners on its payroll, the bureau was constantly scanning the West for new opportunities to develop dams and irrigation projects. Planning and paperwork became a mainstay of the bureau's enterprise. There were Investigations, Preliminary Studies, Progress Reports, Feasibility Documents, Definite Plan Reports, Supplemental Reports. In some cases, these layers of studies helped refine project proposals. But the process of study itself became an independently important aspect of the agency. Once study monies had been secured from Congress, the agency's feet were in the door for more. Studies rarely recommended halting further involvement in a particular project. Gradually, the emphasis of the bureau had shifted from creating a viable reclamation culture in the West to keeping its huge staff busy.

In South Dakota, the bureau had already faltered at Belle Fourche (by 1946, only 2 of the original 580 homesteaders associated with the Belle Fourche project remained on the project), but they were ready to pursue another river valley project in the western part of the state. Their investigations revealed a likely area for irrigation near a prospective dam site in Perkins County. That notion ended up as a proposal in the Pick-Sloan Plan to irrigate sixty-six thousand acres in the Grand River basin. The bureau later reduced its irrigation goal along the Grand River to only twenty-eight thousand acres based on water availability. Apparently, water scarcity had not been part of their initial calculations. The Grand certainly flowed through grand country, with rugged, timbered breaks flanking the narrow, winding channel, but in most years the river was not canoeable by midsummer. Nevertheless, the agency began building an

$11 million dam named Shadehill on the Grand River in 1949. A body of water bigger than that which collects behind a small stock dam is rare in that part of western South Dakota, so there was much local anticipation about Shadehill dam and the lake it would create. The structure built by the bureau was impressive, measuring 12,843 feet in length and standing 145 feet high. Its impoundment, Shadehill reservoir, would have a capacity of 357,382 acre-feet and would cover nearly ten thousand acres.

As construction on the dam neared completion, in 1951, the bureau acknowledged that new uncertainties had arisen. In addition to doubts about adequate supplies of water, it was probable the area's soils could not be irrigated. Later, much of the land that was irrigated was ruined because both the water and the soils that were irrigated had a high sodium content. By the 1980s, virtually no irrigation was happening as part of the Shadehill Unit.

During the development of Shadehill, the bureau's commissioner was a man named Michael Straus. Straus was appointed at the end of World War II and ruled the agency until 1953. These were boom years for the bureau. It was the era of pork barrel aplenty, of unconscious federal spending with hardly a thought about consequences.

The term *pork barrel* has been defined as the government's treasury, into which politicians and government officials dip for funds, or pork, to plan and build projects. Its origin was likely the pre–Civil War South and the practice of plantation owners periodically distributing salt pork from huge barrels to their slaves. The slaves were said to madly rush toward the barrels, scrambling to grab as much as possible. The whites who stood safely to the side found the sight amusing. An 1863 magazine article helped popularize the expression, and by 1870 members of Congress commonly used the term and congratulated each other for securing "pork" for their states and districts. This approach flaunted excess and portended budgets sinking into deep deficits. Former Illinois Senator Paul H. Douglas mockingly described pork-barrel politics: "As groups win their battle for special expenditures, they lose the more important war for general economy. . . . They are like drunkards who shout for temperance in the intervals between cocktails."[7]

Perhaps the most extravagant pork-barrel politicking occurred in the realm of water-project legislation. Members of Congress routinely traded their votes for authorizations and appropriations to deepen harbors, straighten rivers, and develop dams, canals, irrigation projects, and navigable waterways for the folks back home. Some of the projects were useful, but many were wasteful and were promoted by businesses interested only in filling their bank accounts with fresh federal money.

So demanding and hungry for projects was Commissioner Straus that if a certain regional division was not as busy as he liked, he personally scolded those in the office. That was the case with the office for the Upper Missouri basin, located in Billings, Montana. Among the projects handled by the Missouri basin office was South Dakota's Oahe Unit. To rectify what Straus perceived as inadequate performance, he traveled to Billings, rented a movie theater, and demanded that every employee in the office attend a meeting there. According to Marc Reisner, writing in his epic exposé of the bureau titled *Cadillac Desert*, Straus issued a blunt challenge to the startled employees assembled before him. "I don't give a damn whether a project is feasible or not," Straus thundered, "I'm getting the money out of Congress and you'd damn well better spend it. And you'd better be here early tomorrow morning ready to spend it, or you may find someone else at your desk."[8] By Straus's final year as the bureau's leader, the agency was bustling in the scarcely populated upper Missouri basin: 21 projects were under construction, 70 projects were scheduled for construction, and at least 170 projects were being studied.[9]

The political condition fostering pork-barrel water projects was reaching its apex when the plans for Oahe were released in 1960. All across the country, massive water projects were cheered by the public and financed by the Congress. Oahe supporters were undeterred by the bureau's failures at Shadehill and Belle Fourche. They had forgotten Glenn Sloan's exaggeration. *Oahe! Oahe!* South Dakotans spoke the word enthusiastically, reverently. With so much irrigation proposed for its trade area, Aberdeen's leaders welcomed the return of the rainmaker.

There was also excitement in the countryside near Aberdeen. Consider the vantage. From their farms on the level lake plain along the James River, wannabe irrigators looked uphill and west toward Pierre, the Missouri River, and the anticipated beginning of the Pierre canal. They counted on the state's political leadership in Pierre to support irrigation just as they counted on the federal government to tap the Missouri and develop the infrastructure to deliver its water. Both seemed a smooth certainty. Every governor and all the state's congressmen since the adoption of Pick-Sloan had championed the Oahe Unit. And the Bureau of Reclamation's engineering plan to move water from the headworks of the Pierre canal at elevation 1,716 feet to the low-lying irrigation tracts at elevation 1,295 feet seemed a simple proposition. Oahe's development, both politically and topographically, was to be downhill all the way.

5

The Dean of Oahe

I still cherish the pen that President [Lyndon] Johnson used in signing the [Oahe authorization]. I also remember the pleasure I felt in early 1969 when, acting for the United States Government, I signed the repayment contract with the conservancy district in Aberdeen, South Dakota.
Ken Holum, letter in *South Dakota Magazine*, 1994

On 21 October 1961, Texas Congressman Walter Rogers spent a relaxed afternoon hunting pheasants on a farm near the James River, in Brown County, a dozen miles east of Aberdeen. Congressman Rogers, chairman of the House Sub-committee on Irrigation and Reclamation, was also a ranking member of the House Interior Committee, the committee responsible for dealing with reclamation projects such as Oahe. The land he hunted on would likely be part of the Oahe's ultimate irrigation plan. Hosting Rogers that day was a man named Ken Holum. Holum had recently moved from his James River farm to Washington DC to serve as an assistant secretary at the Department of Interior. Holum's post was prestigious and powerful and included supervising the commissioner of the Bureau of Reclamation.

Among those accompanying Rogers and Holum on their pheasant hunt was Nelson "Ned" Hundstad, Holum's cousin and Brown County's representative on the Oahe Conservancy Sub-district board of directors. Ken Holum was as familiar with the Oahe project and the area the project proposed to serve as anyone alive. His Norwegian grandfather homesteaded along the James River and that land remained in the Holum family. As a young man, Holum had diked the James in flood and watched it go dry during drought. Like Bob Hipple, Holum clearly remembered the devastation caused by weather during the 1930s and acknowledged that memories of those days forged his water-development philosophy. Holum's reference point to the beginning of the dust bowl was precise and tragic. In May 1933, Holum was seventeen years old and a freshman at Augustana College in Sioux Falls when it happened. "The heat and the drouth hit on the day my father died," Holum recalled. "And we lived through three years, 1933, 1934, 1936, where we harvested no crops."[1]

Ken Holum's appointment by President John F. Kennedy was no fluke. A tall man with a stern, thoughtful countenance, he had long been a leader in efforts to bring electricity and telephone service to rural areas, had helped organize electric and telephone cooperatives, was a former Democratic state legislator, and had made two bids for the U.S. Senate, although both, it turned out, were unsuccessful. In 1953, Holum served on the Missouri Basin Survey Commission, an important federal task force whose mission was to study water issues in the vast Missouri River watershed. Holum advised expedited development of the Oahe Irrigation Project, and his fellow commissioners agreed.

As a state legislator, Holum participated in hearings about Missouri River development alongside State Senators Frank Ferguson and Roy Houck, but the concerns of those two men never dimmed his enthusiasm about irrigation development in the James River valley. Holum felt federal irrigation was as vital to family farms as rural electricity, and he later said his two primary home-state ambitions while serving in the Interior Department were expansion of electric power for farmers and promotion of the Oahe Unit.

Oahe's outlook could have hardly seemed more promising than on that autumn afternoon in 1961. Holum, Rogers, and Hundstad occupied important positions from which to move Oahe forward. Their camaraderie suggested an auspicious future for South Dakota's unfulfilled irrigation dream. Holum's Oahe advocacy was supported by his boss, Interior Secretary Stewart Udall. Two days before the pheasant hunt, Holum and Udall were in Huron, where Udall addressed a crowded, enthusiastic rally for the Oahe Irrigation Project that was cosponsored by the Oahe Conservancy Sub-district and the Huron Chamber of Commerce. It had been Holum's idea to organize the gathering.

Despite the optimistic climate for irrigation development, Ken Holum faced a formidable barrier to Oahe's continued development as he began his work in Washington. A group of congressmen—including Wayne Aspinall from Colorado, a powerful reclamation booster—was uncomfortable with the lackluster revenues generated by the Missouri River program. Things had not improved much since Glenn Sloan tried to remedy similar problems. Critics said the region's short growing season made it difficult, if not impossible, for farmers to generate the profits necessary to offset the large investment required by irrigation agriculture. It was Ken Holum's responsibility to rewrite and gain political acceptance for a new Missouri basin repayment arrangement. If Holum failed, Oahe and other Missouri River irrigation projects would likely be mothballed.

After months of preparation, Holum presented a solution. His report, issued in December 1963, acknowledged that revenues for Missouri River projects were far below original forecasts. The reasons, Holum contended, included below-average surface water supplies and a shortage of facilities for electricity generation in the region. Holum suggested that interest rates charged to some projects be lowered from 3 percent to 2.5 percent. He advised that a longer and more lenient repayment schedule for certain water projects be adopted and that the rate charged for hydropower sales be increased.[2]

Holum took some heat from his friends in the electric cooperatives, but he held firm and convinced the Bureau of Budget that his proposal was justifiable. Then he surprised many by securing Wayne Aspinall's support. Aspinall, who chaired the House Committee on Interior and Insular Affairs, was crucial. Gaining congressional approval for the new Missouri basin repayment plan would be one of Holum's most meaningful accomplishments while at Interior. His success meant Oahe irrigation planning could continue.

The freshly elected directors of the newly formed Oahe Conservancy Sub-district had met for the first time on 4 January 1961 in Pierre. Fred Holscher, a farmer from Faulk County, was chosen by his colleagues to serve as the first chairman. Lloyd Miller, a businessman who lived on a farm just outside Huron, was chosen to be vice-chairman, Nelson Hundstad was selected as secretary, and Joe Grimes of the state's conservancy district office was appointed treasurer.

Fred Holscher was regarded as an honest man with a keen interest in developing the Oahe project. He had been part of the sub-district's original planning group, along with Bob Hipple, and he believed that local input and support were vital for Oahe to succeed. At the board's first meeting, Holscher was reluctant to accept advice from the Bureau of Reclamation. He preferred that the new board become more knowledgeable about its duties and the district's water needs before outside agencies were allowed to exert their influence. This desire for autonomy was admirable but proved to be unrealistic. Though the sub-district was established to assist local governments and individuals with water needs, the project that clearly dominated the board's time was the Oahe Unit. Because Oahe was a federal project, an intimate relationship with and frequent reliance on the Bureau of Reclamation were inevitable.

Despite its habit of casually spending millions of dollars on irrigation projects that lacked economic and environmental justification, Congress did insist that a verifiable local interest in each project exist. Not only was it necessary for local supporters to form conservancy organizations, but the formation of irrigation districts was essential as well. In a project such as Oahe, the irrigation districts would eventually assume much of the financial responsibility to maintain a project's infrastructure. M. E. VonSeggern, Oahe project manager for the Bureau of Reclamation, suggested the creation of six irrigation districts. The proposed Missouri Slope Irrigation District would be located in Sully and Potter Counties. The lake plain in Brown and Spink Counties would be divided into five irrigation districts. Two of them, the Redfield and Aberdeen Irrigation Districts, containing 75,100 acres and 98,700 acres respectively, would be in the west lake plain, and the east lake plain would contain three districts, Frankfort (87,700 acres), Groton (74,700 acres), and Claremont (106,800 acres).

Sub-district directors argued that fewer districts would be easier to organize. It marked one of the few occasions that the sub-district not only differed with the bureau on a major issue but also managed to prevail. It was agreed that three separate districts would be initially organized: one in Brown County, one in Spink County, and a third in the Missouri Slope area. The districts to be formed in Brown and Spink Counties would include land west of the James River. It was hoped that lands east of the river could be organized in the future.

An effort to form the Missouri Slope district began as early as 1961 with the formation of a water resources committee guided by the local office of the state extension service. Petitions were circulated among affected landowners and presented to county commissioners as proof that sufficient support existed to call an election to form the irrigation district. According to state law, county commissioners were to examine the petitions, approve them if satisfactory, conduct public hearings, determine the boundaries of a proposed district, and, ultimately, set a public election on the proposal.

A critical showdown between Missouri Slope irrigation promoters and their opposition came at a May 1964 joint hearing of the Sully and Potter County Commissions. The petitions had been reviewed, and it was time for the two commissions to establish the district's boundaries formally and endorse a date for a public vote.

Sully County Commissioner Art Wittler said he and others, including some of his county's most prominent farmers and ranchers, opposed the district. Then Wittler made a motion to reject the petitions and sanction no election. Twice commissioners voted to support his motion. It may have been the first time any government body took direct action specifically against the Oahe Irrigation Project. Oahe supporters were incensed by the setback. It was suggested that new petitions be circulated and that those who did not wish to irrigate be deleted from the district. To resurrect the Missouri Slope district, the district's size was cut from 120,000 to 50,000 acres, including only about 25,000 irrigable acres.

A public hearing on 13 September 1965 drew a determined, noisy crowd. Opponents, organized as the Oahe Dryland Farmers, claimed the district's new boundaries were gerrymandered to eliminate opponents from voting. They complained that although the new proposal was substantially smaller than the version rejected earlier, the same system of canals and ditches would be used. ''We were expected to absorb the impacts to our land from canals but they didn't want us to vote,'' recalled Ken Marsh, a leader of the dryland farmers.[3]

South Dakota Attorney General Frank Farrar advised the county commission to approve an election, and a public vote was set for 25 January 1966. But Marsh and his colleagues fought back with a lawsuit that delayed the election. The case eventually landed in the state supreme court, where it was determined that a vote on the proposed district must be held. By the time the election was conducted, in May 1970, a new Oahe plan had been authorized by Congress, and the Missouri Slope district was not included in the project's irrigation areas. Still, 90 percent of the landowners in the proposed district supported formation. The bureau referred to the Missouri Slope as future development.

The process of forming irrigation districts in Brown and Spink Counties also began in 1961 when the extension service conducted landowner surveys. Although most residents in cities and towns favored Oahe, support in the country was not nearly as strong. Residents of rural Brown County were about evenly split for and against the project, though many respondents were undecided. Spink County farmers favored Oahe 55 percent to 35 percent, with about 10 percent unsure.[4]

The effort to organize the districts intensified in 1963. As was the case in the Missouri Slope area, it was a joint effort, linking the state extension service, local volunteers formed into committees, the Oahe sub-district, and the Bureau of Reclamation. Before kicking off the petition drive supporting formation of the proposed 170,000-acre West Brown Irrigation District, supporters placed a series of four articles in a weekly newspaper serving many of the landowners in the proposed district. Bath area farmer Allen Sperry, a friend and neighbor of Ken Holum and chairman of both the Brown County Extension Board and the Brown County Water Resources Development Committee, was quoted extensively in the articles. Sperry and other Oahe supporters realized there were apprehensions about irrigation. Sperry assured landowners that formation of the district did not obligate anyone to the Oahe Unit. "It is to everyone's advantage, regardless of his or her feelings toward irrigation," said Sperry, "to sign the petition and to cast a yes vote for the formation of an irrigation district. . . . Formation of a district will not obligate us to the construction of the [Oahe] project."[5]

In Spink County, a similar campaign was simultaneously conducted to promote a proposed 320,000-acre irrigation district. Three public hearings were held in the summer of 1964 at the county courthouse in Redfield. The first hearing was an orderly affair, attended by about two hundred farmers and others interested in the project. Audience questions indicated that at least some of those at the meeting knew very little about the federal irrigation program and Oahe. Things did not go smoothly at the second hearing, held a week later. Word had spread that the irrigation project was a complicated matter with an abundance of liabilities. An atmosphere of tension filled the room as a speech denouncing federal irrigation was made and questions about tough issues like drainage and the federal law limiting each landowner to 160 acres of irrigation were asked. Many farmers in the James River valley owned more than 160 acres of land in the designated irrigation areas. They would be forced to sell land to comply with federal law.[6]

The Bureau of Reclamation and the extension service suggested that certain landowners faced with losing most of their farms because of the 160-acre limitation be omitted from the project. Landowners who chose to remain in the proposed irrigation district were given the opportunity to remove pieces of their property from the district. They could also request that lands not included in the original proposal be added to the district. Colored sheets of paper were made available to landowners to signify their intentions: if a landowner submitted a green form, it signified a wish to add a tract to the district. A white form demonstrated a wish to have certain land excluded. Within days, Spink County landowners presented ninety-seven colored sheets to their county commission. Only three of the sheets were green. Eventually, about 370 farm families asked that some 80,000 acres be dropped from the proposed district. When the commissioners met on 18 November to set a date for an election to form the Spink County Irrigation District, about 206,000 acres remained.

Brown County commissioners faced a more severe land withdrawal. Approximately 35 percent of the land originally proposed for the West Brown Irrigation District—more than 60,000 acres—was removed following landowner requests. About 150 farmers turned in white sheets. This left slightly more than 100,000 acres in the proposed district.[7]

Because of the removed property, maps of the proposed districts showed disjointed, noncontiguous configurations of land. While this meant that the Oahe project had lost a sizeable chunk of irrigation land, it also meant that opposition to irrigation had been eliminated from the election process. By withdrawing their property from a proposed irrigation district, landowners forfeited their opportunity to vote for or against district formation.

The troubles facing Missouri Slope organizers and the resistance to irrigation along the James River caused irrigation supporters to rethink the project's size. The bureau determined that a 190,000-acre first stage was feasible in terms of satisfying federal cost-benefit requirements and was within what the sub-district could afford. The bureau surmised it could count on the support of landowners representing 190,000 acres on the western side of the James River in Brown and Spink Counties. Missouri Slope organizers were stymied by a legal challenge, and it appeared they would not be able to deliver an officially formed district in time for authorization. Before proceeding with the 190,000-acre approach, the bureau had to convince the sub-district's directors that it was an acceptable plan. In a 14 December 1964 letter to his board, the sub-district's manager, James Lewis, candidly described the situation. "As you are well aware," he began, "in the near future some hard decisions are going to have to be made by the Board of Directors regarding what size the initial first stage development of the Oahe Unit should be. As you know differences of opinion exist."[8] Lewis explained that an analysis had been performed to determine how much irrigation acreage the sub-district could afford. "There are some doubts in the bureau's circles regarding the advisability of the sub-district underwriting anything over the 190,000 acres," he wrote.[9]

Another complicating factor was a law passed by Congress in summer 1964 that prohibited the expenditure of construction funds on any unbuilt Missouri basin project until that project had been reauthorized by Congress. Though Oahe had been initially authorized in the 1944 Flood Control Act, it now faced the scrutiny of a reauthorization process. Oahe's chances for reauthorization, said political insiders, were much better if project scale and costs were reduced.

The issue reached a climax at the sub-district's 18 December 1964 board meeting. Ken Holum, Senators Karl Mundt and George McGovern, South Dakota Governor Archie Gubbrud, and the bureau's regional chief, Harold Aldrich, all endorsed a 190,000-acre project. The directors viewed 190,000 acres as a setback. Each had served on the board since the sub-district's inception, and their earliest expectation had been to provide water for 750,000 acres. Just four years earlier, the bureau had slashed Oahe's first-stage irrigation to 298,000 acres. There was plenty of disappointment acompanying that recommendation. Now the directors were being advised by the state's leading politicians to endorse another drastic reduction.

Ken Holum defended the 190,000-acre first stage by comparing Oahe with other Bureau of Reclamation projects. "Most large irrigation projects were authorized in stages," he explained, calling Oahe's initial stage a "good beginning," and a means to get the project "under construction as quickly as possible."[10] Holum said that receiving congressional authorization for the first stage meant subsequent authorizations were likelier, leading to eventual development of a half-million-acre project. The sub-district's directors reluctantly voted to support a first phase of 190,000 acres. To placate their reservations, the board also voted to begin preparations for a second stage authorization, involving additional acres.

When elections to form the two irrigation districts in the lake plain were held on 5 January 1965, the outcome was not surprising. Many irrigation opponents had been removed from the decision-making process, and those who remained had been assured that by endorsing formation they were not obligating themselves to the Oahe project.

In Spink County, 82 percent of the landowners who voted approved the irrigation district: the final count was 330 for and only 69 against. The irrigation district proposed for Brown County was approved by a similar margin. Of 270 votes cast, 222 supported formation. Following the elections, the county commissions in Brown and Spink Counties officially established the irrigation districts.[11]

Despite the favorable elections, there were signs that all was not well regarding the Oahe project. Opponents pointed to low voter turnout as a sign of indifference or uneasiness. Only 54 percent of the eligible landowners in the Spink County district and 60 percent in the West Brown district participated in the elections. The large amount of land withdrawn and the number of landowners who had opted out of the districts added weight to the warning. C. W. Renz, the sub-district director representing rural Campbell and McPherson Counties, expressed his concern about the low voter turnout and lands withdrawn in a letter to the extension service. "As I read the pulse of the electorate, directly benefiting from irrigation," wrote Renz, "matters do not look good in the sub-district in general."[12]

52

Renz's interpretation was far different from that of most other Oahe supporters. The day after the elections, Ned Hundstad wrote new South Dakota Governor Nils Boe and described the popularity of the Oahe project. "We believe the outcome of this election demonstrates, far greater than words, the tremendous interest local people directly concerned have in the development of the Oahe Unit," said Hundstad.[13] Ken Holum issued a similar observation: "This decision will hasten the day when Missouri River water will be at work stimulating the economy of the fertile James River valley and the entire state."[14] In a boldly worded headline, the *Huron Daily Plainsman* announced: "Brown, Spink in Favor of Irrigation."[15]

And so, despite Allen Sperry's earlier explanation that district formation would not be viewed as a reflection of landowner support for Oahe, project boosters immediately used the election results as proof that farmers wanted Oahe.

To continue developing the Oahe project, the sub-district needed to expand its powers. One necessary new tool was the authority to execute contracts with federal, state, and local entities of government. Such an expansion of power required the approval of voters in the sub-district.

After a series of lightly attended public hearings and a promotional campaign led by the extension service, about 75 percent of those voting in the sub-district on 8 November 1966 approved contract authority. The vote was viewed as another public endorsement of the Oahe project. In addition to its new abilities to enter into contracts, the sub-district could levy taxes up to one mill on personal and real property and had the power to use eminent domain to acquire property. These potent tools would allow the sub-district to sponsor and be caretaker of the Oahe project.

After years of negotiations, the sub-district and the federal government agreed to a master contract on 8 January 1969. The contract obligated sub-district taxpayers to support and maintain the Oahe project for forty years once construction was complete. The sub-district also signed contracts with the two irrigation districts. Under the master contract, repair, maintenance, and operations costs of the project would be the responsibility of the sub-district and the project's irrigators. The federal government was excused from any legal liabilities as the result of damages caused by the project. Irrigation opponents did not hesitate to point out that the contract did not guarantee the availability of sufficient water for the project. In fact, the Bureau of Reclamation specified that "water allocated to the project would be retrievable if higher value uses should arise at some future time."[16]

The master contract also required the sub-district to pay more than $30 million of the project's construction costs, most of which would be paid by irrigators. There would also be a charge for using Missouri River water: the federal government would annually bill the sub-district thirty cents for each acre irrigated.

South Dakota's congressional delegation anticipated that gaining authorization for a 190,000-acre project would be an uncomplicated matter. Senator Karl Mundt noted that President Lyndon Johnson had already asked for $2 million to begin building North Dakota's Garrison irrigation project. "Oahe is next in line," proclaimed Mundt.[17]

Although support for Oahe authorization was organized and strong in South Dakota, there were obstacles, including the federal government's financial limitations because of its obligations to the war effort in Vietnam. A second obstacle surfaced during field hearings on Oahe.

The setting was Huron, where members of the House of Representatives Sub-committee on Irrigation and Reclamation met with South Dakotans on 27 October 1967. South Dakota's Governor Boe had just completed his testimony when Congressman John Saylor—a Republican from Pennsylvania and a leading congressional conservationist, as well as the ranking minority member of the Committee on Interior and Insular Affairs—issued a frank challenge. "Governor," said Saylor, whose support for Oahe was vital, "one of the things that disturbs me—." He then referred to the Oahe project map before continuing: "It seems that there are many areas . . . that are going to be developed for fish and wildlife. I think this a good feature of the project, but I read in the hunting license which I purchased . . . that the [federal] stamp I bought to hunt . . . ducks and geese is not recognized in your State, and those who come from out of the State are not permitted to shoot them."[18] Since 1947, South Dakota had prohibited out-of-state-residents from hunting waterfowl. Such parochialism upset Saylor, especially when federal funds were to be expended for a project that included wildlife benefits in its cost-benefit analysis. He pressed Boe to remove the prohibition.

The following spring, Governor Boe again faced a concerned Congressman Saylor. This time Boe was in Washington testifying in support of Oahe authorization. Boe had already been informed by Congressman Aspinall that, because of the Vietnam War, money was tight. When Aspinall finished, Congressman Saylor asked Governor Boe if the state legislature had agreed to allow nonresident hunters to shoot waterfowl. Boe didn't have good news. "We have had a problem here," replied Boe. Trying to salvage Saylor's confidence, the governor added, "I believe . . . our legislature will . . . come forth with a solution that will be satisfactory."[19] Congressman Saylor was not pleased. Don't be surprised, he warned Boe, if the Oahe authorization bill passed by Congress requires a change in your statutes regarding who can hunt migratory waterfowl in your state. Despite their warnings, Aspinall and Saylor praised Oahe. They were joined by other congressmen, as well as by South Dakotans who attended the hearings.

At each hearing, including the three field hearings in South Dakota, a parade of project proponents came forward to ask Congress to build Oahe. Project opponents made no effort to present their case. If there ever had been a critical occasion for opponents to express their concerns, it was at the authorization hearings. But opposition voices were mostly silent.

At the Senate's Water and Power Resources Sub-committee hearing, held in Washington on 13 September 1967, South Dakota's congressional delegation repeated the time-honored litany of arguments favoring Oahe. Senator McGovern cited the federal government's obligation to South Dakota. "It was the promise of large-scale irrigation development that caused us to accept the sacrifices and the loss of rich riverbottom land that was necessary to make possible the enormous flood [control] potential, navigation, power generation and irrigation reservoirs on the Missouri River," McGovern declared.[20] Senator Karl Mundt, who sometimes had his statements composed by the Bureau of Reclamation, reiterated McGovern's point and also described the benefits the project would have on South Dakota agriculture and the state in general. "The primary impact [of Oahe]," said Mundt, "would be the stabilization of farm production and income."[21] Ken Holum testified that it was his hope, and South Dakota's as well, that eventually the Oahe project would be expanded beyond the initial stage. "Actually, in 1944 we were thinking about a 750,000-acre project. I think the State still is. I think we [the federal government] still are. . . . I think the goal still is to move to the 495,000 acres and then to move to the 750,000 acres."[22]

Less than two months after the Senate's hearing in Washington, a House of Representatives sub-committee conducted a field hearing on Oahe in Redfield, South Dakota. Nearly a thousand people turned out to demonstrate their support for the project. That hearing, however, was marked by an interesting anomaly—an interruption in the procession of Oahe proponents who made their way to the podium. Dr. Russell Berry was an agricultural economist and a professor at South Dakota State University. He bravely stood before the huge crowd and testified that building Oahe was a mistake. His was the only statement against Oahe. Dr. Berry called attention to the small number of farmers who would benefit from Oahe: "We need to remember that it [Oahe] is going to affect something less that 1 percent of the farmers in the State. We have 50,000 farmers [in South Dakota], and there are 500 farmers involved in this first phase of this irrigation project."[23] Then he attacked the project's per-acre costs and accused the Bureau of Reclamation of misrepresenting project benefits.

Before Berry could elaborate on that charge, Congressman Harold Johnson, chairman of the Subcommittee on Irrigation and Reclamation and a California Democat, abruptly interrupted. "The economists and the Bureau of Reclamation people who work on this project with local people under your existing State laws have proved feasibility . . . for this project," he snapped.[24] Dr. Berry did not respond and resumed reading his statement. Again he was interrupted by Congressman Johnson, who asked Berry to submit his complaints in writing. "Now, the time is short," commanded Johnson, "and we have several other people [waiting to testify]. . . . We have given you ample opportunity."[25]

South Dakota Congressman E. Y. Berry then addressed a question to Dr. Berry. "You are employed at the State university at Brookings?" "Yes," answered Dr. Berry. "In what department, did you say?" "Economics," said Dr. Berry. "Well, your views do not agree with other departments of the State University at Brookings, do they?" "That is their privilege," replied the professor.[26]

Next to address Dr. Berry was Congressman Phillip Burton. Like Harold Johnson, Burton was from California and was an ardent defender of federal irrigation. "May I say that I used to teach at a state university, and I think that university salaries are far too low," said Congressman Burton. "I agree," replied Dr. Berry. "I am going back to Washington and hopefully next year get a chance to vote for this project," announced Burton. "And one of the reasons I am going to do it is not because of fish and wildlife and farming and all this that is going to be improved, but for your salary because when you increase the tax base . . . the state has more money to pay its professors. I think you will be glad we did some day."[27]

Dr. Berry's testimony and continued opposition to Oahe would eventually make him a target at South Dakota State University. He soon became embroiled in a battle with the university over pay raises and tenure. Though a special faculty committee at one time supported Berry's claim that he was discriminated against because of his work against Oahe and other unpopular activities, the professor never realized satisfaction in his complaint against the university.[28]

The bill to reauthorize Oahe reached the floor of the House of Representatives on 16 July 1968. The Senate had already endorsed the measure. Congressman Aspinall made the motion to authorize the project but said that such authorization did not guarantee money for construction. Congressman Saylor then insisted that future appropriation of construction monies be contingent on South Dakota reversing its ban on nonresident hunting.[29] The bill passed the House 264 to 128, with Saylor's hunting provision intact. It was signed into law by President Johnson on 3 August 1968.

Despite pressure from the Oahe sub-district, the South Dakota legislature was slow to respond to Saylor's requirement, and the situation remained unresolved during the 1968 and 1969 legislative sessions. Finally, in 1970, the legislature repealed the ban. That opened the door for construction to begin, and the Nixon administration recommended that Oahe receive $500,000 for fiscal year 1971. The Oahe sub-district board, however, requested $850,000; the board wanted the additional $350,000 so the Bureau of Reclamation could begin building the project's pumping plant next to Oahe reservoir.

The administration's resistance to providing additional monies faded in the wake of misfortune. Karl Mundt, facing reelection in 1972, had been stricken by a stroke in November 1969 and was unable to attend to his Senate duties. It appeared that the state's governor would eventually appoint a replacement for him. That meant Republican Governor Frank Farrar's 1972 reelection campaign took on added importance, and the White House offered to help Governor Farrar improve his chances of winning. Farrar was told that the Nixon administration would support funding for three South Dakota projects. Of course, the governor would receive the credit for moving these projects forward. Farrar's choices included an upgrade of nuclear missiles in western South Dakota, development of a satellite research facility (EROS) north of Sioux Falls, and augmented funding for Oahe.[30]

While the House of Representatives balked at the request for extra Oahe money, the Senate supported South Dakota and the bureau. In joint conference, a compromise was struck. It was agreed that the project would receive $850,000, but the additional funds were to be spent on land acquisition, not construction activities. Faced with a slumping national economy and rising inflation, the federal Bureau of the Budget opposed construction start-ups for massive public works projects such as Oahe. But the extra monies were appropriated, just as the White House promised.[31]

Despite the boost given his reelection campaign, Farrar became one of many incumbent Republican governors to fall in 1970, losing to Richard Kneip. Democrats also triumphed in the state's two congressional races, with Frank Denholm and James Abourezk winning the seats vacated by the retiring Ben Reifel and E. Y. Berry. The loss of those two veterans and Karl Mundt's poor health diminished South Dakota's political clout in Washington and portended tough times ahead for Oahe appropriations.

In early 1971, Oahe suffered a setback when the Nixon administration informed South Dakota that construction money for Oahe would not be included in the 1972 budget. To get the project back on track, Senator McGovern and Congressmen Denholm and Abourezk suggested that the sub-district hire Ken Holum. Holum had left the Interior Department when Lyndon Johnson departed the White House, but continued to reside in Washington, where he worked as a lobbyist and consultant for natural-resource developers. At its March 1971 meeting, the sub-district board voted to offer Holum a contract. But it was far from a unanimous decision. Bob Hipple and four other directors opposed the hiring. Holum would also provide consulting services to the West Brown Irrigation District.

In August 1972, during his reelection campaign against the Democrats and Senator George McGovern, President Nixon signed a Public Works Appropriations Act that included $1.55 million to initiate Oahe construction in 1973. Though Oahe's breakthrough was due in great part to Ken Holum, Holum's employment with the sub-district had been terminated by the time the appropriation was secured; earlier in the year, at their 20 January meeting, sub-district directors had voted 7–4 to cancel his contract. It was an odd move, considering Holum's connections and expertise. Apparently, the predominantly Republican sub-district board was not comfortable employing a partisan Democrat like Holum. The board's decision infuriated George McGovern, James Abourezk, and Frank Denholm and prompted an angry letter from them to Fred Holscher. "The Board's action [releasing Holum]," wrote the politicians, "forces us to inquire whether or not we have their [the Board's] support in that effort . . . to see the first phase [of Oahe] completed in the shortest period of time."[32] All three men, along with Governor Richard Kneip, asked the board to reconsider. Their advice, at least for the moment, went unheeded.

Oahe supporters celebrated the news that their project had finally received construction money. In a front-page story in the *Aberdeen American News*, the Aberdeen Chamber of Commerce proclaimed that "virtually every South Dakotan will be touched by expanding irrigation development that should open a new era of prosperity and stability before the State celebrates its centennial in 1989."[33]

Aberdeen, with a population of twenty-four thousand, was the largest community in the irrigation area, and its leaders expected to attract much of the economic and population growth associated with Oahe. The local chamber of commerce reported that the city's population would quickly swell to thirty-seven thousand because of the Oahe project. The project's economic boost to the area was projected to be equally dramatic. Using figures provided by the Bureau of Reclamation, the chamber of commerce proclaimed that retail, service, and wholesale sectors and agricultural processing and production would benefit by more than $71 million for the project's first phase and $185 million for full operation.

These forecasts were exciting news for a remote, often overlooked region of America's outback. Aberdeen's bankers, agricultural suppliers, real-estate agents, and other business interests were ecstatic. There were rumors of a new shopping mall for the community. An ambitious hotel development had already been launched. Plans to build a second hospital were unveiled. Appearing prominently in the center of the *American News* article was a graphic depicting drops of rain falling on a farm scene. The words "WATER OUR GOLDEN FUTURE" accompanied the artwork. That graphic and its text symbolized the newspaper's strong support for Oahe, and they appeared in every newspaper issue during 1972 and for many years after. Similar promotions in other South Dakota newspapers aroused the public and caused a widespread clamoring for the project.

With such euphoria sweeping South Dakota's business and political leaders, how could Ken Holum or anyone else have suspected that the project's greatest challenges lay ahead? It seemed far-fetched to think that the emerging environmental movement would take an interest in a water project proposed for a rural, agricultural state. And who could have predicted that the simmering opposition among farmers in the sub-district was about to erupt into a firestorm?

6

The Dissidents

We were fighting a battle against the Bureau of Reclamation as individuals until United Family Farmers arrived. . . . We weren't organized until George Piper organized us.

Ted Albright, interview

Around the kitchen table in their parents' farm home, George and Bill Piper gathered several neighbors in the summer of 1972 to share with them what they had just learned about the proposed Oahe Irrigation Project. Dressed in overalls and drinking coffee, the farmers sitting in a circle had for many years heard vague stories about a great plan to bring water from the Missouri River to the James River valley. They had heard about ranchers near Pierre fighting against an irrigation district. And they remembered Frank Ferguson's opposition in Sanborn County. But generally, despite an absence of details, enthusiasm in their rural area for the plan was high. The newspaper in nearby Huron constantly reminded them that Oahe meant progress.

The Pipers had been campaigning door-to-door in their farm neighborhood for a friend of Bill's who was a candidate in the 1972 Republican primary for the U.S. Senate when they discovered the startling news. One of the people they called on was a member of the Beadle County Planning Commission. Before the Pipers left his doorstep, the man produced a map he had been given at a recent meeting. It showed the location of a dam to be built as part of the Oahe Irrigation Project. Pointing to elevation lines, the planning commissioner explained what the blueprint meant. An expansion of the existing Byron reservoir would inundate 75 percent of the Pipers' land—about a thousand acres—and drown their parents' farm home on the site homesteaded by their grandfather in 1882. Seven other farm homes and 160 cottages along Lake Byron would also be flooded. To enlarge Lake Byron, the federal government planned to acquire 9,100 acres.

Virgil Gilbert was one of the farmers in the Piper kitchen. Thirty years earlier, Gilbert helped organize the Beadle County Rural Electric Cooperative, and since then he had been a fixture on its board of directors. He thought he understood the issues affecting land and people around him, but Piper's information came as a surprise to him. "I discovered Oahe would ruin half my farm," Gilbert exclaimed. "It would have flooded all my summer pasture, about five hundred or six hundred acres."[1] None of the other men at the table would be as severely impacted as the Pipers or Virgil Gilbert, but learning the bittersweet details about a project they had applauded for so many years stunned them.

Despite the widespread and significant ramifications of a project as massive as Oahe, details about the project had been closely held by the Bureau of Reclamation. Media coverage about Oahe had been devoted to project accomplishments, such as formation of irrigation districts, or the agricultural stability and economic growth the project would bring. So intent were newspapers and other news sources on championing Oahe that investigative journalism was nonexistent. Not only were media outlets reluctant to report the project's possible negative impacts, there was also a loose conspiracy among several of the state's key newspapers to promote Oahe. This conspiracy extended to the Bureau of Reclamation, which provided promotional information and encouragement to the newspapers.

Bureau official George Stapleton, from the agency's regional office in Billings, Montana, spent a week in South Dakota talking to newspapers about Oahe. His conclusions of that tour were shared with an agency official in Washington DC. "I am convinced," wrote Stapleton in his communication, "the media outlets in the state [South Dakota] openly favor the Oahe project and will and do cooperate fully in publicizing material related to the Oahe project."[2] Newspaper publishers in Huron and Aberdeen held strategy sessions with the Associated Press regarding Oahe coverage and how to promote the project.[3] This was irresponsible journalism as well as a public disservice. Already, two Bureau of Reclamation irrigation projects in the state had floundered. The agency's local track record was not good, but Oahe's cheerleaders in the newspaper business were not willing to inform their readers about that.

Early on, the Pipers admitted, they didn't know enough about the Oahe project to be for or against it. "In the beginning," recalled George Piper, "we weren't opposed to Oahe. We simply wanted more information. We had lots of questions. . . . We were no longer going to take Oahe for granted."[4] George

Piper began making regular visits to the bureau's Huron office. The staff there rarely received inquiries from the public, and they could not remember anyone having asked such penetrating questions. It had been only four years since Piper had earned a Ph.D. in zoology from the University of Missouri. After teaching college in Chicago for a year, he had yearned for the quiet and calm of his South Dakota home. He had come back to work with his family on their farm, and he found himself back in school, a student in a self-imposed program with a goal of quickly learning as much as he could about the Oahe project.

Piper's return to South Dakota and his interest in Oahe were fortuitous for their timing. The environmental movement had just started, and a new sensitivity about environmental matters was emerging in Washington and elsewhere around the country. Piper's studies at the University of Missouri familiarized him with environmental concepts, and he was not intimidated by the scientific and bureaucratic jargon that filled bureau documents.

In the early 1970s, a series of significant environmental laws were passed, including the National Environmental Policy Act, or NEPA. This measure, signed into law by President Nixon on 1 January 1970, was arguably the most important piece of environmental legislation the government had ever enacted. Among the act's features was a mandate that federal agencies forecast the environmental consequences of their projects and disclose this information in the form of an environmental impact statement, a document that soon became known by its acronym, EIS. For the first time, the environmental issues associated with federal projects would be identified and would be critical factors in justifying a project. Not only did NEPA require agencies to compile such statements, it also required hearings be held to take testimony from the public about the project and the suitability of the impact statement. Never before had citizens and local government officials been given such an opportunity to participate in federal decision making.

Agencies such as the Bureau of Reclamation resisted NEPA requirements and struggled to fulfill the act's obligations. The bureau's difficulties assembling the Oahe EIS were described by former bureau official Art Moran. Moran had come to South Dakota in 1950 to work on early Oahe studies, and he rose through the ranks to become the project's chief of planning from 1970 to 1979. In the project's earliest days, said Moran, the bureau's emphasis was on locating the most expeditious route for the project's main canals between the Missouri River and the James River. The agency gave little pause to the wetlands that would be drained by the canals, or to the creeks that would be severed or the aquifers that would be pierced. It was not until 1956 that the bureau started taking a serious look at the irrigability of soils in the James River valley. It now seems an illogical sequence: to invest years toward planning a system of canals before determining the practicality of their purpose.

When environmentalists and their new laws confronted the bureau's old-fashioned emphasis on engineering, there was much animosity and confusion in the agency. "The environmental ballgame had started," remembered Art Moran, "and we were trying to play catch-up."[5] Moran recalled that the draft and final versions of Oahe's EIS necessitated research that his agency had not undertaken, despite having planned the project for more than twenty years. "As we started writing this [EIS] statement," Moran explained, "we were learning each day. . . . There were probably quite a few aspects that had not been looked at before on the Oahe Unit which [we were now] required to do." Compounding the uncertainty, said Moran, was the fact that the Huron office had never before prepared an impact statement.[6]

In late November 1972, George and Bill Piper were among a large crowd at a public hearing in Aberdeen to review and discuss Oahe's draft EIS. The document provided the most comprehensive description of the project yet released by the federal government. The meeting was orderly, with time constraints on statements. Surprisingly, testimony was split for and against the project. Most of the opposition came from environmentalists representing fledgling groups in South Dakota or national groups such as the Sierra Club and the National Audubon Society.

While the Pipers had been drawn to the meeting because of the land they could lose beneath Lake Byron, the chief apprehension of environmentalists was for the fate of the James River. They feared that return flows from irrigation would pollute the small river and that channelization would wreck its riparian ecology, destroying fish and wildlife resources and ruining the river's fragile natural character. Environmentalists contended the draft EIS did not adequately address the river's natural values. They wanted the government to describe alternatives that would prevent the river's destruction.

Oahe supporters claimed that channelization would enhance the river. They complained that environmentalists were meddling unnecessarily and threatening a project of great economic importance. Ken Holum had grown up along the river and had spent many hours shoring up dikes to protect farmland from flooding. He also remembered the river running dry. "Some rivers can be improved by man," said Holum, defending return flows and channelization as a means to improve the uncooperative James.[7]

Bud Maher, publisher of the Huron newspaper, portrayed river modifications as an improvement for wildlife. When dozens of fish died in the river from oxygen deprivation, a natural circumstance that occurs periodically in localized reaches of shallow rivers like the James, Maher used the event to slam environmentalists and promote Oahe. Beneath a large photo showing dead, floating fish, Maher inserted a headline that declared "Why We Need Oahe!" In the accompanying text, Maher stated that the Oahe project would make the James a better river for wildlife. "Return flows from irrigation," wrote Maher, "will provide for a continuous flow of water, which will eliminate the type of fish kill witnessed here last weekend."[8] Maher's conclusion found an accepting audience. Most of his readers misunderstood the ecological impacts of channelization and overlooked the environmental values of the James River.

Lacking whitewater rapids, rocky gorges, and clear water, the James was not the subject of flattering photographic essays. What most South Dakotans knew about the river they had learned from newspaper headlines that berated the river's springtime flooding or its dry channel during drought. Not only did the river lack dramatic scenery, it lacked commercial applications. It was too small for shipping, too shallow for motorboats, too irregular and flat for hydropower, and too murky and warm to lure trophy anglers to its waters. As rivers go, it seemed worthless, not worthy.

But the young environmental movement understood what was at stake. They knew the James provided a significant concentration of wildlife habitat found in few other places in agricultural South Dakota. Because of flooding, a substantial amount of land along the river was not intensively farmed, and a corridor of varied habitats, including woodlands, riparian wetlands, and brushy backwaters, followed the winding channel. An impressive and abundant variety of bird species, in particular, benefited. Environmentalists also admired the river's beauty: its circuitous channel meandered beneath towering elms and cottonwoods and through great groves of mature bur oaks, panoramic hillsides covered with grasses and wild flowers gently sloped to the river's edge.

Created and sustained by the topography, soils, and climate of the prairie, the James is a narrow, slow-moving, dark-watered river with an expansive sphere of influence. Its watershed region is inordinately large—some twenty-two thousand square miles—for its small channel, and its length is also considerable. From a birthplace amid a labyrinth of sloughs and potholes in central North Dakota, the James lazily wanders southward to its confluence with the Missouri River near Yankton, South Dakota. A straight line drafted on a map from where the James begins to where it ends would measure only three hundred miles. But that is deceptive, for the curly path taken by the river channel is more than seven hundred miles long. It is the Missouri's longest tributary—longer than other, more storied rivers such as the Platte or the Yellowstone, and it is fondly, or not so fondly, referred to by locals as the longest unnavigable river in the world.

At one time, the James was highly valued by the people who lived on the prairie it drains. The Sioux named the river Cansunsun; its shady forests were attractive to these Indians who called the open plains their home. The earliest whites in the region used its course as a navigational tool and built trading posts and shanty settlements on its banks. Joseph Nicollet, the distinguished cartographer and explorer, was one of the first white men to travel along the James River. In an 1836 expedition, he and his party departed Fort Pierre, along the Missouri River, and set out for the James. The map he produced as a result of that journey used the name Tchan-sansan—meaning river of the white woods. Both the Sioux name and that used by Nicollet refer to the shiny white trees found along the river. Apparently, these trees had perished in prairie fires and their barkless skins were bleached white by the sun. Nicollet also designated the James as the Riviere aux Jacques, reflecting the French name given the river in 1794 by Jean Trudeau, a French trader. Years later, the river became known by this name in its anglicized form. An early Dakota Territory legislature provided the river with a different name, the Dakota River, though this name has rarely been used. In 1907, the United States Geographic Board approved a request by the Rand & McNally mapmaking company to officially adopt the river's name as the James. This was consistent with references by the federal postal service and the U.S. Geological Survey. Today's James River is often called the Jim, a localized slang that is folksier than the river's more formal moniker.[9]

Nicollet's initial destination on the James River during the 1836 expedition was a location in what is now southern Brown County—a large grove called Oak Wood Settlement, or to use its Sioux name, Otuuhu-oju—place where the oaks spring up. Each summer, thousands of Indian people from around the northern plains met in the cool shade of the woods there to conduct a trading fair. While journeying north along the Jacques, the well-traveled Nicollet bestowed a remarkable tribute to the small prairie river, referring to the James and its valley as "perhaps the most beautiful within the territory of the United States."[10]

By the middle of the nineteenth century, aspiring farmers and merchants were moving up the James River valley into Indian country. A band of Yankton Sioux under Chief Drifting Goose harassed white settlers along the river as late as 1879, and the federal government responded by creating a reservation of sixty-five thousand acres for Drifting Goose along the James in what is now northern Spink County. The reservation centered around a large island that had become Drifting Goose's favorite camping and gardening place. Barely a year later, Drifting Goose was induced to abandon his land in exchange for special concessions at the Crow Creek reservation on the shore of the Missouri River. The order creating his James River sanctuary was revoked, and the chief and his band were moved permanently to Crow Creek. Drifting Goose's reservation may have been the shortest-lived reservation in the history of the United States.

When intensive agriculture became an influential presence, the James River and its broad basin changed rapidly. In only a few decades, nearly every square foot of native prairie was plowed under. Eroded soil, blown by winds or carried by tributaries, choked the already limited river channel, diminishing capacity and increasing flooding. After a huge flood in 1920, the South Dakota legislature initiated the first close look at the river. The study, conducted by W. S. Reeves, determined that 94,640 acres of land along the James in South Dakota had been submerged during 1920, including nearly 38,000 acres in Brown County. Reeves suggested that complete flood control was not practical, but straightening and enlarging the channel could diminish flooding.[11] The Reeves report thrust the James River into the engineering age. Whereas Joseph Nicollet admired the river's gentle beauty, Reeves's preoccupation with flood control ignored scenic and ecological values. It would be Reeves's philosophy that would be dominant through the coming decades.

Bureau of Reclamation engineers designing the Oahe project understood from the outset that the James River would be the principal collection point for excess delivered water and return flows. They realized that this would exacerbate flooding along the river and incite local farmers already sensitive about high flows. A plan to minimize flooding was needed, so the bureau sought advice from the federal agency with the most flood-control experience, the Army Corps of Engineers. The corps's predilection for developing inland waterways had them dreaming about transportation applications. The bureau needed a channelized river, agreed the corps, but why stop there? Instead of merely channelizing the river, they asked, why not excavate a canal capable of handling commercial vessels?

Colonel Thomas Hayes, district engineer for the corps's Omaha office, promoted the idea to the Huron Chamber of Commerce in 1957. According to Hayes, the navigation channel could extend up the James River into North Dakota and connect with a navigation/irrigation canal emanating from the Missouri River's Lake Sakakawea, north of Garrison dam.[12] The corps estimated it would cost at least $500 million for just the James River segment. Unfazed by the immense expense and ecstatic at the prospect of becoming an inland port, Huron's city commission and its chamber of commerce endorsed the concept.

Robert Lusk editorialized in Huron's newspaper that navigation and the need to drain Oahe's irrigation return flows made channelization the perfect answer to the economic needs of Huron and the James River basin. "By uniting this navigation development with the Bureau of Reclamation's Oahe irrigation unit," wrote Lusk, "South Dakota could reap double benefits by using the same water twice."[13]

In the bureau's 1960 Oahe report, there was a brief description of what was planned for the James River: "The channel improvements . . . are designed to permit . . . return flows to pass down the James River without causing any more flood damage than now occurs without irrigation. . . . The plan, prepared by the Corps of Engineers, consists of channel enlargements and cutoffs extending from Tacoma Park to the vicinity of Redfield. Levees will not be required. A distance of 121 river miles is shortened to about 54 miles with the cutoffs."[14] Occupying less than one full page in a report containing 175 pages, the bureau's brief description demonstrated the agency's nonchalant attitude about channelizing the river. There was no discussion of the river's ecological values or what would be destroyed by the action.

By the time Oahe's draft environmental impact statement was released, the barge-canal idea had been scrapped, but channelization remained the only plan on record. The river would be "improved" by channelization, stated the bureau document, but "furbearing mammals associated with the reach of the James River to receive channel improvements will decline to about one-half of present numbers with the exception of beaver which will be eliminated." Other than that revealing prediction, the bureau did not address how channelization would impact the river's environment. Nothing was said about the impacts to fish and other aquatic life in the river or about the large deer herd that resided along its banks.

Though neither George nor Bill Piper spoke at the draft EIS hearing, they listened attentively as environmentalists pointed out the draft's shortcomings and articulated concerns that went unmentioned in the document. The Pipers paid close attention as Edward Brigham, a representative of the National Audubon Society, described the James as a priceless natural heritage. Neatly dressed, with a calm, thoughtful manner, Brigham did not look like the sort of environmental radical who raised the ire of the Bureau of Reclamation. But Brigham didn't mince words describing the bureau's plans for the river: "We view with alarm the proposal to channelize 120 miles of the James River, reducing this 120 miles to 54 miles of what most certainly will be a sterile ditch, devoid of the usual stream bank habitat, and the living components which now comprise the James River ecosystem."[15] Brigham called the bureau's plans for the river "environmental surgery" and warned that "such surgery is likely to cause more problems that it is supposed to solve, i.e., siltation, bank erosion, wildlife habitat destruction, loss of scenic beauty."[16]

Unlike many of his fellow farmers, George Piper was comfortable in the company of environmentalists. Though concerns about his family's farm had been the impetus for his interest in Oahe, Piper was also sensitive to the broader spectrum of environmental issues associated with the project. He did not hesitate to seek counsel from people such as Edward Brigham. After studying Oahe's draft EIS, and after listening to what environmentalists were saying, George and Bill Piper decided it was time to move the discussion about Oahe from their kitchen to a larger setting.

Within shouting distance of the Pipers' parents' place was an old, one-room schoolhouse. Because of its proximity to Lake Byron, it was known as the Byron School. Years earlier, George and Bill had been grade-schoolers there. Though it no longer functioned as a school, it remained an important gathering place. Township meetings were held in the plain, spacious room on the main floor, and it served as the township polling place during elections. It was the perfect location for the Pipers to convene a public meeting to discuss the Oahe project.

A group numbering near thirty showed up at the schoolhouse on 9 January 1973. On the walls, where blackboards once hung, the Pipers taped maps and other materials that described Oahe and what lay in store for northern Beadle County. George told the group that despite past references to irrigation, none was planned for their area. We will be impacted by the Oahe project, he told the solemn crowd, not irrigated. As the meeting drew to a close, as the folding, metal chairs creaked while farmers shifted nervously, they arrived at a consensus. A second meeting must be held. George Piper promised to continue researching and to report to the farmers when they reconvened in several weeks.

Although it was disturbing for George Piper to visualize the impacts of Oahe based on reports and maps, it was a visit to the Garrison Irrigation Project in North Dakota that put a face on his fears. Garrison was an Oahe sibling, born of the same Pick-Sloan Plan and nurtured along by the Bureau of Reclamation.

Both projects would deliver impounded Missouri River water from behind namesake dams (Oahe in South Dakota and Garrison in North Dakota) to irrigation districts located in semiarid farming areas that were already productive. The difference was that construction on Garrison had commenced in 1967. When the Pipers visited, it was about 15 percent completed.

Already, environmental organizations had seen enough. To develop Garrison, the bureau would obliterate more than eighty thousand acres of wetlands and forty thousand acres of native grasslands. It would channelize 142 miles of rivers and streams and pollute at least five rivers in eastern North Dakota. Included in this destruction were stretches of the James. Most concerning to environmentalists was the risk posed to a group of the finest wildlife sanctuaries in the nation. A dozen federal wildlife refuges, most of them established forty years earlier, would be destroyed. It is likely that no other public-works project had proposed so much destruction to national wildlife refuges. Garrison also suffered from economic problems. With costs projected to exceed $1 billion, Garrison would provide irrigation to as few as 270 farms, and the price of providing irrigation could run as high as $700,000 per farm.

For all its threats to wildlife habitat and its economic problems, Garrison's most formidable obstacle came from outside the United States. The project's excess water and return flows would drain north, and Canadians worried that undesirable parasites and pollution would be introduced into their lakes and rivers. Until they were assured protection, the Canadian government vowed to oppose the project.

Acting as tour guide for the Pipers was Richard Madson, the young, enthusiastic leader of a group ambitiously named the Committee to Save North Dakota. Madson and others had built a network of local activists and had cultivated a budding force in Congress opposing the project. What the South Dakotans discovered on their tour was sobering. They heard that bureau land-acquisition agents preyed on elderly people to secure property. Farmers were condemned, underpaid, and inconvenienced as the bureau sent bulldozers into action. Standing along Garrison's main water-delivery ditch, the McClusky canal, they gazed into a man-made gorge deeper than a ten-story building and three times that wide. It wasn't difficult to understand the incredible scale of McClusky's impact when they learned the canal would be seventy-three miles long and its right-of-way measured up to a quarter of a mile wide.

The Pipers met Ben Schatz, a patriotic World War II veteran, whose farm would be split into three pieces by the McClusky canal, reducing his cattle herd by one-third. When Schatz complained about the hardships the canal would cause, the Bureau of Reclamation impassively responded: "To us you're just a dot on the map. When you get in the way, we move you."[17] Schatz was so incensed that he erected a large billboard facing a local highway that read: "My farm ruined by the U.S. Bureau of Reclamation."[18] Back home in Oahe territory, inspired by Schatz, the Pipers and others erected their own billboard on a busy road beside Lake Byron's doomed lake cottages. In bold, simple letters, the sign issued a warning: U.S. Bureau of Reclamation Leave Our Natural Resources Alone!

The Pipers now understood that to fight off what would likely be a grim reproduction of Garrison-like impacts required more than erecting signs. They wanted to establish a strong organization based on the premise that the family farm is the basic social and economic unit in U.S. agriculture. It was Bill Piper who recommended the organization be named United Family Farmers.[19] Piper's suggestion constituted a minor name change. Until then, the group had casually called itself the Lake Byron Farmers. On 23 January 1973, the new name and draft bylaws were presented to another gathering at the schoolhouse. Annual membership dues were set at ten dollars. George Piper was elected president, a couple of dozen farmers wrote friendly checks, and the organization was born.

The Pipers next realized that their chances to alter or stop Oahe would be enhanced if they expanded the organization beyond the Lake Byron area. "We began to understand that we had to involve all the farmers in the Oahe project area," explained George Piper. "That meant involving farmers living two hundred miles from us. It also meant we had to go see them, and we did."[20] A crucial area was the western part of the Oahe project area, where the Blunt reservoir would one day force thirty families to abandon their farms and ranches. The bureau hoped to acquire about forty thousand acres to develop the reservoir. Also in the western portion of the project was the proposed Pierre canal. Though not the longest Oahe canal, it would rival the capacity of McClusky canal. To build the thirty-six miles of the canal would require the acquisition of a swath of land sometimes exceeding a quarter of a mile. Using project maps and county atlases to identify landowners in the path of the Pierre canal and the Blunt reservoir, the Pipers and their Lake Byron cohorts traveled west. They were truly starting from scratch. "We drove up to a few farmers' places, introduced ourselves, and asked if they were concerned," is how George Piper explained his early organizing. "We'd contact a few that way and they would direct us to others in their neighborhood who might be concerned. That's how we would set up a meeting and call in all the neighbors."[21]

The process of recruiting members for United Family Farmers, attending meetings, visiting government offices, conducting research, and keeping up with correspondence began to take up more and more time for the Pipers. The family decided that George should be fully devoted to researching Oahe and building United Family Farmers. Bill would continue his involvement in the effort, but he would also make sure the farm ran smoothly.

As the man who must be acknowledged as the primary energy for the first grassroots group to challenge the Oahe project comprehensively, George Piper was a leader quite different from the typical political activist. Piper was a reluctant leader, a modest man uncomfortable in the limelight. That trait was manifested in Piper's approach to dissent. Instead of shiny hyperbole, Piper relied on straight, hard data to question Oahe. He was convinced that the best way to disarm Oahe's proponents was to use research and facts, not fabrication. George Piper brought an unusual brand of political organizing to the rural countryside. He simply set out to secure as much information as he could and share it with as many people as possible. There was no sense of Piper wanting to be the leader, but the more information he obtained, interpreted, and distributed, the more others began looking to him for opinions, for answers, for leadership.

The Pipers' first ally from Oahe's irrigation districts was a man named John Elsing, whom they met at the public hearing on the draft EIS in Aberdeen. Elsing, a landowner from Spink County, was the only farmer from an irrigation area to testify against the project at the hearing. As a young man, Elsing graduated from South Dakota State College and returned home to work the land he loved. His farm was fertile and flat, straddling the Brown County–Spink County border. Elsing, his wife, and their children lived in the house where he was born, sixty-five years before Oahe's environmental impact hearing.

Elsing, a soft-spoken, deliberate man, was a former chairman of the county extension service board, and in 1974 he was recognized as a distinguished farmer by his alma mater. He owned eighty acres in the Spink County Irrigation District and at one time had been a supporter of the Oahe project. "I thought I had it made," Elsing said of his land in the project. Elsing figured he could raise a reliable crop for his livestock on the irrigated land and farm the rest of his land as he had always done. Then he took a vacation to Washington State.[22]

While in the Northwest, Elsing visited a Bureau of Reclamation irrigation project and watched a slide show that documented the destruction of topsoil in irrigated tracts. When he returned to South Dakota, he conducted a soil test on his own land scheduled to be irrigated. He does not recall what prompted him to follow the procedure he followed, but the demonstration he created became an effective tool. Elsing cut away the bottom of a forty-ounce grape juice jar and placed a scoop of soil from his irrigable land into the glass container, compacting the soil to simulate reclamation standards. Before rescrewing the container's wide cover, he poured water on top of the dirt. Since soil permeability is necessary to irrigate successfully, the expected outcome of Elsing's experiment was that the water would seep through the soil. But that's not what happened. "The water would absolutely stand on top of the soil," said Elsing.[23]

Elsing decided to examine the agency's soil classifications throughout the project. By using fine-tipped pens and a magnifying glass, he was able to duplicate the bureau's Spink County soil survey meticulously, color-coding his own map of the lake plain area. Elsing's map identified the soils the bureau called excellent or good prospects for irrigation with green shading. The soils identified as fair would remain white. Those soils with only a poor or unfit prospect for irrigation would be colored red. At meetings, Elsing's large map, mounted on an easel, was turned away from those seated at the gathering. Elsing would explain that his map used three colors to correspnd to the government's soil classifications. Then he asked the audience to imagine which colors would dominate the map. It was a perfect segue, and he would swing his map around to face the audience. "When I showed the map, there were gasps, audible gasps," said Elsing, as he recalled the impact of his presentation. "There was so much red they couldn't believe it."[24] Instead of irrigable soils, nonirrigable lands dominated the map. The patchwork of irrigable land interspersed throughout nonirrigable land was remarkable.

For several years, Elsing carried the jar and map with him to meetings and hearings. During all that time, no water soaked through the dirt and the bureau never challenged the accuracy of his map.

While watching the television news one evening, a Brown County farmer named John Sieh listened closely as a fellow surrounded by feeding cattle described his concerns about the Oahe Irrigation Project. That person, Sieh learned, was a farmer named George Piper, and Piper had started a group that was questioning the Oahe project.

Sieh, whose farm was situated a short distance east of the James River, was unsure about Oahe, but he gave cool support to certain aspects of the project. Sieh's foremost concern was the James River. He was upset that for many years the river had been mistreated and neglected, and he thought Oahe development included river cleanup. But Sieh wanted to meet George Piper, and with the help of local aides for Senators George McGovern and James Abourezk, a meeting was arranged.

When George Piper and several other Lake Byron farmers arrived, John Sieh's home was already noisy and crowded. Piper hesitated on the doorstep, wondering if the group inside was hostile or friendly. But when Sieh came to the door, he extended his hand in greeting and assured them they had nothing to worry about. That night, George Piper's report about what lay in store for the James River especially interested the Brown County group. His description of a dramatically altered landscape and a natural river changed into a channelized chute for polluted return flows put a new face on Oahe. Many of those present owned land along the river, and they were concerned about the fate of that land. By the time George Piper left that night, he had collected membership dues for United Family Farmers from everyone present.

But more than memberships had been gained. That night was a lucky one for George Piper. He didn't know it at the time, but meeting John Sieh was a pivotal happening. The skills and energy Sieh would bring to United Family Farmers would help the organization define itself as strong and combative. Just shy of fifty years of age, John Sieh was a veteran activist. In his twenties he had been a field organizer in Kansas for the National Farmers Union. His personal philosophy was similar to the robust populism that had deep roots in his native Brown County. Sieh believed in government, but only if it reflected the will of the people. The brewing Oahe conflict, born of a government plan conceived without public input, was irresistible to Sieh's fearless style and to his reasoned sense of right and wrong. In terms of personality, John Sieh was nearly a perfect contrast to George Piper. That is probably why they complemented one another so well.

Ted Albright was unimpressed when he first heard George Piper speak at a meeting in the Blunt community center. George Piper's small stature and quiet voice did not provoke Albright's interest. Other farmers and ranchers had their own immediate reservations about Piper. His beard, long hair, and reserved demeanor set him apart. But it did not take long for those reservations to disappear.

Albright and others found Piper's sincerity, humility, and his knowledge of Oahe appealing—even inspiring. Soon United Family Farmers was attracting members from widely different groups. Lifelong Democrats joined straight-ticket Republicans; ranchers joined environmentalists; wealthy landowners joined struggling, small farmers. "We were fighting a battle against the Bureau of Reclamation as individuals until United Family Farmers arrived," remembered Albright. "That's how these sort of government programs get done. People aren't organized to oppose them. You can't win if you're not organized. I've seen other issues where the government divided and conquered. We weren't organized until George Piper organized us."[25]

Among the environmentalists whom George Piper befriended were members of a new group called the Dakota Environmental Coalition, an organization with most of its members in southeastern South Dakota. A founding member of the group was a Vermillion, South Dakota, attorney named Martin Weeks, and Weeks invited the Pipers to Vermillion in March 1973 to discuss Oahe. A respected, experienced Main Street lawyer with a strong environmental ethic and a willingness to use the courts to accomplish environmental protection, Weeks had previously helped block a Corps of Engineers' plan to channelize the Vermillion River. George Piper wanted to ask Weeks about that experience and also about the trustworthiness of the Bureau of Reclamation. Weeks assured his visitors that there were plenty of reasons to distrust government agencies. Keep asking questions and don't accept Oahe as an inevitability, advised Weeks, who quickly became a trusted adviser to United Family Farmers. Three months after meeting Piper, he helped the group incorporate under state law in June 1973.

That the first substantive media coverage of Oahe opposition came from a newspaper outside South Dakota wasn't surprising. The cozy relationship between project promoters and newspapers precluded reporting that would have authenticated the views of United Family Farmers. Oahe supporters were shocked, then, to see the 22 July 1973 issue of the *Minneapolis Tribune*. There, beside a headline that read "Oahe Project: Boon or Boondoggle?" was a photo of George Piper. *Tribune* readers that Sunday learned that thirty-three-year-old George Piper was saying some nasty things about the Oahe project. Oahe was, the article quoted Piper as saying, an "assault on fragile ecosystems" with "detrimental effects on the sociological fiber of the farm unit."[26] Piper was also saying unkind things about government. "This project is a classic example of how bureaucrats make decisions for farmers," he said. "They preach progress, they promise progress, and it fools the farmers."[27]

George was not the only Piper featured in the article. A large photograph depicted George's father, Olie Piper, wearing overalls and a seed-corn cap. Standing in a grain field, the seventy-two-year-old with a burly frame and broad face looked every inch the hardworking farmer. "Back when folks were homesteading around here," said Olie, "there was a lot of skulduggery in land deals. But it was nothing compared with this Oahe." Olie called the project a "big boondoggle" promoted by "finaglers."[28]

Just two months after the *Minneapolis Tribune* article appeared, the student-run newspaper at the University of South Dakota, the *Volante*, published a scathing two-part piece about Oahe that was filled with in-depth, critical analysis. Never before had the project's details been so thoroughly discussed in the media. The paper's news editor, Tim Schreiner, had stumbled onto the subject while home in Aberdeen during the summer. A friend of his worked for Senator James Abourezk, and she invited Schreiner to look through the Oahe files in Abourezk's field office. The young journalist quickly realized he was onto a terrific story.

Schreiner, who later rose to senior editorial positions at two West Coast metropolitan newspapers, remembered the excitement he felt at the time. "Every reporter wants a scoop, particularly in a journalist's formative years," explained Schreiner. "I saw an opportunity to be the first one to raise some questions publicly."[29] Studying the project's environmental impact statement and interviewing George Piper convinced Schreiner that Oahe was not the golden goose his hometown newspaper constantly portrayed it to be. "It was a very negative article," said Schreiner, years later, in describing his piece, which ran to six thousand words. "It was written like an exposé. I felt it was legitimate to do that because up until then no one had printed these questions. No one had raised these questions. The mere fact of raising questions was unusual. Anyone who read it would get a very negative feeling for the project."[30] So delighted were the folks at United Family Farmers that a small contingent drove to the university in Vermillion and went to the *Volante* office to congratulate and thank Schreiner. The farmers offered to pay the gratified student a small fee in exchange for the right to reprint and distribute five thousand copies of the article. Schreiner later cited that experience as one of the reasons he pursued a career in journalism.

The organizing success of the Pipers and their Lake Byron neighbors was evidenced in early 1974 when United Family Farmers celebrated their first annual meeting. Held in the tiny town of Polo, a location selected because of its central location in the sub-district, the meeting attracted more than 150 people and began a tradition of annual potluck feasts that would continue for many years. George Piper recalled that the Polo meeting marked the first time United Family Farmer members from all areas of the sub-district gathered together, and that it was an exciting, reassuring event. "There was tremendous support among all the farmers," remembered Piper. "There was an optimism that something could be done."[31]

Soon, United Family Farmers pursued a more aggressive strategy. The organization's initial attempt at specific political action was a request issued to the state's politicians and the federal government for a moratorium on project development until questions about the project were answered. They flooded the media with news releases about the proposal, sponsored countless public forums to discuss Oahe, and began to confront project supporters at Oahe sub-district meetings. Other organizations such as the state branch of the League of Women Voters, the South Dakota Farm Bureau, and various environmental groups joined United Family Farmers to support a moratorium.

The quest for a moratorium gave United Family Farmers something tangible to support and rally behind, and membership exploded, reaching 665 dues-paying members in the autumn of 1974. Just two years earlier, the organization was a group of neighbors sitting at a kitchen table.

Oahe supporters had come to expect that their project would one day be built. But times had changed, and a host of new faces were entering the farm community in the sub-district area. By 1974, the project's planning had gone on for so long that while one generation of farmers had been educated and convinced about Oahe, another generation of farmers had grown up. The newer generation posed a different challenge for Oahe promoters. Elections forming the sub-district and irrigation districts had occurred years before. Many of those in the new generation of farmers had not been exposed to or involved in those accomplishments.

The appearance of informed and organized Oahe doubters and the contentious conditions they spawned caught Oahe supporters off guard and unprepared. They suddenly found themselves in a bitter grassroots battle. To their rescue came Senator George McGovern, South Dakota's senior senator. McGovern and his staff possessed the shrewd toughness that would be necessary if the rapidly intensifying siege by Oahe's antagonists was to be thwarted.

7

The Defender of Oahe

I was a strong supporter for the Oahe project from the day I got to Congress
until I left. . . . I was convinced that on balance the project was a plus despite some of the environmental losses that it might have brought about.
Senator George McGovern, interview

Everything we faced that tried to destroy our movement, all the efforts to
put us in a bad light, could be traced to Senator McGovern's office.
George Piper, interview

Senator George McGovern did not support Oahe just because it portended a
generous influx of federal money for his home state; he viewed the irrigation
project as genuine conservation of resources. Saving water behind dams in the
Missouri for economic applications justified drowning the river's great valley
beneath man-made lakes. Watering vast ranges of corn justified digging long
ditches across the prairie and channelizing rivers and streams.

Senator McGovern's sentiment regarding Oahe was formed long before he
became a politician. Like his friend Ken Holum and so many others of his generation, McGovern had witnessed and remembered well the ravages of drought
during the 1930s. It was during his teenage years, growing up as a minister's son
in Mitchell, that he experienced the dust bowl. "I saw year after year the crops
wither and die," recalled McGovern. "I've seen South Dakota when the day-
time sky was as black as midnight. I saw middle-aged farmers weeping over the
loss of their crops. I had a lasting impression of South Dakota short on water,
short on rain . . . that drove me harder than anything else in my support for
Oahe."[1]

As a young man, McGovern earned a Ph.D. from Northwestern University
in Evanston, Illinois, then returned home to South Dakota. There, at Dakota

Wesleyan University in Mitchell, he taught history and government for three years until resigning to become the executive director of the South Dakota Democratic Party. This was an immense challenge because the state had been ruled for many years by Republicans. By all accounts, McGovern did a superb job, successfully recruiting candidates for offices, building the party's base, and helping break the stranglehold that Republicans held on the state legislature.

In the 1953 state house of representatives, one year before McGovern became executive director, the Democrats controlled only two of seventy-five seats. On the senate side, the ratio was worse: all thirty-five members were Republicans. When the 1955 legislature convened (in those days the South Dakota legislature met every other year), the Democrats had narrowed the disparity, electing six senators and eighteen representatives. Much of that success was attributed to McGovern. In 1956, McGovern parlayed his political prowess into a victory over a three-term incumbent, Harold Lovre, for the U.S. House seat representing the easternmost part of the state. Two years later, McGovern defeated Joe Foss, a popular war hero and retiring two-term governor, to retain his seat.

McGovern's 1960 bid to unseat Senator Karl Mundt fell short, but he stayed in Washington after being appointed by President Kennedy to direct the Food for Peace program. Two years later, McGovern mounted another Senate campaign and won by a scant 597 votes. The man credited with building South Dakota's Democratic Party had climbed to the pinnacle of the state's political mountain. At age forty, Senator George McGovern was the most important Democrat in South Dakota.

As a senator, McGovern's sympathetic social philosophy and his courageous stand against the Vietnam War endeared him to progressives, including environmentalists. But McGovern was such a staunch supporter of the Bureau of Reclamation that the bureau included him on its list of special friends in the Senate.[2] McGovern warned Oahe supporters in South Dakota that the Council on Environmental Quality (CEQ), the president's official advisory board on environmental matters, had recommended that work on the Garrison project be postponed until certain problems were addressed. The CEQ was headed by an environmentalist named Russell Train, and McGovern expected Train would soon be appointed to head the Environmental Protection Agency (EPA). McGovern feared that from this more influential position, Train would launch an attack on Oahe.

In December 1972, with Russell Train at the helm, the Environmental Protection Agency submitted its comments on Oahe's draft environmental impact statement. McGovern had been right. Train and the agency warned that the draft document did not adequately address several of Oahe's key environmental impacts, including the project's likely detrimental effect on wildlife and pollution of the James River. The following September, Senator McGovern cautioned Jim Lewis, manager of the Oahe sub-district. "We must recognize," McGovern wrote to Lewis, "that the Congress, the Administration and the Judiciary are increasingly responsive to environmental concerns associated with projects of this kind."[3]

To counter EPA, McGovern suggested to Lewis that the sub-district create its own environmental committee. "By taking the initiative," he advised, "we would be in a good position to negate any future administrative attempt on the part of EPA or related agencies to order up a special study of the kind that could result in a suspension of the on-going work on the project."[4] McGovern wanted the new committee to identify the project's environmental issues rather than to have Washington-based bureaucrats and environmentalists doing it. He suggested the new group should conduct its own environmental study, and that the study should be sensitive to Oahe's economic benefits.

It did not take long for Lewis and the sub-district to act. On 13 September, just several days after Lewis received McGovern's letter, a group of forty Oahe advocates met in Redfield to organize the new committee and bolster Oahe's environmental image. The planning group included sub-district directors, government officials, members of the extension service, representatives of the press, and Ken Holum. Appearing the next day in the *Huron Daily Plainsman* was an article celebrating the meeting. "Major strides in solving environmental problems, including a move for immediate creation of an advisory environmental committee, were taken at a meeting attended by approximately 40 people," said the article. The newspaper reported that a broad cross section of South Dakota interests attended the meeting but neglected to mention that no local environmental groups were represented; nor were the federal EPA or the South Dakota Department of Environmental Protection.[5]

George Piper's response was unvarnished. The group, said Piper, is being created to "meet public relations requirements . . . for the benefit of the favorable press."[6] John Elsing was even more direct, calling the committee a "phony environmental organization." Elsing had received a copy of McGovern's letter to Jim Lewis from a state official who requested confidentiality; the man feared he would lose his job if it became known that he had circulated the letter. Thanks to Elsing's secret source, United Family Farmers discovered the role McGovern played in the formation of the new committee.[7] United Family Farmers and the South Dakota Environmental Coalition were invited to join the committee for a subsequent meeting, but both groups resisted. The committee eventually was comprised of four sub-district board members, and the initial intent was lost. Though the committee continued in name, it was impotent to accomplish George McGovern's original vision.

McGovern's next attempt to control Oahe's environmental agenda came in the form of a statewide environmental conference called by the senator and held on 12 January 1974 in Sioux Falls. The portion of the conference that generated the most energetic participation concerned Oahe. Serving as panelists for the Oahe session were Preston Funkhouser, manager of the Oahe project for the Bureau of Reclamation; Dr. Lawrence Fine, of South Dakota State University; Fay Kerr, a water-resources specialist from the state extension service; and Dr. Nels Granholm, an employee at the Electron Microscope Lab at South Dakota State University. All but Granholm were supporters of the project.[8]

Before an audience of several hundred people and the media, Preston Funkhouser dismissed concerns about the James River. He said it wouldn't be necessary to devise a plan dealing with the river until the project was operational for five years. That was plenty of time, said Funkhouser, for his agency to determine a reasonable solution. Dr. Fine defended the irrigability of lake plains soils but acknowledged salinity in the James River would increase. Proper management, said Fine, would make this acceptable. Nels Granholm pointed out that the 1973 report of the president's National Water Commission concluded that "[federal] subsidization of new irrigation projects is not justified on either social or economic grounds . . . and should be discontinued." Dr. Granholm lashed out at river channelization practices, citing a congressional report that accused the Bureau of Reclamation of not adequately considering the adverse environmental effects of their channelization projects. Granholm also defended the notion of a project moratorium, insisting that project development should proceed only after acceptable solutions to pressing problems had been reached.

Ken Holum appeared at the conference and spoke against the moratorium. But his remarks in a letter written to George McGovern several days after the conference were more revealing. "Despite the fact that this was an environmental conference," he wrote, "neither the panel members nor the questioners raised a single question or issue that could be identified as an environmental question or issue."[9] This observation was both telling and curious, considering that critical environmental topics such as soils, water tables, and James River modification had been discussed. Apparently, Holum did not perceive these as matters related to the environment. Holum's service in the Interior Department had helped shape his views about conservation and the environment. Interior managed resources for a number of purposes, including helping rural communities, but also functioned as a clearinghouse for businesses and individuals interested in using or exploiting publicly owned natural resources.

Holum's confidence in the soundness of the Oahe Irrigation Project and the skills of the Bureau of Reclamation were so great that despite publicly testifying in support of Oahe's environmental impact statement, he had never examined the document. "I doubt very much that I [read it]," said Holum in an interview. Shrugging his shoulders, he added, "I suppose I skimmed it."[10] Holum should have known how the bureau struggled to assemble the Oahe impact statement; he should have understood that the bureau's engineers may have been trained in planning, design, and construction, but they lacked schooling and sensitivity regarding the environmental consequences of their actions. From the inside looking out, Holum may not have recognized that the agency took a narrow view of the suggestions and criticisms of environmentalists, seeing them as obstructions.

Meanwhile, Senator George McGovern and his congressional colleagues from South Dakota asked that President Nixon's proposed 1975 allocation of $4.5 million be hiked to $5.5 million, and the Congress concurred. United Family Farmers' attempts to block the appropriation were spurned. Turning its attention from Washington, the group began to pressure the more accessible Oahe sub-district.

For years, sub-district board meetings had been placid, orderly affairs attended only by project supporters. That changed when Piper and United Family Farmers members began attending the bimonthly meetings. Oahe supporters found themselves sitting elbow to elbow in uncomfortable tension with Oahe opponents. Impassioned statements for and against the project were made. Loud arguments between spectators and board members broke out. The decorum of the past deteriorated, and the board and its staff began to dread meetings. Project supporters began to avoid them.

Ned Hundstad remembered one episode at the Holiday Inn in Aberdeen that characterized the hostile atmosphere at many board meetings. Hundstad had arrived early in the morning to help sub-district manager Jim Lewis set up for a meeting. The two men arranged tables and chairs for the board at the front of the room, with chairs for the audience facing the board. Then they left for breakfast. When Lewis and Hundstad returned, the room had been rearranged. The board's table and chairs had been moved to the center of the room and were surrounded by seating for the audience. Not sure what to think of the new arrangement, Hundstad and Lewis left the room as it was. Only minutes after the meeting convened Hundstad realized the configuration presented difficulties. Members of United Family Farmers dominated the audience, and as the board tried to conduct business, heckles and badgering came simultaneously from all directions. It was like being in the middle of a cyclone, Hundstad remembered. "Whenever one of the board would say something that United Family Farmers disagreed with, they'd holler and hiss," he said, his voice rising in anger. "I'd look around to see who said something, but they were all over. They were behind you, they were beside you, they were in front of you."[11] When the board's frustrated chairman, Orville Hill, reached for the gavel to quiet the meeting, he found nothing. John Sieh's sister, Betty Ries, had taken the mallet. When Bob Hipple threatened to call the police, someone from the audience sarcastically offered Hipple a dime to place the call. Confounded and intimidated, the board recessed early.

In the spring of 1974, Jim Lewis resigned after nearly fourteen years as sub-district manager. Lewis said the controversy had become too bitter. Though he had helped guide the project over a number of bureaucratic hurdles, Oahe insiders felt Lewis did not possess the toughness to engage in the kind of fight now confronting the sub-district. Hired to replace Lewis was Robert Raschke, who had been Lewis's assistant. Raschke got his baptism quickly. In an Associated Press story carried in South Dakota newspapers on 18 April 1974, it was reported that the Environmental Protection Agency had sent a letter to the Interior Department expressing its support for delaying construction of Oahe until critical environmental issues were resolved. It was as if a bomb had dropped on Oahe.

Startled sub-district officials and other project supporters had not yet seen the letter, and the newspaper report came as a surprise. To neutralize EPA, George McGovern and Ken Holum set up a 31 July meeting for Oahe supporters with Russell Train. News of the meeting leaked to George Piper, but when Piper contacted Senator McGovern's office, McGovern's staff denied a meeting had been scheduled. They later acknowledged the meeting but refused to allow Piper and John Sieh to attend. The two farmers boarded a plane to Washington anyway, and thanks to Congressman Jim Abdnor were admitted to the meeting. In exchange for being allowed to attend, however, Sieh and Piper agreed that they would refrain from speaking. John Sieh recalled arriving at the meeting and noting those in attendance. In addition to Train, McGovern, and the rest of the state's delegation, Sieh recognized Bob Raschke and James Ruddy from the sub-district and a trio of participants whose presence startled him. Seated at the meeting table were Ellsworth Karrigan, of the *Aberdeen American News*, Bud Maher, of the *Huron Daily Plainsman*, and Vern Laustsen, the publisher of the Aberdeen-based *Dakota Farmer* magazine. Sieh also remembered that although he and George Piper were muzzled for the meeting, Laustsen, Karrigan, and Maher gave presentations. "If there was ever anything that convinced me where the real support of Oahe was, it was at that meeting," Sieh would later say, emphasizing that he and Piper were the only farmers present.[12]

Ken Holum orchestrated much of what was presented at the meeting and in follow-up communications. Before the meeting, he advised the group to press Train for help in solving Oahe's environmental problems. He also suggested that they ask Train to soothe the hostility of South Dakota environmentalists toward Oahe and the sub-district. Train agreed to help.

Senator McGovern was convinced the sub-district was losing ground in the battle for public opinion over Oahe. George Piper had become a press-release machine, and Esther Eide, of the South Dakota Environmental Coalition, regularly issued scathing commentaries on the state's public radio network. The sub-district appeared inept at rebuttal. "I have not found," McGovern told South Dakota Governor Richard Kneip, "that the Oahe [sub-district] board has been so forceful or as responsive to the public 'need to know' as should be the case."[13] Governor Kneip agreed: "The Oahe Conservancy Sub-district does not properly carry the fight, leaving many of us in public office unduly exposed without proper support."[14]

George McGovern himself was feeling politically exposed and vulnerable. He faced reelection to the Senate in 1974 and had lost his home state to Richard Nixon in the 1972 presidential election. Now he faced Leo Thorsness, a Vietnam War veteran angered by McGovern's antiwar position.

Also to be elected in the 1974 general election were five director positions for the Oahe sub-district board. United Family Farmers entered candidates in four of the races. It marked the first time that a slate of candidates presenting an alternative viewpoint to Oahe appeared on the ballot.

In a campaign where every vote mattered, Senator McGovern handled Oahe very delicately. Some Oahe opponents were traditional McGovern supporters, and McGovern did not want to lose their support. McGovern portrayed Leo Thorsness as a supporter of Oahe with a closed mind on the subject, while claiming a more moderate stance for himself. He assured Oahe opponents that their concerns would be addressed, and although he rejected a project moratorium, he declared that the sub-district elections should be viewed as a referendum on the project. During a radio broadcast, McGovern stated that the sub-district elections would reveal how local people felt about the project: "This [the sub-district] election will provide us with a good referendum . . . [about] how the farmers and the people in the affected area feel about [Oahe]."[15] McGovern wrote Virgil Gilbert and indicated he would look to the sub-district elections to establish his position on Oahe. "The people must make the final decision," said McGovern, "for if they strongly favor or reject the plan, then many of us will feel inclined to support that decision."[16]

Simultaneously, McGovern promised Oahe supporters he would speak strongly for the project. Senator McGovern's plan to placate both sides in the controversy—riding the fence is how one McGovern aide referred to the strategy—helped him survive. On election day, he was helped by strong support in the sub-district area and garnered 53 percent of the vote statewide.

The 1974 campaign to elect South Dakota's First District congressman was noteworthy because the candidates presented voters with contrasting views on Oahe. The incumbent, Democrat Frank Denholm, enthusiastically backed Oahe. His opponent, thirty-one-year-old Larry Pressler, appeared to oppose the project. Pressler's position on Oahe had been reinforced by his relationship with Martin Weeks during a tightly contested primary. Weeks, a former chair of the Republican Party in his county, learned that Pressler had reservations about Oahe. The Vermillion attorney soon became a close adviser to the political newcomer. Thanks to Weeks and United Family Farmers, Pressler prevailed in the primary and later shocked the political establishment by beating Denholm. Again, Weeks and United Family Farmers provided much campaign assistance.

Because his chances of winning seemed so slim, Oahe supporters had not worried about Pressler. But his victory prompted Senator McGovern to urge Oahe supporters to convert him. "I regard it as very important," McGovern warned, "that those of us who serve South Dakota in the Congress present a united front on matters of this kind if we are going to have any realistic chance of success. I know that during the primary last Spring, Mr. Pressler appeared to take a contrary view of the project. I have not had an opportunity to visit with Congressman-elect Pressler on this matter, but it seems to me that the Oahe Board, et al., might be well advised to seek a determination of his viewpoint before he takes office in January."[17] Only days after his victory, Pressler met

United Family Farmers leaders in Huron and agreed to introduce legislation deauthorizing Oahe.

Several months later, Martin Weeks inquired about deauthorization during a phone call with the new congressman. Weeks was dismayed to learn that Pressler had had a change of heart. "He explained to me," said Weeks of his conversation with Pressler, "that he'd had conferences with contractors and others . . . and he would not be supporting us."[18] Pressler's abrupt turnaround on Oahe heralded the opportunistic and unreliable behavior he would demonstrate repeatedly during his political career.

After victories in 1970 and 1972, Richard Kneip decided to seek a third term as governor. Beginning in 1974, the state's leader would be elected to serve a four-year term, so Kneip was allowed to run again. Also elected in 1970 and 1972 was Bill Dougherty, the state's lieutenant governor. In those years, the lieutenant governor was elected on a separate ballot from the governor. The men had a strained relationship, and it was not unexpected when Dougherty challenged Kneip in the 1974 primary for the Democratic Party's gubernatorial nomination. As part of his campaign, Dougherty boldly endorsed the Oahe moratorium, and a pro-Dougherty campaign was coordinated by United Family Farmers. On primary day, however, Kneip's popularity, and Oahe's, prevailed in a dominating victory of 65 percent to 35 percent.

Later that summer, environmentalists within the Democratic Party carried their anti-Oahe message into the party's convention and nearly succeeded in placing an Oahe moratorium in the party's official platform. That effort was squashed when pro-Oahe forces, led by Senator McGovern's chief assistant, George Cunningham, repelled the environmentalists. The party instead adopted a position advocating Oahe.[19]

In the general election, Kneip defeated Republican John Olson to win a third term. Kneip's new lieutenant governor was Harvey Wollman, an Oahe supporter and former state senator from Spink County. Wollman, a farmer, owned land in the Spink County Irrigation District. Despite the bruising primary loss, Bill Dougherty was named chairman of Senator McGovern's reelection committee. In that capacity, he helped further McGovern's strategy to mollify both sides in the Oahe fight. Only months earlier, United Family Farmers considered Dougherty a hero; now Dougherty was aiding the Oahe project's most influential advocate. The twists and curves of party politics had swallowed the project controversy, and Democrats were using it for their own benefit.

The local elections for the Oahe sub-district board were nonpartisan contests. Sub-district voters residing outside a municipality voted in rural districts, and nine rural districts were represented on the sub-district board. Residents of cities and towns voted in municipal districts, and they were represented on the Oahe board by only two directors. Conservancy districts elsewhere in the West were not as favorable toward rural residents. North Dakota's Garrison Conservancy District, for example, elected its directors on a countywide vote. The consequence of that arrangement was that the district's power became concentrated in county seats and in chambers of commerce. In other conservancy districts, the directors were selected not by the voters but by a local judge.

United Family Farmers had a long-term goal when the organization fielded candidates in the 1974 election. If a majority of the directors on the sub-district board were supporters of United Family Farmers, the sub-district's agenda could be controlled. The strategy would require victories in the 1974 and 1976 elections. "We were taking a big risk through the first election process," said George Piper. Piper realized that if United Family Farmers candidates failed to win, or did poorly, it would be a setback for the organization. A lackluster showing would reflect badly on the group's platform as well as its candidates.[20]

Surprisingly, United Family Farmer-backed candidates were victorious in all four races they entered. John Sieh ended the sub-district reign of Ned Hundstad in Brown County. Bill Piper challenged Lloyd Miller and won a comfortable victory to become the new director representing Beadle and Clark Counties. Steve Thorson, an Aberdeen businessman, beat Huron's James Ruddy in the at-large director race, joining Bob Hipple on the board as the municipal representatives. Jerome "Bud" Yackley, a Sully County farmer, unseated Bernard "Bud" Beastrom, a farmer from near Pierre. Yackley would represent rural residents in Sully and Hughes Counties. In the fifth race, Mike Madden, a former employee of the extension service and an Oahe supporter, was elected without opposition. Madden would represent Campbell and McPherson Counties, replacing the retiring C. W. Renz. Never before had the board changed so dramatically. In addition to Renz, three of the losers, Hundstad, Miller, and Ruddy, had been on the board since its inception. Bud Beastrom succeeded Geof Garrett as a board member in 1970 following Garrett's death in December 1969.

John Sieh's campaign against Hundstad ignited a grassroots war in Brown County. The most rabid Oahe activists there viewed a person's position on the project as a reflection of their virtue and integrity. Farmers commonly described themselves as being pro-Oahe or anti-Oahe. It was George Piper's prediction that the project would pollute and channelize the James River that had initially soured John Sieh on the Oahe project. Without success, Sieh pressed the bureau to disclose just what the agency planned for the river in Brown County. It seemed ludicrous to Sieh that the agency would build the project without having a firm plan for the river.

But the issue that triggered Sieh's candidacy was the Oahe board's desire to construct the project's pumping facility at Lake Oahe to a size capable of providing irrigation water to nearly half a million acres. This would allow irrigation beyond the project's first phase to include lands east of the James River, where Sieh farmed. Sieh had helped circulate petitions demonstrating minimal support for irrigation in eastern Brown County, but the sub-district frowned on them. He then called Ned Hundstad and asked him to meet for supper. The two men had been friends and political allies on numerous issues. "I asked him [Hundstad] if he wouldn't do something about it," recalled Sieh of the dinner conversation. Sieh wanted Hundstad to appeal to the board to seek smaller pumps. "He said nothing could be done," Sieh explained, shaking his head, "and that the project had to be designed the way it was."[21] Alone in his truck as he drove the dark roads home, Sieh decided to oppose Hundstad. "I made up my mind right then," remembered Sieh. "Nobody asked me to run. If he had given me any indication that we would be listened to I wouldn't have run. But he didn't."[22]

During the campaign, Hundstad cited Sieh's inexperience in water-resource planning and emphasized his own progressive vision for agriculture and water development. Sieh supported a moratorium on the Oahe project and believed irrigation development east of the James River was unwarranted and unwanted. Hundstad's vision was far grander and somewhat far-fetched. He dreamed of extending the Oahe diversion ditch for one hundred miles eastward beyond the James River valley to deliver water to lakes, irrigators, and cities in eastern South Dakota and southeastern North Dakota.[23] When the voters in Brown County cast their ballots, John Sieh carried every precinct east of the James River en route to a 56 percent majority. While Hundstad garnered most of the votes from the irrigation areas, Sieh did very well with those farmers whose lands would be impacted by canals, laterals, and drains.

Bill Piper was one of three candidates seeking to represent Beadle and Clark Counties on the sub-district board. In addition to incumbent Lloyd Miller, Piper was joined on the ballot by a man named Vincent Kennealley. Piper tried to visit every farmer in the two counties personally. That task was an ideal way for Piper to introduce himself to the voters. Those unfamiliar with him would open their door to find a stout man with porkchop sideburns and a broad smile standing on their front step.

Lloyd Miller believed Oahe should be completed as rapidly as possible. Both he and Ned Hundstad clung to the view that most farmers in the sub-district agreed with them. Neither comprehended the changes taking place in the countryside. In defeat, Miller's supporters accused United Family Farmers of recruiting the third candidate to confuse voters. That charge was later revealed as baseless. Vince Kennealley said he had run not at the behest of United Family Farmers, but because his home county did not have a candidate. Even if all of Kennealley's votes had gone to Miller, Piper would still have been the victor.

Steve Thorson was a wild card. Though he had asked for and received support from United Family Farmers, Thorson told the Bureau of Reclamation he did not oppose the project. In contrast to Ruddy's passive campaign, Thorson worked hard, including flying his own airplane pulling a campaign banner. The final tally was not even close: Thorson ousted Ruddy with a 64 to 36 percent victory.

Jerome Yackley's victory over incumbent Bud Beastrom by a count of 53 to 47 percent was aided by United Family Farmers members in the Missouri slope irrigation area.

United Family Farmers happily figured they had four friendly voices on the Oahe sub-district board. A triumphant George Piper reminded Senator George McGovern of his statements made prior to the election. Piper wanted McGovern to live up to his preelection promise and reexamine his views about Oahe. But with victory behind him, McGovern jumped off the fence he had straddled during the campaign and pressed for accelerated project funding.

As 1974 came to a close, hard feelings about Oahe were boiling over the James River valley. People across the state were becoming familiar with the controversy.

In its annual selection of the year's top news stories, South Dakota's Associated Press members voted the Oahe project as the state's third most important story of 1974, behind George McGovern's narrow reelection win and the landslide defeat of incumbent Attorney General Kermit Sande by a political newcomer named William Janklow.

8

Judgment Denied

I knew right away this was going to be a mean project. Whoever fought it
was going to be up to their elbows in alligators.

John Davidson, interview

In a September 1973 letter to James Adams, the dean of the School of Law at the
University of South Dakota, George Piper described the difficulties facing
farmers and ranchers as the Bureau of Reclamation acquired land to build the
Oahe project. He was wondering if the law school could help. James Adams
was a maverick who sympathized with groups like United Family Farmers. He
informed Piper that although the staff of the law school could not directly represent United Family Farmers, faculty members would be available to work with
the group's primary lawyer. Adams routed Piper's letter to John H. Davidson,
the school's instructor in natural-resource law, and Davidson quickly responded with his own letter to Piper. "I hope," wrote Davidson, "you are able
to achieve success in countering this project which is in my mind a waste of
money, an environmental insult and an abuser of the rights of individual
farmers."[1]

There was, perhaps, no lawyer in South Dakota with as profound an interest
in the relatively new field of environmental law as John Davidson. Davidson
had arrived at USD in 1971 after teaching at Washington DC's George Washington University law school. His experience in the East included environmental
litigation. While Davidson was in the nation's capital, several groundbreaking
environmental laws had been adopted by the federal government, including the
National Environmental Policy Act. It was an exciting and momentous time for
environmentalists, and John Davidson was proud to be associated with the
movement. He considered it an honor to apply his skills against the Oahe proj-

ect, and so he joined Martin Weeks to form the legal team assisting United Family Farmers.

Released in December 1973, Oahe's environmental impact statement was, in the opinion of Martin Weeks and John Davidson, the project's last point of legal vulnerability. The bureau had already submitted its draft EIS to public scrutiny, and the final EIS that the agency had prepared appeared to include much more information than the draft version. Although the slender draft document had totaled fewer than seventy-five pages, the final version was nearly four times as thick. Davidson and Weeks were sure, however, that the fat document still fell short of federal requirements. And if United Family Farmers failed to challenge the adequacy of the impact statement, advised the two lawyers, the group's alternatives to slow or stop the project through the judicial system were, perhaps, nonexistent.

When Congress first required environmental impact statements, federal agencies believed the documents should merely be a collection of paperworks that justified development of a project. The agencies did not want the public to use EIS information to criticize their plans, and they did not anticipate that the act would ever be used to block or reshape their projects. During NEPA's first full year in operation, some thirteen hundred impact statements were filed, but nearly all of them lacked penetrating analysis. It became the responsibility of the courts to define the requirements of environmental impact statements.

A landmark case that accomplished such definition involved a nuclear reactor proposed along Chesapeake Bay. Environmentalists charged that the reactor's warm-water discharges would damage the bay's ecology, and they sued the Atomic Energy Commission, the agency that had permitted the reactor. Their suit reached the United States Court of Appeals for the District of Columbia Circuit. The majority opinion in the verdict was written by the distinguished Judge J. Skelley Wright, who scolded the Atomic Energy Commission for failing to consider environmental information in the reactor's EIS. "Perhaps the greatest importance of [impact statements]," stated Wright, "is to require the Atomic Energy Commission and other agencies to *consider* [Wright's emphasis] environmental issues just as they consider other matters within their mandates. . . . Congress did not intend [NEPA and impact statements] to be . . . a paper tiger. . . . We believe that the [Atomic Energy] Commission's crabbed interpretation of NEPA makes a mockery of the Act."[2] It was a victory not only for those opposed to the nuclear reactor but for those interested in a strong and useful NEPA. The cavalier attitude previously taken by most federal construction agencies regarding impact statements had been successfully challenged. A new era in environmental justice had just begun.

To insulate themselves from the demands of NEPA, water agencies such as the Corps of Engineers and the Bureau of Reclamation argued that water projects that were in the planning stages at the time NEPA was passed should be exempt from the tough requirements of the new law. The agencies said that most projects required twenty years or more of planning before actual construction started, and that many projects were well into their planning phases when NEPA was enacted. To subject a project that had already been studied for many years to the scrutiny of an EIS, suggested the water developers, unduly jeopardized years of research.

But the courts were not convinced that sheltering water projects already in the planning process from EIS scrutiny was appropriate. It was decided that projects such as Oahe, with decades of planning already completed, must undergo the EIS process. Suddenly, planning and building agencies could be held liable for their proposals and their actions, and environmentalists began learning how to use impact statements to combat projects they disliked.

John Davidson and Martin Weeks felt the bureau released Oahe's EIS in December in order to allow enough time to move the document through the relevant federal bureaucracies by the beginning of the next construction season. "The bureau was going to try and clear the go-ahead on the project before spring frost was out, and get their shovels in the ground," said Davidson. "It's a lot harder," he explained, "to get a court to stop a project where the dirt is actually being moved. We needed a court order telling the bureau it couldn't start."[3]

That set up a deadline of sorts for the two lawyers and their clients. Oahe and its EIS had to be challenged quickly. A race was on. First out of the gate was the bureau. On 25 April 1974, the agency awarded a $9.9 million contract to construct the project's pumping plant on the shore of Lake Oahe. Just four days later, United Family Farmers counterpunched, filing a complaint in U.S. district court asking for a temporary restraining order and a preliminary injunction. The suit was aimed specifically at blocking any work on the pumping plant. Named in the suit were Secretary of Interior Rogers Morton and the Bureau of Reclamation.

While Weeks and Davidson hoped they could delay the pumping plant and other features of the project, both men realized that a long-term legal and political strategy had to be devised as well. "We hoped we could use NEPA [to question the adequacy of the final EIS, as required by NEPA] in the short term," explained Davidson. "We knew ultimately that if the project had momentum they [the bureau] would eventually prepare a final environmental impact statement that would be suitable and the project would proceed."[4] The long-term tactic, Weeks pointed out, was for the lawyers to win a temporary injunction against the project while United Family Farmers developed a successful political strategy.

Davidson and Weeks struggled to come up with the issues they needed to challenge the federal government. Although both men were knowledgeable lawyers with environmental experience, they were starting a journey through territory unfamiliar to nearly every lawyer in the country. Reclamation law was extraordinarily complex, and how it related to NEPA and other environmental laws was relatively uncharted terrain. The two lawyers were, in essence, bushwhacking through a judicial wilderness.

In their complaint, the lawyers included nine separate issues. Davidson was not sure which one of the issues, if any, might effectively stop the bureau. "We threw everything in there except Oliver Wendell Holmes's casket," remembered Davidson, reflecting on their desperate situation.[5] Davidson was hardly exaggerating. The nine causes of action in United Family Farmers' complaint ranged from alleged violations of NEPA to abuses of citizen rights under the U.S. Constitution. The first and broadest charge alleged that the impact statement was deficient in several areas. The remaining charges spanned a broad expanse of concerns that involved arcane environmental and reclamation statutes. Flooding and polluting the James River, it was contended, violated the Flood Control Act of 1936 and the Federal Water Pollution Control Act. The suit claimed that developing Oahe required the destruction of migratory waterfowl habitat, particularly prairie wetlands, and those deeds, too, broke federal laws. Other charges dealt with bureaucratic procedure and social impacts.

John Davidson believed the bureau was particularly vulnerable in areas related to pollution. He intended to prove that the bureau had never built a project that did not pollute on a massive level. It was inevitable, he claimed, that Oahe would degrade the waters of eastern South Dakota.

The bureau and its allies recognized that United Family Farmers and others fighting reclamation projects elsewhere could make a strong case that irrigation development would likely violate pollution laws. They knew that the Clean Water Act, passed in 1972, provided environmentalists with an important weapon to fight large irrigation developments. During the cycle of the Oahe lawsuit, irrigation supporters convinced Congress to exempt irrigation from Clean Water

Anti-irrigation billboard, Huron SD, 24 April 1974 (*photo courtesy U.S. Department of the Interior, Bureau of Reclamation*). South Dakota farmers opposed to the Bureau of Reclamation's Oahe Irrigation Project erected this billboard near Huron, South Dakota, in 1974. The Bureau of Reclamation's planning office for the irrigation project was located in Huron.

Aerial photo of James River in Brown County SD (*Peter Carrels*). A proposal by the Bureau of Reclamation to channelize the James River in Brown and Spink Counties, South Dakota, to accommodate excess and return flows of the Oahe Irrigation Project galvanized environmental opposition. The Missouri River's longest tributary, the James River originates in North Dakota and flows for 712 miles before entering the Missouri near Yankton, South Dakota. The forest and riparian wetlands along the James's meandering channel provide wildlife habitat types found in few other places on the agricultural northern plains.

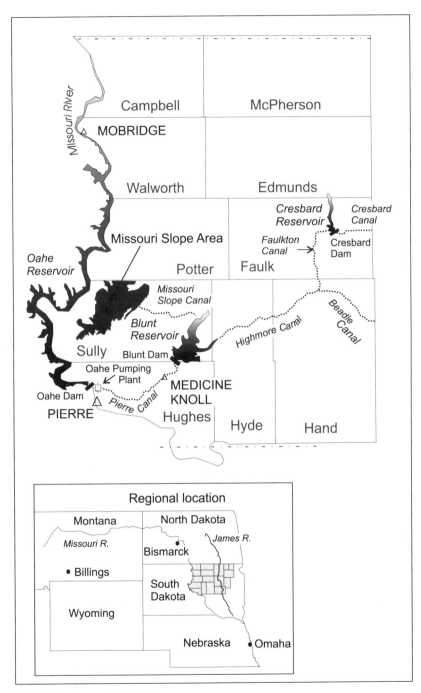

The Oahe Conservancy Sub-district

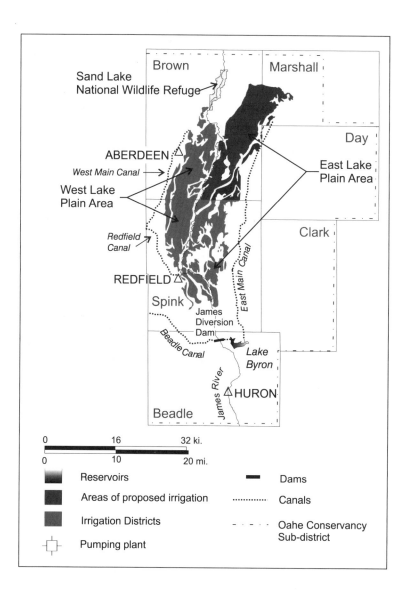

Brown

Marshall

Sand Lake
National Wildlife Refuge

Day

ABERDEEN △

East Lake
Plain Area

West Main Canal →

West Lake
Plain Area

Clark

Redfield
Canal

REDFIELD △

East Main Canal

Spink

James
Diversion
Dam

Beadle Canal

Lake
Byron

James River

△ HURON

Beadle

| 0 | 16 | 32 ki. |
| 0 | 10 | 20 mi. |

Reservoirs   ▬ Dams

Areas of proposed irrigation   ·········· Canals

Irrigation Districts   – · – · – Oahe Conservancy
                                         Sub-district

⊟ Pumping plant

Oahe Dam, Missouri River, near Pierre sd (*Photo courtesy U.S. Army Corps of Engineers*) The Oahe Dam, on the Missouri River near Pierre sd, was completed in 1962. Called the world's largest rolled-earth dam, it is 9,300 feet long and 242 feet high. Ranchers in the Missouri River valley wanted a smaller dam, but the federal government built it large to facilitate development of the Oahe Irrigation Project.

Robert Hipple (*Peter Carrels*) Pierre SD newspaperman Robert Hipple helped convince the U.S. Congress to build Oahe dam (pictured), introduced Lewis Pick to Glenn Sloan (of the Pick-Sloan Plan), and was an organizer of the Oahe Conservancy Sub-district. One of the Oahe Irrigation Project's most ardent promoters, Hipple served on the Oahe sub-district's board of directors from 1960 to 1980.

Pierre Canal, 14 April 1977 (*photo courtesy U.S. Department of Interior, Bureau of Reclamation*) In 1976, contractors began excavating the Pierre Canal. With cuts approaching one hundred feet, this would have been the Oahe Irrigation Project's deepest canal. The Pierre canal was designed to carry water from above the project's pump house near Oahe dam to the Blunt reservoir, a distance of about thirty-six miles.

Intake tube, Oahe Irrigation Project pump plant, 20 August 1975 (*photo courtesy U.S. Department of Interior, Bureau of Reclamation*) More than two thousand gallons of water per second would have been carried through this intake tube to the Oahe project pump facility before making its journey to irrigation fields in the James River valley, a hundred miles to the east. Three other similarly sized intake tubes were part of the pump facility's initial design.

Construction activity on Oahe irrigation pump house, 20 August 1975 (*photo courtesy U.S. Department of Interior, Bureau of Reclamation*) Construction on the Oahe Irrigation Project's main pumping facility began in 1974. Located adjacent to Oahe dam, the facility would have initially housed four 9,000-hp motors and pumps. Additional pumps would have been added later. Water from the Missouri River would have been propelled through the pump facility and up a nearby river bluff to the headworks of the irrigation project's canal system.

Rally of the Oahe opponents at Medicine Knoll, 28 June 1975 (*photo courtesy Rebecca Rosen-baum*) In June 1975, more than seven hundred protesters gathered on the grassy summit of prominent Medicine Knoll to oppose the Oahe Irrigation Project. Medicine Knoll, a hill about sixteen miles northeast of South Dakota's capital, Pierre, was where the Bureau of Reclamation planned to begin digging the deep Pierre canal. Speakers on the rally's makeshift stage included South Dakota legislator Ken Stofferahn (at the oil-drum podium) and Senator James Abourezk. It was at Medicine Knoll that Abourezk first publicly proclaimed his interest in helping Oahe opponents.

John Sieh, George Piper, and Curt Hohn (*Peter Carrels*) The three most prominent leaders of the opposition to the Oahe irrigation project. Sieh, left, was a Brown County SD farmer who became chairman of the Oahe Conservancy Sub-district. Piper, center, a farmer from Beadle County SD, founded and led United Family Farmers. Curt Hohn worked for Senator George McGovern before resigning to coordinate political activities for United Family Farmers. He later served as manager of the Oahe Conservancy Sub-district.

Act jurisdiction. The change meant Davidson and Weeks had lost a potentially valuable tool.[6]

The suit also charged that the bureau's irrigation projects frequently allowed nonresidents and other individuals to irrigate more land than was permitted by reclamation policy. Federal law specified that an individual could irrigate no more than 160 acres in a federal irrigation project. Though it was common that a husband and a wife and even the couple's children could claim 160 acres each, the intention of the policy was to limit the availability of subsidized water to guarantee that small farmers were the primary recipients of federal irrigation benefits. But enforcement had been lax. It was not uncommon for large corporate farms to use irrigation water from federal projects to water thousands of acres. The regulation presented a worrisome scenario for family farmers. Adhering to the policy meant some farmers would be forced to sell lands in the irrigation area to comply with the law. If, for example, a farm couple owned 800 acres in the West Brown Irrigation District, they would be forced to part with 480 acres of their land. It seemed a no-win situation for family farmers. If the law was enforced some farmers would have to sell pieces of their farms. If the law was not enforced, corporate farmers and agribusinesses would begin accumulating lands in the project area and crowd out family farms. John Davidson had an abundance of evidence that showed bureau projects favored corporate farms and harmed small farmers. "I was going to prove that they [the bureau] had never done anything but drive family farmers out of business," said Davidson. "I was going to dare them [the bureau] to take us to a project where family farming had survived."[7]

Davidson admitted that, despite Oahe's deficiencies, persuading a court to grant an injunction was a long shot. "It's extremely hard," he said, "to get a court to issue an injunction on the promise that evils will occur in the future."[8] The courts are also reluctant to pass judgment on political decisions. Projects such as Oahe were creatures of Congress, and it was prudent for the courts to presume that lawmakers closely examined the projects they endorsed.

On 30 April, one day after the suit was filed, Judge Andrew Bogue denied United Family Farmers' requests for a restraining order and a preliminary injunction. Judge Bogue then disqualified himself from further action in the case. The case was assigned to Judge Albert Schatz, of Omaha, and an evidentiary hearing was scheduled for 22 May. For most of the day, Judge Schatz listened to both sides. A month later, on 19 June, Judge Schatz rejected both of the United Family Farmers' petitions.

The crucial testimony came from project manager Preston Funkhouser.

Funkhouser explained that building the project's pump station near the Oahe reservoir would damage no one. It was not necessary, said Funkhouser, for the bureau to acquire any new land or disturb any agricultural soil to complete construction of the pump facility. He also testified that even if Oahe were never built, the pump house would be useful for other water-development purposes.[9]

United Family Farmers decided not to appeal Judge Schatz's decision, but the legal action was far from over. Still to be decided were the nine charges against the federal government. The case would be heard in U.S. district court in Sioux Falls under Judge Fred Nichol—a judge considered to be bright and conscientious. Nichol was a longtime friend and political ally of both Ken Holum and George McGovern. McGovern and Nichol had met while they both lived in Mitchell, just before World War II, when McGovern was a college student and Nichol practiced law. McGovern dated his future wife, Eleanor, while she worked for Nichol. Twenty years later, George McGovern asked President John Kennedy to nominate Nichol for the federal judgeship. Martin Weeks was concerned that the judge's close relationship with McGovern and Holum might affect the trial. In an unusual move, Weeks met with Nichol to discuss the situation. Judge Nichol assured the lawyer he could be fair in the case.

The government immediately sought to dismiss seven of the nine contentions. United Family Farmers dismissed their own charge [count #9] that the project violated the Constitution and substituted an allegation that Oahe's development would violate the 1914 Reclamation Extension Act. This act pertained to the acreage limit imposed on those who wanted to use water from a federal reclamation project for irrigation. Nichol quickly dismissed five of the remaining charges. The surviving allegations included violations of NEPA, the Migratory Bird Act, and the relocation and acreage limitation issues.

In August, United Family Farmers proposed a settlement to the lawsuit. The group said it would drop their suit if several conditions were met by the Bureau of Reclamation, the most important being a public vote on the project. Their offer was ignored.

In October 1975, United Family Farmers again filed motions for a temporary restraining order and a preliminary injunction. The bureau was, by that time, actively pursuing the acquisition of land in order to build the first stretch of the Pierre canal, in Hughes County. Landowners along one reach of the canal had already been given notice that if they declined to sell their property, the bureau would take it by condemnation.

The government's lawyers informed Judge Nichol that the bureau had already built the James River diversion dam near Huron as part of the project. The project's pump house was nearly completed, they said, and construction of a main canal was imminent. Their message was effective: it would be wasteful to halt a project that was already so far along.

Since Judge Schatz's decision, Weeks and Davidson had worked steadily to build their case. Depositions had been taken, interrogatories were filed with the federal government, and documents had been studied. But the two men suspected that there was much vital information in the bureau's files they had never seen. Through the court, they asked the agency to supply them with any documents that might be used during the upcoming trial. Arrangements were made for documents and files to be delivered to the federal courthouse in Sioux Falls, where Davidson and Weeks could review them. When they went to the courthouse to find out what new information had been made available to them, they were shocked. "It looked as though they'd unloaded a fullsized pickup with documents we'd never seen before," recalled Weeks.[10] Stacked about were volumes and volumes of data and figures, piles of reports, and many boxes of studies. Weeks began working day and night to study the new documents. He was so consumed by the work that he spent the Christmas holidays preparing the case instead of traveling with his wife to their daughter's Utah home.

Lead lawyer for the government was Andrew Walch. Walch was assigned the case out of the Department of Justice's Land and Natural Resources Division. Though he had graduated from law school only five years earlier, Walch was no youngster. Before deciding on law as a career, he had spent a dozen years working as a petroleum geologist. He was considered a very capable attorney.

Walch remembered being eager for the trial to begin. "I was ready to take on all comers, like a gunslinger on Main Street," recalled Walch of his confidence.[11] Teaming up with Walch to take on Oahe's seditious opponents were Robert Hiaring, an assistant U.S. attorney, and Al Bielefeld, a veteran from the Interior Department's Solicitor Office who had worked on Bureau of Reclamation cases. Bielefeld had already been involved in a variety of legal and congressional issues related to Oahe. The Oahe Conservancy Sub-district, both irrigation districts, and the Friends of Oahe assigned lawyers to the case as well.

The Bureau of Reclamation viewed the Oahe case as extremely important. Al Bielefeld later said it was one of the most significant cases his agency had faced in the Missouri River basin. An unfavorable outcome for the bureau, said Bielefeld, would have affected reclamation programs throughout the West and possibly halted the large irrigation projects being developed under the Pick-Sloan Plan.[12]

95

Martin Weeks quickly discovered how seriously the government viewed the case. Whenever Weeks conducted a deposition, he found himself facing a troop of government officials. There were lawyers, technicians, administrators, economists, scientists; sometimes as many as twenty of them. Each was taking notes and carefully watching and listening to Weeks. It was an impressive display of authority and power, recalled Weeks. And it was, he admitted, intimidating.

Two days before the trial began, a rally for Oahe supporters was held in Aberdeen. The event served as the first annual meeting for a newly organized group of Oahe proponents called Friends of Oahe, and it attracted about five hundred people from around the state to celebrate Oahe's progress and to downplay the threat posed by United Family Farmers and the approaching trial. A number of government officials attended the event, including the bureau's regional director, Robert McPhail, and the Oahe manager, Preston Funkhouser, plus attorneys Andrew Walch and Al Bielefeld. The rally's principal speaker, Ken Holum, told the audience that once the Oahe Irrigation Project was built there would be no opposition.

On 29 March 1976, Martin Weeks delivered the trial's opening remarks and asked for an injunction on project construction until the Bureau of Reclamation satisfied the complaints of United Family Farmers. The first witness for the plaintiffs, George Piper, explained the origins of his concerns. During cross-examination, Piper acknowledged that his family would lose land to the Byron reservoir and would receive no irrigation. The implication was that Piper opposed Oahe not so much because he judged it to be inappropriate, but because he would be damaged without benefit.

Davidson and Weeks argued that the environmental impact statement did not fully describe the phased, or segmented, approach to developing the entire Oahe Unit. They charged that the impact statement failed to analyze, adequately, the project's potential impact on the James River, on project soils, and on wildlife. United Family Farmers was well prepared to convince the court about the threats to irrigated soils. They had hired a photographer to document lands ruined by irrigation in Wyoming, and they gathered data proving that soils in the government's Columbia basin project, in Washington, were salting up at a rapid pace.

Their best evidence came from a study conducted by the bureau itself. Martin Weeks discovered that a board of three experts had been convened by the bureau in 1954 to study Oahe soils and drainage and make recommendations. Their report was the basis for the drainage design initially adopted by the bureau. When Weeks first asked the bureau for a copy of the report, the agency said they no longer had one. Weeks didn't believe them. He discovered that each of the consultants was deceased, but through relatives he learned that the papers of one of the men had been donated to a library in New Mexico. A librarian told Weeks that among the donated files was the document he sought. Weeks was ecstatic when he reviewed the report. "The report," he recalled, "was dynamite. It was a strong condemnation of the project."[13]

In the report, the three experts warned that project subsoils would be difficult and expensive to drain. They expressed concerns about irrigating the lake plain. To prevent waterlogging irrigated soils, they recommended a costly design for subsurface drains. The design would prevent the water table from rising to a height of 4 feet below the surface. To achieve this, they specified that drain spacing not exceed 330 feet (one consultant recommended 225 feet) and drain depth be about 9 feet.[14] Although the bureau initially adopted the recommendations, by the time the environmental impact statement was released, they had been discarded for a less effective, less expensive design that would permit the water table to rise to 3 feet below the surface. The new plan called for drain spacing at an average of 620 feet and at depths ranging from 6 to 12 feet. The reason the consultants were ignored, said John Davidson, was a matter of simple economics. "Drainage is a principal cost of an irrigation project," he explained, before adding that the bureau decreased the project's drainage capacity to reduce the overall cost of the project and to enhance the project's chances of being funded by Congress.[15] George Piper now had an official repudiation, or at least a conflicting opinion, of the bureau's contention that Oahe's soils could be drained adequately by the existing design, and he circulated hundreds of copies of the report.

During questioning by Martin Weeks, the bureau's chief of drainage for the Oahe project defended the decision to change the design and allow the water table to climb within three feet of the surface. "Does [the change] increase the risk [to the soil]?" asked Weeks. "I am not going to answer your question," responded the bureau official. "If the boss says do something, we do it."[16] The bureau claimed that using modern sprinkler irrigation instead of water distribution by gravity flow allowed for a new drainage design. But an expert hired by United Family Farmers refuted that. "Using the sprinkler method of irrigation," said the scientist, "may only delay the number of years in which the soil would become waterlogged."[17]

Walch and the government planted doubts about United Family Farmers' expert witnesses. When one testified that the Oahe's wildlife plan was inadequate, the defense informed the court that the plan was being reevaluated. They pointed out that the witness had evaluated at least one hundred other impact statements and found none to be satisfactory. The implication of this, said the government, was that the witness was impossible to satisfy.

Just before the government opened its defense, Judge Nichol dismissed the complaints about excess lands and migratory birds, leaving only two counts to be decided. The government and its lawyers reminded Judge Nichol that no one had as much experience as the Bureau of Reclamation in developing irrigation projects. The agency, they contended, had been communicative with the public throughout the project's development, and more reports were forthcoming. Environmental concerns were being addressed, they told Judge Nichol, and alternatives to the original plan were being examined.

The trial took nine days, and four months later, on 18 August 1976, Judge Nichol issued his ruling. Although he agreed that the project's environmental impacts would be substantial, he defended the bureau and declared that the requirements of NEPA had been fulfilled. "The purpose of NEPA [and impact statements] was to insure that environmental degradation would occur only after such effects were brought into the decision-making process," the judge declared. "The FES [final environmental statement] has served its purpose and fulfilled the goals set forth in NEPA."[18]

United Family Farmers' contention that relocation assistance had been inadequate was denied by Nichol on the grounds that the farm group's evidence included an admission that the bureau was improving in the area of relocation. Nichol said his court could not concern itself with the political process, and the best way for the farmers to secure relief was in the political arena. Andrew Walch agreed with Nichol's rationale. "I thought United Family Farmers was contesting a congressional decision that had to be attacked through the political process, and not through litigation," he said later.[19]

In a letter written immediately after the ruling, Al Bielefeld explained what victory meant: "[United Family Farmers] was a difficult and important case and its successful completion was critical to continued resource development in the Great Plains area."[20] Victory also meant that construction on Oahe's massive pump house, a vital component in the bureau's plan, could continue. This monolithic, concrete structure, the size of a spacious community auditorium, would house four 9,000-hp motors and pumps. Using electricity generated by Oahe dam turbines, each giant pump could power 2,250 gallons of water per second to the top of river bluffs. High above Oahe dam, the water would gush from the tubes into the headworks of the proposed Pierre canal. To quench the needs of Oahe's first stage, the government planned to divert about 450,000 acre-feet of reservoir water each year. That was the equivalent of 147 billion gallons of water, or enough to satisfy Aberdeen's annual domestic and commercial water needs for 180 years. But nearly all the diverted water was intended to serve one purpose: irrigation. Less than 6 percent would be available for municipal and industrial purposes.

The defeat notwithstanding, United Family Farmers derived significant benefits from the case. The Bureau of Reclamation was forced to produce data and documentation previously unexamined by project opponents. Materials uncovered in matters related to soils and drainage proved especially useful to United Family Farmers. The new information affirmed the suspicions of project skeptics and was used to recruit new opponents in South Dakota and in Washington. United Family Farmers was not pleased at the outcome of the trial, but defeat forced the organization to rethink its strategy. Judge Nichol had advised that the farmers seek relief not in courtrooms but in the political arena. United Family Farmers decided to do just that.

9

The Shifting Debate

I really don't want you people to believe you're on the outside looking in, thinking that nobody cared and is concerned.
Senator James Abourezk, Medicine Knoll speech, 1975

The evolution of James Abourezk's position on the Oahe project mirrored the maturation and growing influence of United Family Farmers. Abourezk, a Democrat who was elected to the U.S. House of Representatives in 1970 and to the U.S. Senate in 1972, brought an appealing blend of strongly held convictions and spontaneity to politics. He had a penchant for populism and wasn't bashful about breaking with conventionality.

Abourezk represented South Dakota's second district, the state's western district, which included most of the Oahe sub-district. When Abourezk first entered Congress, his strong support for the project was not surprising. For advice on Oahe, he sought out George McGovern and Ken Holum.

Despite United Family Farmers' strong showing in the 1974 sub-district elections, the organization's chances to stop Oahe appeared remote. Of the sub-district's eleven directors, only John Sieh and Bill Piper were defenders of United Family Farmers' positions. Steve Thorson surprised United Family Farmers shortly after the election when he announced that the Bureau of Reclamation had calmed his misgivings. Bud Yackley did not reverse his preelection position as conclusively as Thorson, but he was not reliable.

In Washington, South Dakota's delegation continued to promote the project. Piper and other project opponents decided to seek satisfaction through the state legislature. After losing to Richard Kneip in the 1974 gubernatorial primary, Bill Dougherty became a lobbyist. It seemed fitting that among Dougherty's first clients would be the farmers opposing Oahe. Dougherty offered access to the political establishment and lobbying know-how, both of which the farmers desperately needed. The issue that United Family Farmers campaigned for in the 1975 legislature was the one Bill Dougherty had endorsed in the primary: a moratorium on the project.

Ken Stofferahn, a farmer and a Republican legislator from Humboldt, emerged as the moratorium's chief sponsor. Stofferahn was acquainted with Bill Piper through the National Farmers Organization. It was while campaigning for Stofferahn in the 1972 U.S. Senate primary that the Piper brothers learned about plans to expand Byron reservoir. Stofferahn had connections to a politician who had his own relationship with United Family Farmers—Larry Pressler, who grew up several miles from Stofferahn's home. Stofferahn had served as campaign treasurer when Pressler made his first run for Congress in 1974. The relationship between Stofferahn, Pressler, and others in the Humboldt vicinity was known as the "Humboldt kitchen," reflecting on political ideas hatched in Stofferahn's home. As the 1975 session approached, United Family Farmers was ready. They had a bill to promote, a lobbyist to help them, and a gutsy legislator to champion their cause.

On the Sunday preceding the start of the session, a program promoting Oahe was broadcast on South Dakota television stations. Financed by Charles Kearns, an equipment dealer for the Caterpillar company, a half-hour film titled *Why Oahe?* was shown before and after the screening of the Super Bowl. Kearns also paid for the air time. Kearns's film made no pretense at being impartial. Featuring statements by Oahe supporters, the film was essentially an advertisement for the project. Kearns himself spoke, urging the development of Oahe. "If South Dakota is to avoid becoming the Appalachia of the Midwest," warned Kearns, "we'd better get on with Oahe."[1] Kearns was prominent in state politics, having been appointed by Governor Kneip to serve on the commission overseeing the Department of Game, Fish and Parks. Based in Sioux Falls, Kearns was a perfect target for United Family Farmers since he lived outside the Oahe area but stood to profit enormously if Oahe was built.

To combat United Family Farmers, Senator George McGovern had encouraged formation of a group that was named Friends of Oahe. Though the organization was touted as a grassroots equivalent of United Family Farmers, most of its contributors were businessmen from across the state, not farmers from the subdistrict. The organization's first director, a man named Ed Glasgow, lived in Rapid City, some 350 miles from Oahe's irrigation districts. From his home base in the Black Hills, Glasgow directed a variety of organizations that promoted resource development. Among Glasgow's clients was the South Dakota Water Development Association, a pro-irrigation group affiliated with a national water-development association that served the wishes of the Bureau of Reclamation. With its membership roster loaded with influential businessmen, Friends of Oahe had instant credibility among the state's political establishment, and the group's rivalry with United Family Farmers was immediately vicious.

Several weeks into the legislative session, a confidential state report was leaked to Oahe opponents. Authored by South Dakota's department of environmental protection, the report listed numerous concerns about Oahe and concluded by stating that "serious disruption of and damage to the environment will result from construction and operation of the . . . Oahe Project."[2] For years, the official position of South Dakota had been to support the project. It was now clear that within certain segments of state government there was serious apprehension. Bill Dougherty gave a copy of the report to Tim Schreiner, the former *Volante* editor who was working as a reporter for KELO-TV, and Schreiner described the report during a newscast. Dougherty also distributed copies to every member of the legislature.

Governor Kneip was incensed about the report reaching the public, but he was unable to ward off the wave of pressure from legislators and Oahe opponents urging him to release other state reports related to Oahe. At first Kneip resisted, but later he released additional documents, including another report containing unflattering analysis about Oahe. Wielding this new information, United Family Farmers strengthened their status and began making inroads with legislators. In an unusual move, and reflecting Oahe's rising controversy, the house state affairs committee set a public hearing on the project, with both legislative bodies scheduled to be present. The fate of the proposed moratorium hung in the balance.

A half dozen speakers represented project opponents at the hearing on 25 February 1975. Along with Oahe proponents, they addressed legislators from the high podium facing the house chamber. George Piper testified that too many aspects of the project's design would be unfinished until after irrigation water was applied to the land: "Can we plunge ahead and expect that we will have answers when the project is built? . . . The build now, plan later procedure won't work."[3] Tony Dean, speaking on behalf of the South Dakota chapter of the Wildlife Federation, urged caution: "Assume for a moment that the environmentalists are right. Can we undo the damage that would result if they are right and the project goes ahead anyway?"[4]

Mike McHugh, a Brown County farmer installed as president of the Friends of Oahe, emphasized his respect for the Bureau of Reclamation: "The Bureau of Reclamation has the qualified experts on irrigation . . . we must rely on those who know what they are doing."[5] E. C. Pieplow, a banker and state senator from Aberdeen, made an ominous prediction. "A moratorium," warned Pieplow, "would sever the jugular vein of the Oahe project."[6] A letter from Governor Kneip concluded the hearing. His position, the letter reiterated, was absolute opposition to a moratorium.

During the hearing, the gallery was crowded with farmers protesting Oahe. Oahe proponents, mostly businessmen from cities and towns, milled about on the main floor. Before and after the hearing, citizens thronged the capitol's corridors. Legislators found themselves surrounded by determined faces. No other day of that year's session was as tense.

On 4 March, the moratorium resolution was defeated by seven votes to five in the state affairs committee. But several days later, Ken Stofferahn and his legislative allies maneuvered the proposal to the house floor for a vote. For nearly three hours the moratorium was vigorously debated before losing by four votes—thirty-three to thirty-seven. Most legislators from the project area opposed the moratorium, but two future governors, George Mickelson and Walter Dale Miller, supported it. Despite the defeat, United Family Farmers made immense gains in terms of new political friends and statewide coverage of the controversy. The group came close to victory because of its ability to convert those legislators who had been uncertain about the project when the session convened. Throughout the session, members of the group swarmed the legislature in orchestrated shifts. Ed Glasgow observed that United Family Farmers outworked and outlobbied Friends of Oahe. "I estimate there were ten times as many contacts with legislators by those wanting the moratorium than by those of us that opposed the moratorium," noted Glasgow, in a memorandum to the Friends of Oahe board of directors. "Our friends that came in to help were effective, but there just were not enough of them."[7]

Senators McGovern and Abourezk were troubled by the shrinking public and legislative support for the project, and they admonished the Oahe sub-district for failing to promote the project effectively. "If the Board does not take the direct responsibility of 'selling the project' to the people," scolded the two senators, "then we cannot do it for you."[8] McGovern was especially concerned that neither the sub-district nor the Bureau of Reclamation was handling the public relations challenge facing the project. "Who will speak for Oahe?" he asked sub-district manager Robert Raschke. "For over two years now, I have been urging a strong public relations effort in relation to the project—not only in the project area, but throughout our State."[9]

Senator Abourezk continued to support Oahe publicly, but there were signs that his feelings were changing. The press reported that staff in Abourezk's and McGovern's offices wanted the senators to reconsider their positions on Oahe. At the senators' shared field office in Aberdeen, aides Steve Blomeke and Curt Hohn, working for Abourezk and McGovern, respectively, had become skeptical about Oahe. McGovern's Washington staff remained committed to Oahe, but Abourezk's aides there were split over the project. Most wanted Abourezk to fight the project, and they were making headway with the senator.

It is unclear who first proposed a public referendum on Oahe. George McGovern had described the 1974 sub-district elections as a referendum on the project, but he backed away from that assessment when opposition candidates scored victories. United Family Farmers offered to drop their lawsuit against the federal government if a public vote on the project were held, but that suggestion was spurned.

A referendum on Oahe was a chancy proposition for United Family Farmers. While the group had convinced many farmers to oppose Oahe, the prevailing sentiment among town and city people was favorable toward the project. Losing a referendum could halt the group's rising influence and end their movement. But with their options to block further development of Oahe dwindling, United Family Farmers decided that a public vote was a risk they were willing to take, and the group's next major campaign was launched.

To dramatize their opposition to Oahe and their support for a referendum, the organization staged a summertime rally on a remote, windswept hilltop in northern Hughes County called Medicine Knoll. In the hummocky Missouri River coteau, Medicine Knoll rises prominently above the surrounding countryside. Travelers bound for Pierre from either the north or east cannot help but notice it protruding from the rolling plains. The site was chosen because, in addition to its topographical prominence, it was where contractors would begin excavating the deepest stretch of the Pierre canal. From lofty Medicine Knoll, they would dig the ditch in two directions: west toward Oahe dam, and northeast to the proposed Blunt reservoir. Royal "Roy" Runge operated a successful ranch on Medicine Knoll. He had been born on the ranch in 1922 and had lived and worked there nearly all his life. He had already joined United Family Farmers when the Bureau of Reclamation began negotiating with him for his land.

Roy Runge was not the first area landowner to be visited by the bureau's land-acquisition specialists. More than ten thousand acres had already been secured for the proposed Blunt reservoir. Acquisition of land to allow canal construction would spark greater resistance. Forty-nine different landowners stood between the bureau and completion of the entire Pierre canal route. Many ranches would be severed and crippled by the canal; even the acquisition of small parcels would seriously impede ranching operations.

That the bureau planned to initiate canal construction on Roy Runge's 4,500-acre Medicine Knoll Ranch proved a public relations blunder. Runge was respected by his neighbors, and his plight quickly drew many sympathizers. Eight farm and conservation groups joined United Family Farmers to help sponsor and promote the rally, and advertisements were placed in newspapers and on radio stations across the state. Newspaper ads showed a photo of Roy Runge holding his young son, looking out over a peaceful prairie setting. "This man is inviting [South Dakota] to his ranch," said the ad's text, before describing the threats of Oahe: "The Oahe Canal is more than a charted line on a government map. It means farm families who will be forced to move, farm land that will be lost from production forever, natural wildlife areas drained and destroyed, and underground water supplies disturbed. Unchecked and unreviewed it can mean destruction for South Dakota."[10]

Two days before the rally—scheduled for 28 July—a bloody gunfight on the Pine Ridge reservation claimed the lives of two FBI agents and an Indian man. The incident dominated the news for several days while a manhunt was under way. As the state and its media looked west, pondering the circumstances of that tragedy, farmers and environmentalists gathered on the lofty plateau at Medicine Knoll. Roy Runge made the accommodations as comfortable as possible by pulling cactus and trimming grass. To shade the day's speakers, he fastened a canvas tarp to a hay fork and hoisted it over the flatbed hay wagon serving as the stage. In the middle of the makeshift stage, Runge placed an empty oil drum for use as the podium. A U.S. flag was hung on the upraised arm of a tractor.

As the rally's noon starting time approached, so did the traffic. Over the gravel roads and the dirt trail leading to the rally site came hundreds of vehicles, including busses arranged by George Piper to carry United Family Farmers. People spread their blankets, ate picnic lunches, and listened to a folksinger beneath a hot, bright sun. Sales of soda pop were brisk, reported the Blunt Altar

Society. With John Sieh serving as master of ceremonies, the speakers came forward, one by one lashing out at Oahe, its political supporters, and the Bureau of Reclamation. Sieh indicated that all four members of the state's congressional delegation had declined an offer to address the rally.

Roy Runge told the crowd that the ranch had been in his family for fifty-seven years. He and his twin brother bought the place from the rest of their family in 1940. The brothers were still in their teens when they began buying the ranch, too young to sign legal documents or purchase papers. But they had worked hard and had done well, and as the years passed had built it up to 4,544 acres. "Where we're sitting now," said Runge, referring to the picnic area and stage, "is the center of the ditch cut." The rancher swung a long arm from his side and pointed toward flags outside the rally area. Those markers, he explained, showed the width of the corridor to be acquired by the government.[11] Although Runge would lose only about 244 acres to the government, the 1,900-foot-wide right-of-way containing the ditch would split Runge's ranch into two large segments. Some 1,000 acres south of the ditch would be marooned from the remaining 3,500 acres. Runge figured he would have to sell the smaller tract and revamp his ranch operation.

The afternoon's highlight was the unexpected appearance of Senator Abourezk. The senator happened to be traveling by small airplane in the area. On a whim, he landed at Pierre and drove out to the rally. Abourezk's presence sent a ripple of excitement through the crowd, and John Sieh invited the senator to the stage. Abourezk was perhaps the only Oahe supporter in the crowd of some eight hundred people. "It's kind of awkward for me to be up here," said Abourezk, "especially since a great many of you are my friends, and have been for a long time. But I've come here because of my own background. I have all of my life been on the outside looking in. People who are associated with the Oahe project as supporters are considered to be the establishment. Well, I do support the Oahe irrigation project, but I don't consider myself to be any part of the establishment. That's why I'm here, to tell you that I really don't want you people to believe you're on the outside looking in, thinking that nobody cared and is concerned."[12]

What Abourezk said next caught everyone off guard: "I think the best thing to do is for a district-wide [i.e., sub-district] referendum to be held to determine whether or not the people out here, who are affected [really want the project]."[13] Cheers and applause erupted like a long burst of thunder. Abourezk then reiterated his support for Oahe and left the stage, shaking many hands extended to him as he moved through the crowd.

At the rally were South Dakota filmmakers Judi and Doug Sharples. The couple had just completed a documentary film entitled *Oahe: A Question of Values*. The Sharples became interested in Oahe when they produced radio and television advertisements for George McGovern's 1974 reelection campaign and noticed that Oahe had been delicately handled by McGovern. The premiere of their film had drawn rave reviews from both the Bureau of Reclamation and United Family Farmers. The auspicious reaction pleased the Sharples because a difficult balancing act had been achieved. Funding for the film came from the South Dakota Committee on the Humanities, an organization affiliated with the National Committee on the Humanities. The South Dakota committee felt the film contributed intelligent discussion to a complex public-policy issue and congratulated the Sharples for their fine work.

The film's first major exposure came at the 1975 South Dakota State Fair, held in late summer in Huron. During fair week, more than fifteen hundred people viewed the film, and comments continued to be favorable. The National Committee on the Humanities was so impressed by the film that it ordered a copy to show affiliated groups in other states what filmmaking could accomplish.

When Doug Sharples attempted to obtain public-service air time for the film on South Dakota's leading television station KELO-TV, the film's honeymoon came to an abrupt halt. The station had previously sold time to Charles Kearns's thirty-minute commercial for Oahe and was selling advertising to Friends of Oahe. The Friends group had also purchased time to rerun Kearns's promotion, timing its broadcast to coincide with the beginning of the 1976 legislative session. KELO-TV refused to show the Sharples's film on the grounds that it was a news documentary. Doug Sharples countered by offering to buy air time. Again, the station declined the request.

The Sharples were dumbfounded. They had already shown the film on two other South Dakota stations. Purchasing air time from the other stations, they reported, had been quickly and routinely concluded. The filmmakers complained to the Federal Communications Commission that KELO's refusal violated the fairness doctrine. Only one side of a controversial public issue, the Sharples charged, was being presented by the television station. In April 1976, the FCC ruled in KELO's favor, saying the station had complied with the fairness doctrine: KELO had, in fact, allowed United Family Farmers to appear on a special broadcast to explain their opposition to Oahe. In the aftermath of the FCC ruling, Senator McGovern and Friends of Oahe lodged a complaint with the National Endowment for the Humanities. The Friends group described the

Sharples film as biased and poorly made and asked the national organization to suspend all grants to the South Dakota Committee on the Humanities. They also requested restitution for Oahe supporters. To "untangle the confusion caused by the film," they wanted money to create another production.[14]

The Sharples defended the objectivity and quality of their film. On a modest, $18,000 budget, they had traveled to five states to film federal reclamation projects. They showed ruined land, blighted boomtowns, and the domination of federal irrigation by corporate farms. The fifty-five-minute film did not ignore the claims made by project proponents: included in the more than two dozen interviews were statements for and against the project. The Sharples film was certainly a more professional production than the Kearns film, but no taxpayer monies had been used to produce *Why Oahe?* And that was the crux of the complaints. Doug and Judi Sharples later said that the research they conducted while making the film soured them on the Oahe project. That perspective, though not blatantly presented in the film, was a subtle theme through much of the production.

Oahe proponents had initially underestimated the film's ability to spark doubts about the project. Setting aside the murky issues regarding the film's objectivity, or lack of objectivity, one thing was clear: within the context of the film, the contentions of project opponents were elevated to at least a level of parity with the contentions of project proponents. This provided viewers with an opportunity to gauge the benefits and drawbacks of the project and to make an informed decision. The film also lifted a mystique that had for years encouraged the public to accept Oahe simply because their political leaders favored it.

Not surprisingly, the film's controversy attracted bigger crowds to its showings and increased its influence. United Family Farmers was grateful for the film and showed it at dozens of meetings across the sub-district. The Sharples may have been rejected by KELO, but their desire to create a film that played a role in the public debate over Oahe was fulfilled. Eventually the South Dakota Committee on the Humanities and the Friends of Oahe reached a settlement. Oahe proponents were granted money by the committee to produce a slide show. That project floundered and had no impact on public opinion.

Though he continued to proclaim his support for Oahe, Jim Abourezk discussed the mechanics of a referendum with Martin Weeks. George Piper quickly spread the word. "Abourezk is wavering," Piper told a local leader of the Sierra Club. "He [Abourezk] should be encouraged to support a delay in the project until a referendum is held."[15]

Soon, letters and phone messages began to flood Abourezk's office. Curt Hohn, a former aide to George McGovern, wrote a particularly effective letter. Hohn knew Abourezk because he had worked at the field office shared by McGovern and Abourezk in Aberdeen. Hohn thanked Abourezk for attending the Medicine Knoll rally and posed a poignant analogy by asking the question: "If Jim Abourezk were living in Aberdeen and working as a welder or farming near Aberdeen, or ranching in the valley south of Blunt what would you do and where would you stand?" Then Hohn answered his own question for Abourezk: "You'd be leading the charge my friend . . . there's no doubt about it. When the digger moved out to Medicine Knoll, you'd be there. When the bureau told one thing to elected officials and another to farmers, you'd be pissed. . . . In short, you'd do just what we're going to do."[16] Hohn told Abourezk that United Family Farmers was preparing to launch an effort in the 1976 state legislature calling for a referendum. Anticipating much resistance, Hohn asked Abourezk to help the group. "All it would take from you," Hohn suggested, "is a couple of news releases and maybe something in a newsletter." Hohn mailed the letter on 31 July 1975.[17]

Less than two months later, Abourezk announced his support for a referendum in a letter to South Dakota Governor Richard Kneip and members of the South Dakota legislature. The letter was followed by a news release to South Dakota media outlets and a constituent newsletter devoted to Oahe that included a section titled "Arguments against a referendum on Oahe are not convincing."[18]

The backlash was ferocious. An angry Ken Holum quickly wrote to Abourezk: "Your actions . . . have placed in jeopardy the Oahe Irrigation Project and the same activities have embarrassed and endangered the South Dakota Democratic party and many of its leaders. . . . I have followed the activities of South Dakota's delegation to Congress for over 40 years. I have never been more displeased."[19] Oahe supporters told Abourezk that elections to form the sub-district, to grant contracting authority to the sub-district, and to form the two irrigation districts amply demonstrated public support for the project.

But Abourezk would not retreat, declaring that opposition to the project had increased and that Congress needed to know how the state felt about the project before proceeding with further development. He pointed out that the earlier elections had been conducted before the project became controversial and had not offered the voters an opportunity to oppose or support Oahe. At the time, Abourezk personally felt that Oahe could withstand a public vote and would be politically stronger after winning at the polls.

In preparation for the 1976 legislative session, Governor Kneip departed Pierre to garner support for his budget package. At several stops in the Oahe area, Kneip encountered abnormally large crowds. The governor quickly discovered that his budget was not what drew them to the meetings. United Family Farmers dominated the sessions, and they angrily disagreed with the governor about the referendum. Kneip wrote to Mike McHugh, president of the Friends of Oahe, about the hostile crowds and the lack of Oahe allies: "I must commend [United Family Farmers] for marshalling forces to get so many people to attend . . . these meetings," he said, adding: "It sure made it tough to stand before those crowds and almost alone defend the merits of the project."[20]

United Family Farmers was doing more than loading local meetings. To prepare for the 1976 legislature and the next round of sub-district elections, the group began an aggressive effort to educate the public. They formed a speakers' bureau, created a slide show, and started an advertising campaign in newspapers and on radio. The group's treasurer, Roger Schuller, began an ambitious fund-raising effort in the fall of 1975. Schuller, who had grown up listening to his father, George, criticize the Oahe project, proved superb in building the treasury.

Not long after the 1976 session opened, Ken Stofferahn and nineteen other legislators introduced a measure calling for a referendum on the Oahe project, with voters in Brown, Spink, Day, Marshall, and Sully Counties—the counties most effected by the proposed project—eligible to cast ballots. Stofferahn's bill excluded most city and town residents from voting, leaving farmers to decide the question. Bill Dougherty was again the United Family Farmers lobbyist. He urged his clients to rewrite the bill to allow more residents of the sub-district to vote, but Stofferahn and United Family Farmers disagreed. The Oahe sub-district board, while uncomfortable with the idea of a public vote, indicated they would support an election involving the entire sub-district. Governor Kneip also opposed a vote but said that if one were to be held it should be statewide. Senator Abourezk thought the state legislature should determine the appropriate election area. Stofferahn's restrictive bill was tabled by nine votes to four in the house state affairs committee, but he successfully appealed to the entire house for a vote of all members. There was a catch, however. Stofferahn compromised his measure, amending the voting area to include the entire Oahe sub-district, comprised of fifteen and one-half counties.[21]

On 6 February 1976, the *Aberdeen American News* carried a front-page headline that horrified Oahe supporters: "House Okays Referendum." By a vote of thirty-nine to thirty-one, the house had approved Stofferahn's bill. Pro-Oahe forces roared into Pierre to derail the proposal in the senate.

Heading up the team for Friends of Oahe was Jeremiah Murphy, a savvy, veteran lobbyist from Sioux Falls and one of the most influential people in state politics. In his testimony, Murphy challenged Oahe opponents to concentrate on the upcoming sub-district director elections or to circulate petitions to bring an election to dissolve the sub-district. "The legislature," advised Murphy, "should not be involved in this."[22] Twice there were motions to send the bill to the full senate. Each motion died. Then the committee killed the bill on a six-to-three vote. Aberdeen Senator Peg Lamont attempted to circumvent the committee decision, but her motion to bring the referendum to the senate floor failed by twenty-one votes to thirteen. United Family Farmers had lost.

The intense debate claimed more than just the referendum. Tim Schreiner lost his job as a television reporter because of the controversy. Schreiner certainly was not new to the Oahe issue when he came to Pierre to cover state government for KELO-TV. As a reporter, Schreiner was resourceful and talented. Despite his feelings about Oahe, Schreiner balanced his reporting on the issue, but his interest in exposing the problems and controversy associated with Oahe was evident by his stories.

Apparently, Schreiner's demise was triggered by complaints from Governor Kneip and other Oahe backers. Schreiner asked tough questions at news conferences, and his story about the leaked report from the environmental protection agency embarrassed the governor. Kneip's concerns reached KELO's owner, Joe Floyd, who enthusiastically supported Oahe. The station tried to remedy the problem by asking Schreiner to stop covering Oahe. Schreiner objected. Then KELO asked another reporter, Bryan Bjerke, to cover the Oahe issue. Bjerke refused to replace his friend. Schreiner was then told by his supervisor to refrain from reporting anything except legislative vote totals in matters related to Oahe. Schreiner again protested, pointing out that the referendum was approaching its dramatic climax in the legislature. To clear up the mess, KELO brass traveled to Pierre and demanded that he avoid controversial Oahe stories. At that point, Tim Schreiner quit.[23]

It is likely the complaints about Schreiner extended beyond the stories he reported and his alleged bias. At the time, Schreiner was sharing a house in Pierre with several people. When George Piper and other United Family Farmers came to town, they often used an empty room in that house as their lobbying headquarters or as a place to get some sleep. United Family Farmers did not come by this arrangement because of Tim Schreiner, however. Piper and other United Family Farmers came to the house because one of Tim Schreiner's housemates was none other than George McGovern's former staffer Curt Hohn, the young man just hired by United Family Farmers to serve as its first executive director. Schreiner's friendship and living arrangement with a United Family Farmers leader may not have compromised his abilities to be an effective and balanced reporter, but it was certainly a red flag for Oahe supporters. Here was the legislative correspondent for the state's most influential television station sharing a house with a leader of the group that opposed the project they coveted.

10

The Young Defector

You can't work for someone if you have a strong difference of opinion.
It's almost like stealing if you do.
Curt Hohn, interview, 11 October 1988

Curt Hohn had a reputation for intelligent thoroughness—for a capacity to
focus, simultaneously, on both the big picture and its most minute details. This
talent served Hohn well, first in his position as an aide to Senator George
McGovern and later as he worked against the Oahe project. When Hohn resigned his position with George McGovern, his friends were puzzled. Those
who knew him felt he had a fine career stretching out before him. It was envi-
sioned that Hohn would end up as a top policy staffer working in Washington or
maybe become a politician himself.

Politics, it was apparent, came to Hohn naturally. He had snatched up the
McGovern job not long after graduating from Northern State College, in Aberdeen. And he had done well for McGovern, providing constituent services and
organizing the northeastern part of South Dakota during McGovern's successful 1974 election. Hohn was well-liked, mature beyond his young age, and he
loved the workings of government and politics. Shortly before Hohn left the
senator's employ, he declined a promotion. He had been asked to relocate to
Washington to serve as McGovern's environmental and water policy aide.

Curt Hohn admired George McGovern's intelligence and compassion, but
Hohn's growing reservations regarding the Oahe project sharply contrasted
with the feelings of his boss. Hohn repeatedly encouraged McGovern to reexamine his position, but nothing could dim the senator's enthusiasm. He remembered McGovern repeating the same theme over and over. "He told me many

times," Hohn later said, "that it was South Dakota's turn for water development. He said that we've got to take Oahe and make the best of it."[1]

On one occasion, Hohn and Steve Blomeke, Senator Abourezk's aide in Aberdeen, set up a meeting for McGovern with a group called the Lake Byron Farmers (this was the first name used by the Pipers and their neighbors, before Bill Piper suggested the name United Family Farmers). Hohn expected the farmers to focus their complaints on the land they would lose to the expanded Byron reservoir. Instead, the group's spokesman, George Piper, presented sophisticated reasoning against the project, including concerns about soil irrigability and cost benefits. Hohn also arranged for McGovern to tour the proposed Blunt reservoir and talk with farmers and ranchers unhappy with the treatment they had received from the Bureau of Reclamation. These meetings had a strong impact on Hohn. McGovern seemed unaffected.

George Piper challenged Hohn and Blomeke to visit the Garrison Diversion Project, and the two staffers arranged tours with Richard Madson and the Bureau of Reclamation. During discussion with the bureau, Hohn raised concerns that he had heard earlier from farmers. A bureau engineer became highly agitated, dismissed the farmers' complaints, and accused Garrison opponents of deceit. Hohn was surprised at the outburst. "I expected [the bureau] to be reasonable," explained Hohn. Instead, he found the government employee to be strident and unsympathetic.[2] "I had no bias against engineers," said Hohn, "but I knew farmers." He recalled his days growing up on a farm near Plankinton, South Dakota: "The people I met along the [Garrison] canal route were just like the people I grew up with."[3] Hohn agreed with something many of the farmers told him: that the biggest problem facing farmers was not occasional drought but the perennially low prices for crops. "One of the worst years we had, when I was a kid, was the year we had the best milo crop and the best corn crop," explained Hohn. "We worked hard to harvest those great crops, but to our astonishment we made less money that year than the year before."[4]

Senator McGovern's fence-riding Oahe strategy during the 1974 reelection campaign especially bothered Hohn, and he realized it was time to quit. "You can't work for someone if you have a strong difference of opinion," explained Hohn. "It's almost like stealing if you do."[5]

After leaving McGovern, Hohn took a position with South Dakota's Highway Safety Division. Moving from Aberdeen to Pierre, however, did not isolate Hohn from the Oahe issue. He began to assist United Family Farmers as never before, helping organize events and meetings and advising United Family Farmers on political tactics. It had been John Sieh's idea to hire Curt Hohn as

United Family Farmers' first paid executive director. Sieh recognized that Hohn possessed abilities and experience in electoral politics. Hohn had many contacts throughout the sub-district because his area assignment for McGovern almost exactly coincided with the sub-district boundaries. These attributes, Sieh knew, would be helpful as United Family Farmers prepared for the 1976 sub-district elections.

Hohn left his state job on Halloween 1975 and began his duties for United Family Farmers while living in Pierre. The effort to convince the legislature to allow a referendum on the project dominated his first months in 1976. Once the session concluded, Hohn returned to Aberdeen, to be nearer the struggle raging through the James River valley. Throughout the campaign, Hohn's apartment in Aberdeen served as the organization's office. The phone and doorbell there rang at all hours, and Hohn became addicted to his mission, working up to eighteen hours a day, day after day, week after week. Once a month, he would collect his $964 paycheck.

On 2 March 1976, twenty-two days before the trial began in the United Family Farmers' lawsuit against Oahe, the Bureau of Reclamation opened bids to begin construction on the Pierre canal. Hohn and the Piper brothers went to Huron to protest the event. While a government official announced bidders on the project, George Piper stood nearby and read a prepared statement asking that Oahe construction be delayed until a plan was identified for the James River. Ten days later, the bureau awarded a contract to Bechtold Excavating, a construction company from Minot, North Dakota. Bechtold would be paid more than $2 million to excavate a short segment of the Pierre canal classified as Reach 1B. This stretch was where the canal's depth would reach nearly 100 feet. Bechtold's assignment included digging .5 of a mile of unlined canal and .8 of a mile of earth-lined canal. Part of Roy Runge's ranch had been condemned, and this canal segment would sever his land. Landowners in the area were seething, worried about their own land and angry for what had happened to their neighbor. Law-enforcement officials, the Bureau of Reclamation, and Bechtold feared demonstrations or vandalism: radio-equipped patrols were dispatched to the site and preparations began to deal with any protest rallies. Considering the tension gripping the canal area, it was remarkable there were no incidents.

The same day Bechtold won its contract, United Family Farmers held their third annual meeting and banquet. The occasion had already become festival-like, with bountiful potluck feasts. Long cafeteria tables were lined with serving platters and bowls bearing a multitude of meat dishes and a variety of salads. There was corn and other vegetables, served hot or cold, in two dozen different recipes. Loaves of bread were stacked like hay bales beside a tub filled with tabs of butter. Desserts covered one entire table: pies of all kinds, fruit jello, crisps, and cookies. Large urns of coffee and Kool-Aid steadily emptied. People filled the gymnasium at Northwestern High School in Mellette, where the meeting took place. Some five hundred diners occupied all available seats around tables on the floor and another two hundred found seats in hastily added chairs or on the gym bleachers. Featured speaker James Abourezk told the crowd that if public officials were required to endure the election process, then so should a public-works project. As they had done at Medicine Knoll, members of United Family Farmers cheered as Abourezk reiterated his support for a referendum. John Sieh delivered a rousing speech; not unexpected, as Sieh had earned a reputation as a sharp, fiery speaker. It was time, Sieh announced, for United Family Farmers to invade Washington DC. The trip would be timed to coincide with Oahe's appropriation hearings.

Three weeks later, Oahe supporters and Governor Richard Kneip appeared before a congressional sub-committee, where Kneip declared the project would transform the James River valley into an "abundant garden." Kneip asked Congress to increase the Ford administration's Oahe budget recommendation for 1977 from $16.6 million to slightly more than $17 million. Oahe's 1976 appropriation had been $7.25 million.[6] Several days after Kneip's presentation, two hundred United Family Farmers arrived in Washington on a chartered plane and began lobbying against Oahe. At each congressional office they left a reminder. Before departing South Dakota, United Family Farmers members placed soil samples from fields scheduled to one day be irrigated by the Oahe project inside clear, plastic baggies. The dirt in the bags wasn't fine, and it wasn't coarse, but when a solid clump of that rock-hard gumbo was dropped onto a congressman's polished desk, there would sound a sharp knock, like bare knuckles on a door. Can this soil be irrigated? the farmers asked.

In a hearing room packed with their comrades, six members of United Family Farmers presented testimony to a Senate appropriations sub-committee panel. Art Fischbach, a farmer from the Spink County Irrigation District, introduced himself by proclaiming, "I never thought I'd see the day when I would come to Washington to ask Congress not to give me something, but here I am." Fischbach then told the senators that "we really should all be back in South Dakota planting crops but we had to come to Washington to talk with Congress to protect ourselves and give back a project that we were not fully consulted on and don't want."[7] Watching United Family Farmers closely was George Cunningham, Senator McGovern's chief legislative aide. Cunningham despised the farm group and helped carry out much of Senator McGovern's strategy to undermine Oahe opponents. When the plane carrying United Family Farmers left the nation's capital, George Cunningham had already mailed a list of the people who had lobbied against the project to Friends of Oahe. "I thought you would like to have, for your files," wrote Cunningham, "the attached list of those who came to Washington . . . in opposition to the Oahe Irrigation Project."[8]

Despite their creative display of opposition, United Family Farmers failed to block the 1977 appropriation. In addition to President Ford's original recommendation, Congress appropriated $2.7 million for the year's transitional quarter, meaning Oahe would receive more than $19 million during fiscal 1977. The money would be spent on activities such as land acquisition and construction work on the Pierre canal. Oahe supporters hailed the 1977 appropriation as a huge victory. Not only had United Family Farmers been thwarted again, but major canal construction could finally begin. No large project in the history of federal reclamation had been halted against the wishes of the Bureau of Reclamation once such construction had commenced.

No one smiled more broadly at Oahe's new funding than L. J. "Bud" Maher, publisher of the *Huron Daily Plainsman*. Not even Bob Hipple used his newspaper to promote Oahe as aggressively as Maher. Long before United Family Farmers existed, Huron's newspaper championed water development. The newspaper's love affair with Oahe started under the direction of Bob Lusk, the man who hired Maher. It had been Bob Lusk who called Glenn Sloan's vision for federal irrigation in the James River valley the greatest boom central South Dakota could hope to experience. During the 1930s, Huron had struggled to survive, and Bob Lusk did not want that to happen again. In 1938, he authored a story for the *Saturday Evening Post* that described a farm family recovering their lives and their farm after grueling drought.[9]

In his campaign for irrigation, Lusk created the pro-Oahe dam and pro-irrigation newspaper editions that infuriated Roy Houck and Frank Ferguson. When Houck and Ferguson demanded, in 1952, a public debate with irrigation supporters, they sought as their adversaries a representative of the Bureau of Reclamation and Bob Lusk. In 1946, after graduating from South Dakota State University, Bud Maher had reluctantly gone to Huron to visit with Bob Lusk about selling newspaper advertising. Maher was skeptical about living in Huron. He had grown up on a farm not far south of Huron, remembered how the dust bowl decimated the area, and planned to make a career far away from Huron. When he told Lusk of his apprehension, Lusk described the irrigation project that would one day transform the James River valley into a prosperous paradise. Huron will thrive, predicted Lusk—and Maher took the job. After Lusk's death in 1962, Maher became the paper's point man—and Huron's—on Oahe.[10] By that time it had become apparent there would be no irrigation from the Oahe project close to Huron. That did not diminish Maher's desire for the project. With the completion of Oahe, there would be a water-conveyance system between the Missouri and the James Rivers, assuring additional flows in the James. Because Huron relied on the unpredictable James for its water, the community needed a more reliable water source to promote community growth. Maher also anticipated that new agricultural processing plants would spring up in Huron if Oahe were built.

Bud Maher needled Curt Hohn when Hohn boldly announced that United Family Farmers hoped to take over the Oahe sub-district board by winning the sub-district elections in November 1976. "We were just a little surprised," editorialized Maher, "at the candor with which Curt Hohn . . . outlined the plan to take over the Oahe Sub-district Board."[11] Maher warned his readers that if United Family Farmers triumphed, Huron would forever lose its opportunity for water development.

It was inevitable that Bud Maher and Curt Hohn would clash. The two men were sharply contrasted not only by their philosophies toward Oahe but by the tactics they used to advance their position. Bud Maher had begun a newspaper career based on his employer's support for Oahe, while Curt Hohn abandoned a promising political career because his assessment of Oahe did not concur with that of his boss. Hohn continued United Family Farmers' tradition of working directly with landowners to organize a grassroots army. Maher believed that bank presidents, newspaper publishers, construction interests, and the state's business establishment could win the fight. With his ear to the ground, Curt Hohn heard the discontent that was sweeping the countryside. Bud Maher either failed to recognize it or chose to ignore it.

11

The Public's Crucial Decision

We tromped over hundreds of people to get the Oahe dam in and we'll tromp over hundreds more to build the Oahe project.
Robert Hipple, quoted in a United Family Farmer ad, 1976

By the summer of 1976, United Family Farmers was motivated by a sense of desperate urgency. The group had failed to block Oahe in the courts and had been foiled in Pierre and Washington. Their opportunities to stall or stop the project were vanishing, and the Bureau of Reclamation was building as fast as its appropriations allowed.

Oahe supporters held a comfortable plurality on the sub-district's board of directors—of eleven board members only John Sieh and Bill Piper were stalwart project opponents—and all of the six board seats up for election in November 1976 were occupied by men favoring the project. If United Family Farmers could win four of the six contests, they would possess a board majority and be in position to dictate sub-district policy. The implications of this scenario had the group pouring most of its energy and resources into the elections.

Senator George McGovern was wary of the sub-district elections. He recognized Curt Hohn's political skills, and he pressed Oahe supporters to prepare for serious competition. "It would be very difficult, if not impossible," McGovern warned, worried about United Family Farmers winning the elections, "to continue the project if the very Board that was established by State law to work with the Bureau of Reclamation in its development was opposed to completion."[1]

McGovern's concerns were justified. John Sieh and Curt Hohn had already prepared a detailed blueprint for United Family Farmers to follow during the election campaign. The plan established a board of operations within the organization and delineated individual and committee responsibilities. Under the plan, Hohn would be the political field-worker. His working relationship with the rest of the operations board would be close, including daily contact with George Piper, John Sieh, and Roger Schuller. Hohn would travel frequently throughout the sub-district, and he was assigned a tight timeline to organize election committees in each of the voting areas. In addition to advising individual candidates, he would devise a public-education campaign about Oahe that would be unleashed through newspapers and radio in the fall. This media effort would function independently of candidate advertising.

Because of the tremendous workload facing United Family Farmers, the organization hired a young man named Jay Davis. A 1974 graduate of Brown University, Davis had worked summers on congressional campaigns for Democrats in South Dakota. He disliked the Oahe project and eagerly accepted the job with its meager weekly paycheck of $75 plus room and board. For the first two months, Davis's "room" was a bedroom in the Piper home and his "board" was served alongside his hosts at the table where United Family Farmers was born. As the election neared, Davis moved to Aberdeen to help Curt Hohn.

John Sieh's role was to create and critique short-term and long-term campaign strategies. Sieh emerged as the organization's taskmaster, pushing everyone to work harder as the elections grew nearer. Roger Schuller continued as treasurer. The organization's budget was cautiously frugal, reflecting Schuller's vigilance, and members trusted their contributions would be wisely spent. Schuller, who also advised on political tactics, lived just twenty miles from John Sieh, and it was only a forty-five minute drive to Aberdeen from his home near Claremont. Having Hohn, Sieh, and Schuller living in proximity to each another was a great advantage for United Family Farmers. The three met regularly to steer the organization through the campaign.

George Piper managed United Family Farmers' headquarters, based in the one-room schoolhouse. Eighty miles from Aberdeen, Piper's role in helping formulate campaign strategy was limited, but he continued working with members, researching the Oahe project, and coordinating the distribution of information, press releases, and the newsletter.

It was during the 1976 campaign that the shrewd, tenacious, and cohesive character of United Family Farmers was best demonstrated. Not only was the group's leadership attuned to the membership's feelings about Oahe, they were bound by a spirit of camaraderie and focused purpose. Grassroots organizations have often been impaired by divisiveness among their leaders. The harmony of United Family Farmers was manifested by the smooth rhythm of decision making. Before anything else could happen, suitable candidates had to be recruited. That task was Curt Hohn's.

In the sub-district's area #3, which included rural Day and western Marshall Counties, a farmer named Leonard Naessig challenged incumbent director John Schwab. Naessig entered the race because of his concerns about wildlife mitigation. Under federal law, any wildlife habitat destroyed during construction of a project such as Oahe must be replaced, or mitigated, by equivalent habitat. Oahe's mitigation plan involved the acquisition of approximately forty thousand acres of privately held land from across the Oahe sub-district. Day County, where Leonard Naessig farmed, contained thousands of shallow ponds and marshes that provided excellent wildlife habitat. It was likely that Day County would host more mitigation than any of the other counties in the sub-district. Although many wetland areas in the county had already been drained and destroyed by farmers, it was an ideal place for the federal government to locate surviving or repairable wetlands that could be used to mitigate for wildlife habitat destroyed elsewhere by Oahe development. Ironically, various federal programs had encouraged the destruction of the potholes and sloughs that were to be restored, and the federal Fish and Wildlife Service was already active in Day County purchasing wildlife lands for purposes unconnected to Oahe mitigation.

In March 1976, Naessig received a letter from the Bureau of Reclamation informing him that three hundred acres of his farm were part of Oahe's mitigation plan. The letter identified marshy areas Naessig had drained twenty years earlier. Naessig called his friend John Schwab and asked for an explanation. Schwab explained that mitigation was necessary, and he assured Naessig that he would receive a fair price for his land. It was not what Naessig wanted to hear. When Naessig filed his election papers, John Schwab asked him to withdraw his candidacy. Naessig refused. Neassig's campaign was given a boost by the unrest sweeping Day County regarding Oahe mitigation. The Day County Commission adopted a resolution opposing the acquisition of wildlife lands in the county. County commissioners wrote Senator George McGovern and said mitigation in Day County was not welcome. The county chapter of the Farm Bureau also opposed mitigation in the county. John Schwab must have cringed when the local newspaper editorialized against Day County farmers losing land to mitigation and printed a lengthy article about mitigation under the headline: "Bureau bats zero with farmers."[2]

Another sub-district area holding an election was Spink County. Bisected by the James River, with irrigation proposed within its borders, Spink County was deeply embroiled in the Oahe debate when Glenn Overby, a farmer living in the irrigation area, decided to challenge incumbent Dwayne Kettering. Kettering, a farmer who had once worked for the Bureau of Reclamation, had served on the sub-district board since 1965. Overby was chairman of the Spink County chapter of United Family Farmers. Despite their differing opinions on Oahe, Overby and Kettering were lifelong friends and neighbors. As youngsters, they had been schoolmates, and later they served together on their township board. In Oahe's early days, when Overby circulated petitions to form the sub-district, they had been allies on Oahe. But Overby's feelings changed when he accompanied Kettering to visit a reclamation project in Nebraska. While his traveling companion continued to support Oahe, Overby became concerned about the suitability of the soil for irrigation and withdrew his land from the Spink County Irrigation District.

Farmers in Edmunds and Walworth Counties would also be selecting a representative to the sub-district board. As was the case in Spink County, the contest pitted neighbor against neighbor. Arnold Schurr's first exposure to Oahe politics came in 1960 when he accompanied Melvin Roesch to a meeting of area farmers interested in irrigation. Schurr had just started farming, and his home place in sparsely populated Edmunds County was only two miles from where Roesch lived. At that meeting, Roesch agreed to be a candidate in the very first sub-district election. He was unopposed in that race and for sixteen years was the only representative to serve his area on the Oahe board. Schurr was uncomfortable with the new taxes portended by Oahe development, and he had heard that wildlife mitigation was likely for his county. He also knew that his area would receive no irrigation despite those impacts. Roesch, he felt, had become too cozy with the Bureau of Reclamation and could not be counted on to defend local interests. Not long after sharing his apprehensions with several members of United Family Farmers, Curt Hohn paid a visit and convinced him to challenge his neighbor.

The election to represent rural Faulk and Potter Counties featured Dan Cronin and Siegfried Swanhorst. Cronin was an irrigator who had been selected by the Oahe board to replace Fred Holscher, the district's original director and former sub-district chairman. Holscher had resigned in January 1976 because of poor health. Sieg (pronounced *Zeke*) Swanhorst loved John Deere implements, and his home and farm buildings were painted green. In the 1960s and early 1970s, Swanhorst had been attracted to the green crops promised by Oahe promoters. He looked forward to the day when an Oahe canal would pass by his farm in Faulk County and empty into the proposed Cresbard reservoir. Even though the reservoir would claim some of his land, Swanhorst supported Oahe.

In 1973, Swanhorst accompanied other South Dakota farmers on a tour of the Garrison project that was sponsored by the Bureau of Reclamation. Swanhorst noted that at least half the North Dakota farmers he met during the tour were skeptical about the project. Later, he attended a meeting of United Family Farmers and met George Piper. Then he went to an Oahe sub-district board meeting and met John Sieh. Piper and Sieh convinced him that Oahe supporters on the sub-district board had not asked the right questions and could not supply the public with adequate information about Oahe. That tilted Swanhorst to run for the board.

In January 1976, Orville Hill had been named chairman of the Oahe board. Representing farmers and ranchers in Hyde and Hand Counties, Hill was another director who had served since the sub-district's inception. He was offended by John Sieh's firebrand behavior, and as chairman declined to appoint Sieh to any of the sub-district's working committees. Sieh protested the exclusion—it was the first time a director had been excluded—but Hill's decision was upheld by the executive committee. At the board's March 1976 meeting, a group of Brown County farmers complained they were being deprived of adequate representation. Hill ignored them. At the next board meeting, a writ of mandamus, requiring Hill to appoint Sieh to a committee, was presented by the local sheriff. An embarrassed Hill quickly appointed Sieh to a committee.

Hill himself was facing a challenger. His opponent, a young rancher named Doug Beckett, had willingly sold his ranch to the Bureau of Reclamation in the proposed Blunt reservoir area and then relocated to Hand County. When Hill attempted to connect Beckett to United Family Farmers, his tactic backfired. Although Beckett had been recruited to run by United Family Farmers, he later repudiated his ties to the group and refused their campaign assistance. Beckett said that he supported the project but was more cautious than Hill.

The sixth sub-district seat open for election was for one of the board's two municipal director positions. Challenging Bob Hipple was thirty-five-year-old Curt Johnson, a high-school teacher from Huron. Johnson was supported by environmental and sportsmen groups, and a popular outdoors commentator, Tony Dean, served as chairman for his campaign. Several years earlier, Dean had been hired to describe Oahe's wildlife benefits in Charles Kearns's film called *Why Oahe?* Since then, Dean had changed his position on Oahe. One of Johnson's chief worries was the damage Oahe would cause to wildlife.

Of the six challengers supported by United Family Farmers, Curt Hohn thought Naessig and Schurr had the best chances to win. Naessig's concern about mitigation fitted well with farmers in his area, and Schurr's politics—he was a Republican and his opponent was a Democrat—coincided with a hefty majority of the party registrations for farmers living in Edmunds and Walworth Counties. Curt Johnson faced the most difficult contest. Huron, his hometown, was headquarters for the project, and hundreds of well-paid Bureau of Reclamation employees had long been part of the community. Johnson's supporters there were hesitant to associate themselves publicly with his candidacy. Bob Hipple's editorials attacking Johnson and promoting his own candidacy were reprinted in the Aberdeen and Huron newspapers. Jay Davis was assigned the formidable task of running Johnson's campaign.

In September, United Family Farmers' hard-hitting media campaign hit the newspapers and radio. It was the beginning of a two-month advertising blitz that caught Oahe proponents flat-footed. The ads, which mentioned no candidates, hammered away at the Oahe project and the government institutions supporting it. They appeared every week in more than three dozen weekly newspapers serving the sub-district and were heard many times each day on radio stations heard across northern South Dakota. Curt Hohn orchestrated the ad campaign so that different areas received different ads at different times, and some ads were tailored to specific areas. Altogether, there were nearly fifty different themes. It was impossible for Oahe proponents to respond to this information barrage in a timely way.

Each newspaper ad was similarly designed. This included a bold heading such as "Blank Check for Bureaucrats" or "Government Cheats Farmers" or "For Marshall County, Oahe Means Taxes." Supporting the headlines was tightly written text that provided compelling details. For example, beneath the headline "One Thing the Oahe Board Can't Guarantee Is Water" was the statement: "They can guarantee that you'll be paying taxes for Oahe. They can guarantee that 500 farmers will lose their land. But they can't guarantee water. The Oahe Board signed a contract that says irrigators can't hold the government responsible for any shortage in the quantity of water . . . on account of drought or other causes. A lot of our interests were sold down the river when the Oahe contract was signed. Maybe we need to review that contract."[3] Readers were referred to page nine of the sub-district's master contract to confirm the ad's charges. Another headline stated: "The Bureau's Errors Will Be Your Responsibility." The succinct text included: "According to the master contract the Oahe Board signed with the U.S. government . . . the Bureau . . . shall not be responsible for the control, carriage, handling, use, disposal, or distribution of water." The ad continued: "If a dam breaks, a ditch cuts a farmer's underground well, or the project pollutes the James River, or any other project feature goes wrong, your taxes will be responsible." The ad then declared: "The present Oahe Board committed you to that contract."[4]

A provocative statement attributed to Robert Hipple was integrated into another ad. "We tromped over hundreds of people to get the Oahe Dam in," Hipple had declared, "and we'll tromp over hundreds more to build the Oahe project."[5] United Family Farmers used Hipple's comment as the headline and then asked a question: "What will the Oahe Board do to protect the farmers in South Dakota whose land is to be taken for ditches and reservoirs and wildlife refuges? Tromp over them? The Oahe Board is all that can stand between the Bureau's condemnation and the farmer."[6] Another ad began with the headline "Now Boarding" and went on to describe junkets taken by Oahe incumbents to places like Honolulu, Phoenix, Palm Springs, and Las Vegas."Maybe all these trips to exotic fun places provide Board members with insight into South Dakota water problems," stated the ad. "Maybe it's time," the ad concluded, "to tell the Oahe board that the party is over."[7]

At the bottom of every ad, below the headline and its supporting text, and beside United Family Farmers' trademark logo that showed a farmer standing beneath a weather vane and beside his mailbox reading his mail, was a simple statement that reduced resolution of all the bitter and complicated issues in the Oahe controversy down to the simple act of voting. "November 2nd you have a choice," declared each ad. "You can elect a director who will represent YOU on the Oahe Board." The organization's radio ads ended similarly.

Fund-raising for both sides intensified as the election neared. Rumors and misconceptions regarding contributors for either side swirled about without substantiation. Though Friends of Oahe accused United Family Farmers of being funded by large farmers and out-of-state interests, the opposite was true. More than 90 percent of United Family Farmers' money came from farmers in Brown and Spink Counties. In 1975, when the group raised $36,000, the contributions included 300 donations of under $100 and 111 of more than $100. A handful of out-of-state contributions totaled less than $100. That trend of raising money from sub-district farmers, especially in the proposed irrigation areas, continued through 1976, when Roger Schuller and other volunteers worked even harder and brought in nearly $70,000.

The organization was especially adept at raising money during large rallies. At one rally, with hundreds of United Family Farmers present, John Sieh growled about the bureau's miserable treatment of farmers in the Pierre canal and Blunt reservoir areas and reminded everyone that the future of their farms was at stake. Jay Davis circulated through the crowd collecting contributions as Sieh implored the farmers to dig deep for the cause. Davis remembered checks and cash piling up and then overflowing from the large bowl he carried. When he counted the night's take, he began to tremble. "There was more than $15,000," recalled Davis.[8] Another fund-raiser drew six hundred people to a chicken dinner held in a high-school gymnasium. So much chicken was consumed that the caterer had to return to Aberdeen to get more. The bill that night for chicken and fixings exceeded $1,000. But the diners were generous. Some $10,000 was collected for the campaign.

Fund-raising at Friends of Oahe was entirely different. Most contributions came from nonfarmers. Charles Kearns and his heavy-equipment sales company, for example, gave more than $20,000. An association of contractors contributed at least $10,000. Bankers and business interests in Huron, Sioux Falls, Aberdeen, and other cities pitched in, too. The budget during 1975 for Friends of Oahe was at least $43,000. For 1976, that figure jumped to more than $70,000. Lacking volunteers, Friends of Oahe relied on consultants and paid staff to perform most of its functions. While Curt Hohn ran the campaigns for United Family Farmers out of his apartment in Aberdeen, Friends of Oahe hired Mid-America Communications, a Sioux Falls public-relations firm, to handle some of its campaign chores. Owned by Rollyn Samp, an aide to former Governor Frank Farrar, Mid-America was paid nearly $16,000 in 1975 and more than $36,000 in 1976. Bill Riechers, executive director of Friends of Oahe, also worked on the elections from an office on Aberdeen's Main Street.

Rollyn Samp hired a Sioux Falls graphic artist to produce a media campaign for incumbents. "Drought is a terrible thing," headlined one ad. It continued: "It robs our money, steals our dreams and damages our spirit."[9] Another ad was headlined: "Remember the Dust Bowl days of the 30s?"[10] Below that was a photo showing a forlorn prairie shanty and a dusty sky. Each ad contained in large type the words "Vote For: Water, Re-elect," and below this request was the candidate's name. Though these ads were designed for Friends of Oahe, some appeared in newspapers with a disclaimer that identified a different organization. Virgil Ellwood, a former professor at Northern State College in Aberdeen, was listed in some of the ads as the contact person for the "Committee for Water Conservancy."[11] Ellwood later admitted that he had been a front man for a group that did not exist. The money for at least some of the ads had come from a prominent Aberdeen businessman whom Ellwood refused to name.[12] Apparently, the man feared being linked to the Oahe election.

126

The evocation of drought and the "dirty 30s" was a timely tool for Oahe proponents during the 1976 elections. Dry conditions during 1976 were the worst in parts of South Dakota since the 1930s. Not only did Friends of Oahe highlight the drought in its campaign, the *Aberdeen American News* placed stories and headlines about the drought alongside advertisements or news releases from United Family Farmers.

Friends of Oahe also stressed another theme in its campaign. Many South Dakotans feared that other states would appropriate Missouri River water before water projects could be developed in their state. Oahe supporters capitalized on this anxiety by promoting the expression "use it or lose it." They circulated a story about wealthy Texans who were planning to divert Missouri River water to the Southwest. In his newsletter to constituents, Senator McGovern reinforced the paranoia about Texas. "'Use it or lose it' is not an idle slogan," said McGovern.[13] The newsletter portrayed Texas as a water predator with its eyes on the Missouri River. McGovern's worries were not without a shred of credence, but the threat was exaggerated and used as a scare tactic to influence an election that should have hinged not on the purported aggression of Texas, but on the appropriateness of a plan to use Missouri River water in South Dakota. "Use it or lose it" was a slogan used by water-project promoters all over the West to gain public support for projects.

Senator McGovern wanted to showcase the Oahe project and remind South Dakotans of the crucial sub-district elections, so he scheduled a statewide water conference for Sioux Falls several days before election day. United Family Farmers derisively referred to McGovern's conference as a rain dance, and they criticized McGovern for holding his Oahe rally outside the sub-district area. The group decided to present retaliatory statements during the main session.

John Bieber, an elderly farmer from Brown County, was a loyal, lifelong Democrat who had supported George McGovern in every election McGovern had entered. But Bieber was mad that McGovern was meddling in Oahe politics. Gathered in a downtown Sioux Falls hotel room were Bieber and others, including Jay Davis and John Sieh, who helped Bieber compose his speech. Bieber had suffered a heart attack several months earlier and he regularly popped nitroglycerin pills, but he assured his friends that he was fit enough to present the speech before a large, hostile crowd. By the time Sieh and Bieber entered the hotel's convention hall, the big room was teeming with more than five hundred Oahe supporters, and the main forum was about to convene. Most everybody knew who John Sieh was, and his presence was not appreciated.

Looking across the throng, Sieh was relieved to find several unoccupied chairs at a table where an old friend was seated.

Fred Simonton had been Sieh's boss years before, when Sieh worked as a field organizer for the Farmers Union. Now Simonton was the executive director for the Mid-West Electric Consumers Association, a Denver-based organization that supported rural electric users. The association's first office had been in Aberdeen, and its first president and executive director had been none other than Ken Holum. When they had worked together, Sieh and Simonton had been more than fellow farm organizers. Sieh had been the best man at Simonton's wedding and had loaned honeymoon money to Simonton. But as Sieh sat down, Simonton left the table without saying a word and moved to a place along a wall. Bieber took the chair beside Sieh.

Earlier in the day, McGovern had met with Oahe board incumbents. Now he was seated at the main table with the conference moderator, Harvey Wollman, South Dakota's lieutenant governor. Among the crowd were Bureau of Reclamation employees, including Commissioner Gilbert Stamm. Stamm had come to Sioux Falls to present an award from the Bureau of Reclamation to Robert Hipple.

When Wollman finally acknowledged Bieber, the farmer stood, appearing small in the sea of faces and business suits. Without glancing down at the page in his hands, Bieber looked straight at McGovern and started to speak. "There comes a time when something needs to be said," opened Bieber, his voice crisp and louder than his frail stature should have allowed. "Maybe the language is harsh," he continued, "but still it needs to be said, and I'm going to say it right now." Suddenly, all attention in the vast room was focused on the bent, gray man with the German accent. Bieber's speech began like the many constituent letters he had sent McGovern over the years, except that this one would attack the senator, not praise him. "Dear Senator McGovern," rang out Bieber, "It's time we reviewed the record on Oahe, for us to understand this conference and water issues."[14] Quoting extensively from newspaper articles and radio interviews, Bieber accused Senator McGovern of manipulating sub-district politics, and he demonstrated that McGovern's position on the Oahe referendum had been contradictory. At the conclusion of his remarks, Bieber said he would turn over corroborating evidence to be placed in the conference record. And then he introduced John Sieh.

Wollman quickly interjected, warning that he would not tolerate further attacks on the senator. McGovern said nothing, though later, in a statement made at the conclusion of the conference, he acknowledged the accuracy of Bieber's charges and defended changing his mind on certain issues. John Sieh stood as Wollman completed his warning. Surrounded by the buzzing crowd, trying to gather his composure, Sieh described the need for government to involve the public in water-project planning. Relying on government bureaucrats and political institutions, he said, was one of Oahe's principal flaws. Fred Simonton had not moved from along the wall. John Sieh was now his enemy, and their positions were irreconcilable. It was the same for nearly every other person in the room. Simonton had traveled from his Colorado office to attend the meeting. He was not a farmer, but he was part of the political apparatus that supported Oahe. McGovern's conference drew a roomful of Simontons. They were living examples of the condition John Sieh described in his brief speech. Two years later, when Fred Simonton had his own chance to serve as the best man at a wedding, the groom was Ken Holum.

McGovern's gathering failed to generate momentum for pro-Oahe candidates. It was too late in the campaign for new money and publicity to have much impact.

Throughout the sub-district area, the Oahe controversy was a major issue in legislative and county races. Pro-Oahe candidates for the legislature held joint campaign meetings with incumbent Oahe directors to promote the project and themselves. Contests for seats on the West Brown and Spink County irrigation districts were intense. The Bureau of Reclamation's role in the campaign was mostly behind the scenes. They helped with political meetings designed to promote pro-Oahe candidates running for the sub-district or the state legislature.

A large group of United Family Farmers gathered on election night in the aptly named Farmers Bar, near the town of Brentford, in Spink County. In the early evening hours on 2 November 1976, the mood inside the big tin building was tentative. No one knew how much hope to risk. Curt Hohn was tired but relaxed. He was satisfied he and the organization had done all they could.

With members of United Family Farmers stationed at the various county courthouses and regularly phoning in the sub-district election numbers, bar patrons were kept apprised of the races. A television set brought in for the occasion was tuned to a local station. In addition to covering the Gerald Ford–Jimmy Carter presidential contest and other political races, South Dakota's broadcasters regularly provided information about the sub-district. This was unusual attention, considering the fact that these were nonpartisan, local elections, but by then people from throughout the state were following the Oahe controversy. On the wall was a tally sheet, and members of United Family Farmers began hollering and whistling as each update was reported and posted. By midnight, there was a full-fledged celebration going on. Project incumbents were being ousted by wide margins. Only the Curt Johnson race was in doubt, and that race was too close to call.

Arnold Schurr won by the largest margin, garnering 72 percent of the vote. Farmers in Edmunds and Walworth Counties gave Schurr 1,495 votes, while Melvin Roesch received only 577. Sieg Swanhorst was selected on 70 percent of the ballots in his race against Dan Cronin. Swanhorst collected 1,189 votes to Cronin's 510. Leonard Naessig's campaign against mitigation and sub-district taxes led to his lopsided victory over John Schwab. Naessig tallied 1,728 votes—64 percent of the total. Schwab finished with only 24 percent of the votes. A third candidate who campaigned as an Oahe opponent finished third. In Spink County, Glenn Overby surprised Dwayne Kettering by taking 61 percent of the vote. Overby's total of 1,270 votes included many from the irrigation area. Doug Beckett's moderate positions prevailed over Orville Hill in Hand and Hyde Counties, 61 percent to 39 percent. Hill's defeat ended his long, dedicated career on the Oahe board.

Bob Hipple was the lone incumbent to survive—and even though Hipple symbolized Oahe and irrigation development, Curt Johnson collected 49.5 percent of the votes and lost by only 18,656 votes to 18,321. Despite being constantly blasted by newspapers in the sub-district's major cities, Johnson carried Aberdeen and came close in both Huron and Pierre.

There were other victories for United Family Farmers to celebrate. State Senators Ted Lerew and E. C. Pieplow, leading Oahe supporters in the state legislature, had been defeated as part of the anti-Oahe siege. Lerew, an especially rabid Oahe supporter from Faulk County, whose rancorous debates with John Sieh disrupted more than one public meeting, had been targeted early by United Family Farmers. Pieplow, an Aberdeen banker, lost to Robert Williams, a local telephone company employee and union activist whose campaign was given a boost by United Family Farmers. With Williams's election, both of Aberdeen's state senators—Peg Lamont was the other—backed United Family Farmers.

Election watchers at the Farmers Bar also learned that Jimmy Carter, a Democratic governor from Georgia, had beaten Gerald Ford. Based on correspondence between United Family Farmers and the Carter campaign team, the new president would probably be more sympathetic to them than the Ford administration had been.

The milestone sub-district election results were not entirely attributable to United Family Farmers. It was not just a beating meted out by their candidates and by Hohn, Sieh, Schuller, the Pipers, and the rest of the farm group; it was a beating that Oahe proponents invited upon themselves.

Throughout the campaigns, United Family Farmers contended that Oahe supporters were not genuinely interested in local input. United Family Farmers understood that voters, particularly farmers, wanted the sub-district to acknowledge local opinions and not simply be a rubber stamp for a federal agency or for special interests. One reason the incumbents lost was because they had earned such a label.

Issues such as Vietnam and Watergate had battered the trustworthiness of big government, and this sentiment also influenced voters in the sub-district. Men like Arnold Schurr, Glenn Overby, Leonard Naessig, and Sieg Swanhorst loved their country, but they had come to realize that federal programs and bureaucracies often ignored local concerns. They knew that in pursuing certain condemnation cases, the Bureau of Reclamation had been ruthless and insensitive to farmers. They disliked the way Oahe's mitigation plan had been sprung on the unsuspecting public. They believed the bureau was mistaken about fundamental issues such as soil irrigability, drainage, and the project's cost-benefit economics. And they were convinced that the bureau had intentionally withheld information about Oahe from those who would be directly impacted by its development.

Oahe proponents failed to comprehend a movement of dissatisfaction that was sweeping the sub-district. It had been thirty years since the passage of Pick-Sloan, a decade and a half since formation of the sub-district, ten years since the irrigation districts were created, and seven years since the project was reauthorized by Congress. Those were Oahe's halcyon days, when few in the countryside knew much about the project but expectations were great. With the release of Oahe's environmental impact statement, the education of the farm community about the project began. Oahe's once glittering facade dimmed as more and more farmers learned about the plan.

In preparing for the crucial 1976 elections, Oahe supporters mistakenly discounted the strength of United Family Farmers. Though he had warned Oahe supporters not to be complacent, George McGovern was privately confident that the project's popularity was broad. "I thought the opposition," said McGovern, "was confined to a handful of ideologues."[15]

The bureau's Preston Funkhouser had earlier dismissed an offer from United Family Farmers to settle the Oahe lawsuit and had also rejected the notion that

United Family Farmers participate in the Oahe planning process. "We cannot," announced Funkhouser, "drag our feet in construction of this project and countermand the directions of Congress because of a vocal minority group which has had continuing opportunities . . . to delay development of this project."[16] The election results revealed a surprising occurrence. Among farmers in the five sub-district areas who had voted, board incumbents were overwhelmed by a margin of 7,240 votes to 3,371 votes. Project supporters like George McGovern had completely overlooked the possibility of such a huge shift among rural residents. Perhaps just as remarkable was Curt Johnson's near victory over Robert Hipple. Apparently, the project's popularity in cities and towns had drastically declined. Adding together the rural and municipal results showed that Oahe's "vocal minority"—to quote Preston Funkhouser's words—had become a majority. Election totals from all six sub-district races showed that board incumbents received 22,087 votes, and their challengers tallied 25,562.

Thrown into an unfamiliar position, Oahe proponents began counterpunching with a vengeance.

12

The Daring New Majority

We played by the rules of the game. We won. They lost. And now they're trying to change the rules.

George Piper

The remarkable vote totals from the sub-district elections had barely been tabulated, and Senator George McGovern was already in touch with the Bureau of Reclamation seeking advice on how to dislodge John Sieh and his allies from their positions of power.[1] McGovern realized that in the spring of 1977, only a few months away, the sub-district board would be testifying before Congress regarding 1978 funding for Oahe. If new board members would not support ongoing appropriations, or if some other organization could not be recognized or appointed to represent South Dakota on Oahe matters, the project would be wounded, perhaps permanently.

Before the election, McGovern had endorsed the importance of the sub-district board. "Frankly, I would hesitate to substitute my judgement for their's [the sub-district's] in relation to the future development and/or termination of this project," stated McGovern, before adding: "I hope that I can apply this criteria for so long as I am privileged to serve our State in the Congress."[2] Now that the makeup of the board had changed, so, apparently, had McGovern's philosophy on the importance of local control. McGovern phoned Sieg Swanhorst and tried to convince the new director to support continued funding for Oahe. Swanhorst, viewed by Oahe supporters as the director most apt to soften his position, resisted McGovern, saying it was premature for him to commit to any position. Ted Lerew and Charles Kearns pressured Swanhorst during a lunch meeting in Faulkton. Again, Swanhorst wouldn't budge. Bureau of Reclamation officials invited Swanhorst and the other new directors to Huron for an

Oahe orientation, but the full intent of the meeting was spoiled when an uninvited John Sieh accompanied the group.

Preston Funkhouser and the Bureau of Reclamation soon learned that with the takeover of the Oahe sub-district board, United Family Farmers would not rest on its laurels for more than a celebratory moment. The farmers were fashioning their own agenda and hoping to keep the bureau, Friends of Oahe, and Senator McGovern off balance and backpeddling. Sieh and Bill Piper gathered together the new board members—except Doug Beckett—to discuss strategy. It was agreed by the group that Sieh should be the next chairman of the Oahe sub-district and that a new staff was needed. Sieh knew that sub-district manager Bob Raschke was attending a meeting in Wyoming, and he phoned Raschke there, told him about the new board's intentions, and convinced Raschke to resign. To expedite the matter, Sieh and Glenn Overby hopped in a car and made the long trip west, carrying with them a resignation letter for Raschke to sign. That letter's contents, as approved by Raschke in a hotel room, stipulated that Raschke's last day on the job would be 31 December. Once they had collected the signature, Sieh and Overby set out for home. No one ever accused John Sieh of procrastination.

A letter written by Sieh and Curt Hohn and signed by eight of the eleven men who would be directors on the next sub-district board was sent to South Dakota's congressional delegation, the Secretary of the Interior, and the White House. The letter asked that construction and land acquisition on the Oahe project cease until the new board was officially seated and could take a formal position on the project. When Sieh, Bill Piper, and several of the new directors personally delivered the letter to Governor Richard Kneip, an eyes-blazing argument erupted between Sieh and the governor. Sieh pounded his fist on the governor's desk as he pointed to the sub-district elections as proof that Oahe's popularity was waning. Kneip skirted that by claiming there was much support statewide, and he refused to endorse the moratorium. Sieh and Curt Hohn soon realized that their letter to politicians and bureaucrats achieved nothing. Landowners along the Pierre canal route had reported a burst of land-acquisition activity in the days leading up to and immediately after the sub-district election, and only three weeks after the election, new contracts for canal construction were awarded. When digging on the canal started before 1976 ended, it was clear that the bureau was uninterested in heeding the wishes of the next sub-district board.

The bureau was also exploring ideas that would remove the sub-district from the decision-making process. An internal faxogram from Robert McPhail, the bureau's regional director in Billings, to the agency's Washington headquarters suggested that the Oahe sub-district could be relieved of its authority in regard to the project's master contract. The project's contractual obligations, proposed McPhail, could be shifted to the more supportive irrigation districts.[3]

In their last weeks at the helm, several members of the sub-district's lame-duck board attempted to counter the election victories of United Family Farmers. Their weapon was a public-opinion survey, purportedly mailed to forty-two thousand households in the sub-district, that asked recipients if they favored construction of the Oahe project. The survey results, showing strong public support, were released to the press on 30 December, just days before proponents surrendered control of the sub-district.

When the new sub-district board met for the first time, on 6 January 1977, a large, noisy audience listened as important housekeeping matters were handled. The previous board's chairman, Orville Hill, was unable to attend, so he had asked Bob Hipple to run the meeting until new officers were elected. Hipple graciously guided the early proceedings, including conducting the swearing-in ceremony for the new directors. But when it came time to elect officers, Hipple's differences with the new board majority became apparent.

As expected, John Sieh was nominated to serve as chairman. Hipple and the other staunch Oahe supporters on the board, Mike Madden and Steve Thorson, did not want the outspoken, assertive Sieh in such a powerful position, but nominating one of their own was sure to end in defeat. Hoping to tempt several of the new directors away from Sieh, Mike Madden nominated Bud Yackley. Yackley was not as devoted to Oahe as Hipple, Madden, or Thorson, but he certainly was not as hostile to it as Sieh. As a director, Yackley had developed a cordial relationship with the Bureau of Reclamation and was friendly with Bob Raschke. Project supporters hoped that if Yackley was chairman, Raschke's return was possible. When the votes were counted, however, Yackley lost by six votes to five, and the board's two factions had been distinguished. It appeared that Beckett and Yackley would align themselves with Hipple, Madden, and Thorson on crucial votes. If Sieh, Piper, Schurr, Overby, Naessig, and Swanhorst stuck together, they could control the sub-district.

The big audience was stunned and silent when Sieh's victory was announced. Project proponents had just witnessed the election of their archenemy to the most powerful position in the Oahe sub-district. After so many frustrations, opponents of the project could hardly believe their good fortune. They would soon see one of their own grasp the chairman's gavel. One by one, the board's executive committee was elected. Glenn Overby would be the vice-

135

chairman, Bill Piper would be the secretary, and Sieg Swanhorst would serve as treasurer. It was a complete sweep for United Family Farmers.

But the rout wasn't over. Curt Hohn, who had resigned as executive director of United Family Farmers barely twenty-four hours before the meeting, was hired as the new sub-district manager by a one-vote margin, despite Bob Hipple's efforts to stall the decision. The board also hired Tom May, an assistant city attorney in Huron, to serve as the sub-district's first in-house lawyer.

New chairman John Sieh startled the crowd when he announced his desire to move the sub-district headquarters from Huron to Aberdeen. Huron had hosted the office for many years, and an amicable relationship existed between the city and the water agency. Moving the office was unthinkable, impossible, Oahe supporters fretted. But Sieh argued that an Aberdeen office would be closer to the irrigation areas and more centrally located in the sub-district. Bud Yackley contended that the office should remain in Huron, to be near the Bureau of Reclamation's Oahe headquarters. It was vital, argued Yackley, that the sub-district and the bureau continue to communicate. "Our problem," countered Sieh, "hasn't been access to the bureau. The problem this board has had is access to the people."[4] There were other factors, too. With the sub-district office in Aberdeen, Sieh and most directors who were his allies would be able to meet more conveniently at the office, use its facilities, and consult with the new sub-district manager. Despite their age difference, John Sieh and Curt Hohn had become close friends and had developed a collaborative and creative chemistry that was proving to be a powerful force against Oahe. Their mutual admiration had developed during brainstorming sessions that could be explosive but almost always were productive. Sieh's farm was only twenty miles from Aberdeen. A one-way trip to Huron measured eighty miles.

Only minutes into his chairmanship, John Sieh was determined to prevail. Too much was at stake for the office to remain in Huron. Again, Bob Hipple led the effort to stop Sieh. Hipple inquired about a lease for the office. It was reported that the office space in Huron was rented on a monthly basis, and that the lease expired 1 February. If the previous board had anticipated Sieh's maneuver and had signed an agreement committing the office to Huron, it would have been more difficult for Sieh to win his motion. But without the lease, Hipple lacked a pragmatic argument capable of convincing the new board members to respect Oahe's tradition. Twice, Hipple's motions to prevent the move were defeated. Then the Oahe board voted to end its historic association with Huron. Beginning 1 February 1977, the sub-district's new address would be Aberdeen.

John Sieh and Curt Hohn were interested in gathering public input about

Oahe, but their plan was more sophisticated than a mailed survey. They proposed holding a series of seven public hearings across the sub-district, and each hearing would address a specific aspect of the project. "Our responsibility," said Sieg Swanhorst, defending the need for the hearings, "is to the people. We need to find out what they want. I don't think the old board knew what the public wanted."[5] Sieh and Hohn also felt that the hearings would be an educational experience for the board of directors. It was especially important, the two men believed, that the newest directors quickly learn about the project. They realized that pressure on the new directors had begun not long after election day, and that if project supporters managed to nudge just one of the new majority directors into their camp, United Family Farmers would lose their tenuous hold on the sub-district. After protracted debate, the board agreed to sponsor the hearings.

Then John Sieh turned his attention to the public-opinion survey. It had been at the previous board meeting, held on 16 December and before the new majority could take office, that Bob Raschke first informed the entire board about the survey. At that meeting, Sieh, Bill Piper, and Bob Hipple complained that the entire board had not participated in the decision to fund the survey. But it was too late. A check for nearly $10,000 had already been delivered to the survey printer and the survey had been mailed. When Sieh sought to review the taped minutes of previous board meetings to discover what specific actions, if any, had been discussed regarding the survey, it was discovered that board member Steve Thorson had taken the tapes from the sub-district office and had not returned them.

Bud Yackley claimed the survey was necessary to clear up any confusion that the sub-district election had caused about Oahe's popularity.[6] To the public, it may have appeared that the survey was endorsed by the sub-district and professionally written. Bud Maher's newspaper reported that 80 percent of the survey respondents favored Oahe. Maher also reported that of the 2,300 landowners in the irrigation districts who had filled out the surveys, nearly 1,700 supported Oahe. How could that be? protested Glenn Overby. There were, Overby pointed out, fewer than 1,400 landowners in the irrigation districts. Although Thorson claimed that 25 percent of the surveys had been filled out and returned to the sub-district, the survey design and responses lacked credibility. The surveys had been mailed using bulk-mail postage during the postal mayhem of the Christmas season, and thousands of them had been improperly addressed and were returned unopened. While many farmers in the sub-district reported that they never received a survey, some city residents said they had received as many as five surveys. The more that was learned, the more it became apparent that the survey was a bungled, biased fiasco. The instigators had been Thorson and Raschke, with Bill Riechers, the executive director of Friends of Oahe, and Vern Laustsen, an Aberdeen publisher and printer who was a leading Oahe supporter. Laustsen's firm had printed the survey and mailed it. At least one Bureau of Reclamation employee helped tabulate the survey's results.

Bud Yackley had assisted with the survey, and now he feared he had broken the law. Board approval had never been secured; neither had bids for printing the project. In a rare moment of agreement, both Bob Hipple and John Sieh denounced the survey as a public-relations stunt. Though the surveys were sub-district property, Steve Thorson informed the board he had delivered them to the state office of water and natural resources. New sub-district manager Curt Hohn pondered all the improprieties and later described the survey as a sordid matter, hastily and sloppily carried out by project supporters who were frantic because they had lost control of the sub-district.

On 7 January, when Hohn arrived at the office for his first day as manager, the sub-district staff walked out in protest. "I didn't even know where the coffee-maker was," remembered Hohn. But that was just the beginning of his welcome. As he began exploring the office, the phone rang. It was Bud Maher, and the newspaper publisher began blurting obscenities. "It was the most foul, bitter language I've ever heard," Hohn said.[7] Maher grumbled that having Hohn and John Sieh in charge of the sub-district was like having Russell Means and Dennis Banks running the Bureau of Indian Affairs, and then he hung up.

Soon, the phone rang again. This time it was Ben Radcliffe, powerful leader of the South Dakota Farmers Union, calling from his organization's headquarters in Huron. Radcliffe coldly informed Hohn that he and the sub-district board could be sued if they did anything to endanger Oahe. Wherever Hohn went in Huron he felt unwelcome. At the grocery store, he noticed cold stares. At the post office, while others exchanged greetings to start their days, Hohn saw people turning their eyes away from him.

The notion of suing the sub-district if it opposed the Oahe project likely originated with the Bureau of Reclamation. In responding to Senator McGovern's inquiry about how to retaliate against Sieh and the new sub-district, the bureau's commissioner, Gilbert Stamm, suggested that the project's irrigation districts and "other beneficiaries of the Oahe Unit may have just cause for complaint."[8] Stamm's analysis circulated through the pro-Oahe community in

South Dakota, and South Dakota's attorney general, William Janklow, publicly questioned the authority of Oahe board members to oppose the irrigation project.[9] Two of Commissioner Stamm's final acts in office were advising Senator McGovern about Oahe and awarding contracts to extend digging on the Pierre canal. Stamm's appointment was ended with the election of Democrat Jimmy Carter as president.

Senator McGovern had his own ideas about stripping the sub-district of its power. As the 1977 South Dakota legislature convened, McGovern suggested that Governor Kneip pursue legislation that would circumvent the sub-district's role in the decision-making process. "The Sub-district board," declared McGovern, "is a creature of the legislature. . . . [The legislature can] amend the law granting authority [over Oahe] to the Sub-district board."[10] Governor Kneip wasted no time launching an assault on the sub-district. He asked state lawmakers to pass a law that identified the governor as South Dakota's voice on matters related to Oahe. The law also mandated the Oahe sub-district to support federal funding for the Oahe project. If passed, the legislation would deprive the sub-district of its traditional role of representing South Dakota on Oahe. Kneip's bill was welcomed by Oahe supporters but blasted by project opponents and by those who disliked such a blatant power grab. United Family Farmers had cultivated friendly legislators during battles in the 1975 and 1976 sessions, and they doggedly fought to preserve the sub-district's authority. To garner support from some Republicans west of the Missouri River, Kneip promised to ease his opposition to a contentious proposal from Energy Transportation Systems, Incorporated, or ETSI, involving the issuance of a state permit to a project that would move water from Oahe Reservoir to a Wyoming coal-slurry pipeline.

George Piper reacted angrily to Kneip's tactics. "What they're trying to do," growled Piper, "makes a sham of the [sub-district] election and of the democratic process. We played by the rules of the game. We won. They lost. And now they're trying to change the rules."[11]

The 1977 session of the South Dakota legislature was dominated by Oahe. Not only did lawmakers consider Governor Kneip's proposal, they also had to decide the fate of a measure to protect the James River that was sponsored by the state's Department of Game, Fish and Parks (GF&P).

More than two years earlier, in the summer of 1974, GF&P had initiated an ambitious study of the James River. The agency wanted to document what resources might be lost if Oahe were built and the river system channelized.

GF&P faced a delicate task as it dealt with the channelization issue. The agency wished to remain loyal to Governor Kneip, who supported Oahe, but as steward of the state's wildlife resources it could not passively allow the James River to be transformed into a dull ditch. A young wildlife biologist named Kay Cool was assigned to study the potential losses of wildlife and habitat that would occur if channelization took place. One aspect of his study involved a census of whitetail deer near the river. The results did not surprise Cool. "What we found was exactly what we expected," he later said. "Of the deer we observed, about 90 percent were associated with the James River."[12]

Cool explained that the James River was a premier habitat area for whitetail deer. He cited statistics indicating the nation's most successful archery hunting for deer occurred along the James River in Brown and Spink Counties. "If channelization of the James is completed," Cool warned, "we could expect a 90 percent reduction of the habitat types necessary to produce and maintain the deer population." But that was not all he forecast. "We could eventually expect," Cool concluded, "a 90 percent reduction in the deer population."[13] Cool surmised that populations of other wildlife species would be similarly weakened. He cautioned that channelization would severely reduce fish populations in the river, depleting food sources for many types of wildlife. He noted that about 150,000 ducks were born on the James and its tributaries each year. If these watercourses were modified, warned Cool, their productivity for waterfowl production would be lost. Other biologists in GF&P concurred with Cool's dire findings, and the agency decided to publicize the study.

On 4 July 1976, Cool's blunt assessment of channelization was the lead in an interview with him in the *Aberdeen American News*. "The worst thing that could happen to wildlife in South Dakota," declared the biologist, "would be the channelization of the James."[14] Oahe proponents went ballistic. Cool faced a hostile bunch of bureau employees when he discussed his research at a meeting in Huron. Efforts to suppress the GF&P's public-education campaign failed.

Cool's research contradicted reports previously issued by the bureau. The bureau had, intentionally or erroneously, underestimated the impacts of channelization. In its 1960 Oahe report, the bureau stated that "deer will be little affected by development of the Oahe Unit."[15] The project's environmental impact statement did a better job, although the bureau's dispassionate descriptions vastly understated the coming ecological destruction. The U.S. Fish and Wildlife Service, the federal agency responsible for evaluating Oahe's impacts to wildlife and for recommending a mitigation plan to replace destroyed habitat, had also overlooked the consequences of channelization. Because of Cool's study, the service rewrote its mitigation proposal. It is also likely that Cool's work promoting the James had something to do with Curt Johnson's near victory over Bob Hipple. Voters in Aberdeen and other sub-district cities read Cool's newspaper interviews in the months before the 1976 elections and their perspectives about Oahe were broadened.

On the national level, concerns about channelization were mounting, and the Bureau of Reclamation was forced to develop new approaches to James River management. Of the alternatives advanced by the agency, the so-called "green belt" alternative was considered channelization's opposite. Under this concept, the river would be left in its existing state. An easements program would compensate landowners for flood damages, and a select number of unique riparian areas would be purchased by the government to preserve environmental values. The bureau announced it would be unnecessary to decide on a specific plan for the river until five years after irrigation was under way.

The five-year postponement did not calm GF&P officials or others concerned about the river. They viewed the delay as a way for the bureau to stall environmentalists while pursuing construction for the remainder of the project. John Popowski, director of GF&P, decided his agency could oppose channelization without opposing Oahe by supporting the green-belt alternative. Popowski and his staff also pursued a more direct strategy to protect the James.

South Dakota law allowed rivers or stretches of rivers to be designated by the state legislature as wild, scenic, recreational, or a combination of the three. A designation as "wild" preserved and protected rivers that already existed in a primitive condition. The James, even on its most preserved stretches, did not qualify as a candidate for wild river status. The intent of a "scenic" designation was to preserve a river's aesthetic character and its recreation opportunities. Although impoundments were not, and are not, permitted on stretches of river classified as scenic, access by roads and the development of public access was allowed. Agricultural development was not limited unless it detracted from the river's scenic qualities. Rivers and stretches of rivers classified as "recreational" could contain impoundments, diversions, and agricultural development, and public access was mandated.

GF&P decided to seek scenic and recreational designation for the entire reach of the river that would be impacted by Oahe development. All 127 miles of the river between Sand Lake National Wildlife Refuge, in northern Brown County, and U.S. Highway 212, in central Spink County, were nominated as recreational, with four separate areas of the river within that stretch proposed for additional protection under scenic designation.

Kay Cool helped lead the agency's effort to gain scenic and recreational status for the James. It was a demanding role for a young man destined to make his mark in wildlife management. Years later, he would direct state outdoor agencies in Montana, North Dakota, and Michigan. The James River would be his baptism in the treacherous waters of biopolitics.

Knowing its rationale would be scrutinized, GF&P carefully selected the areas it nominated for "scenic" status. Among them was a riverine wetland complex along the river in southern Brown County called the Stratford slough. On no other stretch of the James was the channel so crooked and shallow and the gradient so flat. This was floodplain that flooded frequently, and the result was a several-thousand-acre marsh containing diverse and dynamic habitat without equal elsewhere along the river. Stratford slough was the site of the largest colonial bird rookery in South Dakota. Hundreds of herons, egrets, and cormorants would gather each spring in a long grove of willow trees that bordered the river's main channel. Nests made of sticks and twigs, some of them as big in circumference as a bicycle tire, were used season after season. It was a noisy, active avian community that flourished for many years. For wading birds like great blue herons, there was ample food in the James River stew. Not only were frogs, salamanders, and crawfish abundant, so were fish. Most of the fish reproduction in the entire upper James River could be traced to the emergent vegetation so plentiful in Stratford slough.

Only a modest area within the Stratford slough complex, including three miles of main channel and 471 acres along the channel, were nominated for protective status. Included were the important nesting colony and the mouth of Mocassin Creek. All the nominated land belonged to one farmer, a man named Herman Hansen. GF&P had selected this stretch of river for scientific reasons, to be sure, but the agency also knew that unlike some of his neighbors, Hansen was sympathetic to the designation.[16]

Not far downriver from Stratford slough was a reach of river quite different but also noted for wildlife activity. Canoeists paddling the Rondell area found themselves beneath a dense hardwood canopy that shaded the coffee-colored river. The forest at Rondell created important deer browse and served as a vital wintering area for part of the river's large deer population. Rondell had been the site of Oak Wood settlement, where Joseph Nicollet had camped. This was also the site of the Dakota Rendezvous, the great Indian trading fair. In the Rondell area, GF&P hoped to designate as scenic some fourteen miles of winding channel and 1,200 acres of adjacent land.

A short distance downriver from Rondell was the third area proposed for scenic designation. Armadale Park contained large meadows surrounded by thick woods and supported a deer herd that rivaled Rondell's. Impressive oak trees, some of them more than two centuries old, clustered along the river's main channel and concentrated on a two-hundred-acre island. At one time, Armadale Island had been a locally popular summertime center for recreation and entertainment. Baseball and horse racing were popular, children rode wooden horses on a carousel, and after sunset couples danced in an impressive pavilion to lively bands such as Lawrence Welk's. By the late 1950s, however, the parties at Armadale had ended, a victim of better roads and highways that led to nearby Redfield and Aberdeen. Armadale had another claim to fame. The same gleaming night sky that inspired romance among the farm boys and girls had also shone down on the island's most famous resident. Drifting Goose, the Sioux chief who resisted white settlement along the James River, lived on Armadale Island, also known as Drifting Goose Island, and the island served as the hub of his short-lived reservation. To protect Armadale, GF&P wanted scenic status for five miles of river channel and 520 acres, including the entire island.

A fourth area to be protected by scenic designation was called the Turton grade. "Away from the road, the river meanders through an unspoiled environment of timber and grasses," wrote GF&P in its nomination of Turton grade. "The uniqueness of this area," the agency continued, "is the dense timber and canopy." At Turton grade, GF&P proposed designation for five miles of channel and 370 acres of land.[17]

GF&P did not hide its intentions. "Quite openly, candidly, and honestly," recalled Jack Merwin, who served under John Popowski as the agency's public-affairs chief, "we pursued the designation as a legal mechanism to preclude the channelization of the James River and, hopefully, turn the direction toward some of the other alternatives that would not have had the same devastating impacts on wildlife."[18] The battle over the proposal evolved into one of the most controversial aspects of the Oahe conflict. Although they were not normally sympathetic to plans that enhanced recreation opportunities at the expense of agriculture, many farmers backed GF&P. They viewed the designation as a means to block the irrigation project.

At public hearings to discuss the proposal, Kay Cool's slide program and presentation quickly cut to the heart of the debate. "Channelization," declared Cool, as he projected slides showing ruined rivers elsewhere in the nation onto a large screen, "consists of tearing the guts out of a river . . . resulting in a sterile ditch of no use or benefit to anyone other than as a massive drain."[19] Bureau of Reclamation officials attempted to deflect Cool's warning, reminding the audience that a final decision about the river had not been made. At the conclusion of each hearing, an audience survey was conducted. More than 94 percent of the estimated 294 individuals attending the three hearings expressed support for the designations. Many of those attending the public hearings were members of United Family Farmers.

Further strengthening the proposal was the fact that every landowner along the four stretches proposed to be protected as "scenic"—twenty-six landowners in all—supported the plan. Landowner support for the "recreational" stretch, involving several hundred landowners, was not unanimous but was substantial. GF&P surveys indicated that 75 percent of the affected farmers favored the recreational designation.

By the time the proposal landed in front of legislators for their consideration, Jack Merwin was the new leader of Game, Fish and Parks. Merwin's passionate feelings about the river and the importance of protecting it were soon apparent. "All of these people, and some at great personal sacrifice, are saying: It's our James River, wet or dry, fair or foul," announced Merwin, defending his agency and members of the public who supported designation. "It's our river, and we do not want it crucified upon the cross of channelization."[20]

Despite the evidence submitted by GF&P that the James was a valuable source of habitat for many species of wildlife, Oahe proponents continued to portray the river as a useless resource. During the 1977 legislative session, an array of unflattering adjectives about the river followed GF&P lobbyists as they solicited support for the designation. One legislator typified those who doubted the values of the river when he called the James "a mudhole."[21] Most legislators opposing the designation were concerned that it would imperil Oahe. At an emotional hearing held by the agriculture and natural resources committee, Senator Peg Lamont, a Republican from Aberdeen and a sponsor of the measure, said the designation would not necessarily affect the Oahe project. Concurring with GF&P, she testified: "We can have both water and birds."[22]

Peg Lamont came from one of Brown County's most prominent families. In 1914 her father-in-law had been an investor and cofounder of Wells-Lamont, the glove manufacturer, but most of the family fortune derived from investments in land and farm management.[23] Her father had been a bank president in Aberdeen for twenty-five years and had served as a president of the chamber of commerce. Her husband was a partner in one of Aberdeen's major banks. With such a background in business, large-scale agricultural development, and banking, it would seem that Peg Lamont's preference would have been to support the Oahe project. Lamont's opposition to Oahe stemmed from several influences. She remembered that her husband's grandfather had attempted to irrigate, using groundwater and James River flows, beginning in 1888. Four or five years later, he stopped irrigating. "He discovered he was salting up his land," explained Lamont. She was convinced that the lake plain's mix of soils made it impossible to locate sizeable, contiguous tracts of land that could survive long-term irrigation. "My views on Oahe were strongly influenced by my understanding of geology," said Lamont, many years later. "I was familiar with the pattern of soils and gravel and clay that dominated the lake plain."[24] Lamont was pressured by Aberdeen businessmen to switch her position on Oahe. She was frequently warned that her opposition to Oahe would destroy her politically. Unfazed, Lamont continued to be a card-carrying member of United Family Farmers and a contributor the organization counted on.

At the hearing, the Bureau of Reclamation's Preston Funkhouser did not agree with Lamont's assessment of James River designation. He said the designation would prevent his agency from considering the full range of river-management alternatives. It was likely, he said, that a combination of the alternatives, including both channelization and green-belt measures, would eventually be implemented. "If the James is designated," Funkhouser warned, "it would inhibit full use of combination plans."[25] As the crowded hearing room hushed, committee members explained their positions. Preston Funkhouser looked on anxiously as the votes were tallied. Peg Lamont was counting, too. Soon she smiled. Her measure was passed out of committee to the full senate with a do-pass recommendation.

Pierre was soon swarming with alarmed Oahe advocates. The governor's personal lobbyists made the rounds to disagree with their fellow state officials at GF&P. When the senate votes were counted, their efforts had been rewarded. Lamont and her fellow senator from Brown County, Bob Williams, were two of only twelve senators approving the designation. With two members absent, twenty-one of Lamont's colleagues in the body refused to endorse the designation.

Meanwhile, Governor Kneip's proposal to shrink the powers of the sub-district and remand them to the governor encountered a snag. Lawmakers, both Republicans and Democrats, were not comfortable shifting the power from a group of elected officials to one official, even if it was the governor. Oahe supporters submitted a compromise measure that would create a new state board, the so-called Oahe Task Force. Task-force supporters intended for the new organization to function as the state's voice on Oahe. Its members would be the governor, four legislators, and two representatives of the Oahe sub-district board. The bill also declared that construction of Oahe was state policy and urged full funding of the project. This proposal was enacted. Although Kneip lost his bid to serve as Oahe's sole spokesperson, Oahe supporters were pleased at the formation of the task force.

Bud Maher vigorously defended the task-force concept, referring to the sub-district board as a "subordinate board" inappropriate to "set policy and speak for the state of South Dakota."[26] For sixteen years, Maher had worked closely with the sub-district to promote Oahe. He had often cited the sub-district's key role in the development of the project. Now he was ready to abandon the organization.

John Sieh and Glenn Overby were selected by their fellow directors to serve as the sub-district's representatives to the task force. Both men understood the hazards of the assignment. For them to participate on the task force would, to a certain extent, validate its purpose. And that could undermine the sub-district's traditional role as representing South Dakota in matters related to Oahe. Sieh and Overby also understood that the other members of the task force would be aligned against them. John Sieh remembered the challenges and the dividends of being an outcast on the sub-district board. During the two years he and Bill Piper were a minority of two, they had often been ignored and almost always were outvoted. But there had been benefits. Not only were Sieh and Piper able to monitor the proceedings of their adversaries and disrupt or delay the majority's agenda, they were able to make and second motions to force board votes. As minority members of the task force, Sieh and Overby could serve the same role.

13

The District of Columbia

Courage: the attitude or response of facing and dealing with anything recognized as dangerous, difficult, or painful, instead of withdrawing from it.
Webster's New Universal Unabridged Dictionary

In the Deep South, where building dams and creating man-made lakes was a sacred obligation for politicians on all levels, Jimmy Carter's antipathy toward the water-development status quo required a special fortitude. Carter, an avid outdoorsman, loved free-flowing rivers. Because he had graduated from the U.S. Naval Academy with a degree in engineering, he was also familiar with the lexicon and methods of engineers. While serving as Georgia's governor, Carter analyzed the plans prepared by the Army Corps of Engineers for a huge dam on a wild Georgia river that was promoted by powerful business interests. Dismayed at the inaccuracies he discovered, Carter accused the corps of lying to the public, called the dam unnecessary, and blocked its construction.

By the time Jimmy Carter took his presidential oath, in January 1977, nearly fifty thousand dams had already been erected by public and private interests on rivers and streams across the country. There was hardly a river that had not been dammed; many were dammed multiple times. Carter believed the economic waste and environmental destruction should stop. One of his first acts as president was to order an aggressive, high-level analysis of the nation's water-development programs. For the first time in the nation's history, a process steered by the president himself would critically and comprehensively examine the impacts of federal programs on water resources.

A federal official who served under Carter later said that even as he defended the president's ambitious agenda, he worried about its efficacy. Guy Martin, an Interior Department official under Carter, was awestruck when he first learned about the scope of the president's proposal. The president, explained Martin, was eager to review and reform "everything that had to do with the federal role in water management and water development."[1] Martin, a native Coloradan who had gone to Alaska after finishing law school, was one of the many environmentalists who had stormed Washington as part of the Carter administration. He had first come to Carter's attention during the presidential campaign when he was summoned to Plains, Georgia, to brief Carter on oil issues. At the time, Martin, only thirty-four years old, was serving as Alaska's commissioner of public lands.

Carter appointed Martin to serve as an assistant secretary in the Interior Department. Although it was the same post Ken Holum had once occupied, including supervision of the Bureau of Reclamation's commissioner, Martin's outlook on natural-resource management was quite different from Holum's. Martin recognized serious flaws in the federal water program and accepted the job of upholding President Carter's plan.

Carter's political strategy, Martin pointed out, was to initiate the reform process by sending a powerful signal to water developers that the old days were over and that it was time to enter a new era of federal responsibility with respect to water. That signal, Carter decided, would be best achieved by compiling a list of the nation's worst water projects, based on economic, environmental, and safety criteria, and defunding them. It was an extraordinarily bold approach.

The notion of assembling a formal list of wasteful water projects had probably originated several years earlier when Brent Blackwelder, a prominent Washington environmentalist, tacked a roster containing what he considered the worst Corps of Engineers projects to the main door of the agency's Washington DC headquarters. His inspiration for that renegade act, Blackwelder fondly recalled, came from Martin Luther. In 1973, Blackwelder's Environmental Policy Center joined other public-interest groups to produce another list of dubious projects.[2] Their report, titled "Disasters in Water Development," offered damning vignettes of thirteen Bureau of Reclamation and Corps of Engineers projects. North Dakota's Garrison Unit, where considerable construction was under way, was among the projects described. Oahe, where ground had not yet been broken, was not. Several years later, on a summerlong automobile expedition to learn more about water projects, Blackwelder visited George Piper at the Piper farm and reviewed Piper's files in the schoolhouse headquarters of United Family Farmers. Impressed by Piper's information, Blackwelder added Oahe to his personal list of unwarranted water projects.

Among other water-development critics already in Washington when Jimmy Carter ascended to the White House were Bob Lane and David Weiman. Lane's first experience in reclamation policy came as a staffer for a congressional committee that held hearings on the Garrison project. Weiman worked for the Farmers Union before becoming a freelance legislative consultant specializing in water and natural-resource issues. According to Lane, Weiman made significant headway unraveling the byzantine and misleading economic formulas and figures used by the bureau to justify Garrison. As their alliance and friendship deepened, Lane and Weiman delved further and further into bureau calculations, and they found an abundance of questionable and faulty conclusions. Their concerns helped launch an investigation by the General Accounting Office that cast doubt on the economic data used by the bureau to promote Garrison. Weiman and Lane recognized that Garrison was not an isolated case. They discovered that exaggerated economic forecasts were used to justify many bureau projects.[3]

Shortly after Carter's election, Lane was hired away from his committee position to serve as a special assistant in the Interior Department.

Oahe activists, pro and con, must have been overwhelmed by the flurry of activities in early 1977. On every political front, national, state, and local, momentous events were unfolding. Locally, the Oahe sub-district area was extremely volatile. The recent sub-district elections heightened the controversy in South Dakota, and the situation remained explosive as Sieh and his allies took control of the sub-district board. Held concurrently with President Carter's water-projects review and the intense fights in the South Dakota legislature over the James River and how much power the Oahe sub-district should wield, the sub-district's series of seven public hearings had the potential to be a pivotal part of the Oahe debate.[4]

The first hearing was certain to attract a feisty crowd. Held 3 February in the small town of Blunt, the hearing topic was land acquisition. With major canals and a large dam and reservoir planned for the Blunt vicinity, there had already been plenty of condemnation activity in the area, and animosity toward the bureau was intense. When the hearing convened at 9:00 AM, some three hundred people had assembled in the community's school gymnasium. The crowd's predominant sentiment was quickly made evident when John Sieh, chairing the proceedings, asked Preston Funkhouser to take an oath before opening the hearing with his testimony. Flanked by nine other representatives from the Bureau of Reclamation, Funkhouser questioned the need for such an oath. My agency, he rigidly declared, always tells the truth. Instantly, the gymnasium reverberated with howling, disdainful laughter. Sieh urged quiet, and Funkhouser endeavored to assure sub-district directors and the audience that the Bureau of Reclamation operated fairly and within congressional guidelines. "There has been an accusation in the recent past," stated Funkhouser, "that the Bureau of Reclamation has been accelerating acquisition of land for the Pierre canal. This is completely untrue."[5] A buzz of skeptical whispering and the motion of many heads shaking swept through the crowd.

It was easy to doubt Funkhouser. Landowners reported that the bureau's land-acquisition agents had been particularly busy in the days immediately before and after the sub-district elections in early November. For several months, the agency had been pressuring Helen Metzinger and her husband to sell their land. Two days after United Family Farmers trounced project supporters in the elections and took control of the sub-district board, the bureau came to the Metzingers with their final offer. "They seemed to be in a hurry," recalled Helen Metzinger.[6] Then there was the letter John Sieh and seven other Oahe board members sent to politicians and federal bureaucrats asking that land acquisition and project construction be halted until the new board had formulated a position on the project. Although the Bureau of Reclamation claimed that the letter surfaced in its Washington office "several hours" after bids to build a twenty-one-mile stretch of the Pierre canal had been awarded,[7] it appeared that the bureau had simply ignored the sub-district's request. For years, the federal agency basked in the sub-district's support for the project, citing that support as proof that local people wanted Oahe. Now that the sub-district's position had changed, the bureau was prepared to defy the sub-district.

A barrage of testimony from unhappy landowners followed Funkhouser's remarks. Roy Runge testified that during a series of negotiations, he had been frustrated by a confusing array of bureau representatives and contradictory statements and promises. "Every month or two I had to deal with a different person who didn't seem to have knowledge of what the previous person had told me," Runge complained.[8] Though Runge was asked to sell only 101 acres and grant a permanent easement on an additional 143 acres, the Pierre canal would split his 4,500-acre ranch into two uneven pieces. Runge figured he would have to sell 1,000 acres isolated by the ditch and drastically reduce the scale of his ranching operation. Bureau negotiators chuckled when Runge countered their $34,500 offer with an $82,000 request. Runge then revised his price to $57,000, and the bureau raised its offer to $40,000. Nope, replied Runge. If you want my land today, said the rancher, you pay me $57,000. Too high, said the bureau's representatives, and they headed toward the front door of Runge's home. "When I come after you the next time," warned the rancher, "it's going to cost you considerably more money."[9]

Shortly after that failed meeting, the government took Runge's land through condemnation. That meant a judge and jury would eventually decide whether the government's offer was fair. But in the meantime, before litigation could commence, earthmovers began excavating the deep canal on Runge's former property. Runge discovered that when he had been presented with the government's condemnation papers, he had lost his rights to the land, despite the unresolved compensation issue. When Runge told his story to the Oahe board at the Blunt hearing, his case had not been settled. When it was, several years later, Runge was awarded $89,696. His warning to the bureau's land-acquisition experts proved prescient.

Also testifying at the sub-district's hearing was Earl Briggs, another landowner whose land lay in the path of the Pierre canal. Briggs earned a reputation among bureau personnel for his irascible behavior, but he had not always been so ornery. For more than a decade, Briggs and his wife Marilou had cooperated with the government, allowing bureau canal surveyors access to their land. But then bureau personnel trampled a wheat field and carelessly discarded a metal cable in high grass that later damaged Briggs's mower. When the ranchers asked the government for $200 to cover the damages, an amount they considered reasonable and fair, the bureau offered only $50. No further communication took place until the following spring when the bureau again asked permission for its surveyors to enter Briggs's land. This time Earl and Marilou refused. Twice, a bureau representative came to their home, and each time offered the couple progressively higher but still unsatisfactory settlements. On yet another visit, the bureau's offer reached $182.50. Frustrated and disturbed by the government's time-consuming efforts to shrink their request, the Briggs accepted the settlement. By paying $182.50, the agency may have conceded making mistakes, but it had managed to avert the original claim requested by the Briggs. It was not just to save a whopping $17.50 that the bureau had invested countless hours and travel expenses. The Briggs were convinced that the agency was more interested in demonstrating its authority over landowners than behaving responsibly.

Although the bureau needed only 64 acres from the Briggs, the Pierre canal would slice their 560-acre ranch into two segments, destroy both stock dams on the ranch, and separate an important calving area from the rest of the ranch. The bureau tried to entice the Briggs to support the irrigation project by suggesting that excess water from the canal would be available for them to start a truck farm, growing onions, potatoes, and cabbage. Provisions in the Oahe plan for canalside landowners to use water for irrigation had no legal basis in the Oahe plan, and the notion of high plains ranchers becoming commercial vegetable growers was improbable. "They wanted to make willing sellers out of us," said Marilou, laughing at the idea of becoming a vegetable farmer. "They tried to lead us down a garden path."[10]

By the time the bureau offered them $37,590 for their land, Earl and Marilou had had enough. They quickly rejected the offer and requested $350,000, a fantastic figure that was, no doubt, amplified by their anger. The bureau countered by raising its offer to $40,000. When the Briggs again refused, the bureau served condemnation papers, and Earl Briggs went on a rampage, running over survey stakes, glaring at bureau personnel he encountered on back roads, and bumping a bureau vehicle with a tractor. After discovering a survey crew had left a fence gate open, he argued with the crew and hurriedly drove away, ripping an open door off a government vehicle. The county sheriff served a peace bond on Briggs, requiring him to stay away from federal employees. A local jury later found Briggs innocent of hit-and-run. At one point, Earl and Marilou wrote Senator George McGovern and asked for his help. Several days later, a bureau official came to their home and complained about the letter. The Briggs had not yet heard back from McGovern.

As was the case with Roy Runge's final settlement, the Briggs's condemnation trial several years later revealed that the government's offer was drastically inadequate. The court awarded $73,000 to the Briggs.

Curt Hohn had been escorted through the proposed Blunt reservoir by Doug Beckett. Although his family had willingly sold their ranch there, Beckett had misgivings about the bureau's land-acquisition practices. During the tour, he introduced Hohn to people who had been intimidated and shortchanged by bureau agents. Eugenia Schmitgen, for example, owned about 1,400 acres in the Blunt reservoir taking area. Bureau land-acquisition specialists repeatedly visited Mrs. Schmitgen, despite being told by the elderly woman's daughter that she was ill and did not understand the situation. The bureau's agents warned Mrs. Schmitgen that she would be condemned if she resisted their offer. Mrs. Schmitgen, an immigrant from Germany, thought condemnation meant losing land without compensation. She remembered the government doing that in the old country, and so she reluctantly sold her land for $90 an acre, a fraction of its true worth. The Beckett ranch, some of which shared a fence line with Schmitgen's land, was purchased for $150 an acre. Beckett's family received more money for identical land, said Curt Hohn, because the Becketts were more assertive and more astute. It was, said Hohn, a vivid example of how the bureau operated. "Those guys were like bounty hunters," Hohn complained. "They went out in the name of the U.S. government and took advantage of widows and the elderly."[11]

Schmitgen's daughter, Mrs. Margaret Pope, later described the tension her mother felt because of constant pressuring by the bureau. "She about had a nervous breakdown over the situation," Mrs. Pope explained. "They came to see her every day. She was sick when they started coming to see her, and they wore her down. She was afraid they weren't going to pay her anything if they condemned her. They knew she didn't understand. She was admitted to the hospital the day she sold the land. It bothered her until she died."[12]

Eugenia Schmitgen's large holding was among the first tracts acquired by the bureau, and it gave them a sizeable foothold in the proposed reservoir. But it was not so easy for them to acquire additional land. So antagonistic were some landowners in the reservoir area that the bureau had to condemn land just to conduct surveys and test soils. Sub-district directors at the Blunt hearing learned that 212 landowners would lose property to the project's three main reservoirs and the thirty-six miles of the Pierre canal. As many as 43 families would be forced to relocate because of those project features. The project's overall impacts, including project construction and mitigation, involved taking about 110,000 acres of land from more than 500 farmers. Their sacrifice would make irrigation possible on 190,000 acres for about the same number of farmers. United Family Farmers ridiculed the ratios. Of the 33 landowners who had already lost land to the project, 11 had been so displeased with the government's offers that they forced the bureau to condemn them. Many of those who willingly sold were absentee landowners. Pushing the bureau to condemnation was a gutsy, defiant step, but it demonstrated that people distrusted the agency and disliked the Oahe project.

Many landowners complained that the bureau refused to show them the detailed appraisal that had been prepared for their property, depriving them of important information during their negotiations with the agency. Preston Funkhouser stated that it was Department of Interior policy not to reveal appraisal details to landowners. John Sieh then read from a congressional report condemning this bureau practice. The report explained that the bureau's rationale in withholding information was to increase its opportunities for favorable settlements if condemnation was necessary.[13] After hearing this, Funkhouser admitted he was mistaken about federal policy. He agreed to work with the sub-district to correct the situation.

The hearing lasted eleven hours, with badgered, frustrated bureau officials explaining and reexplaining information to a persistent group of board members and staffers Curt Hohn and Tom May. Late in the hearing, and long after supper, attorney May asked a weary bureau representative if he would like to go home. The government employee eagerly said yes, and May responded, "I don't think we will let you do that just yet."[14] May then continued asking questions.

The hearing offered landowners a chance to speak directly to the bureau and vent their anger. "We lost our respect for our government," sighed Marilou Briggs, as she summed up her feelings about Oahe and the Bureau of Reclamation. "I was brought up to believe that mother, God, and our government were all in the same league. We found out that isn't so. The bureau treated us poorly. They treated many people poorly."[15]

During this frenzied period, no one's life could have been more hectic than Curt Hohn's. Between lobbying trips to Pierre, phone calls to President Carter's staff in Washington, researching for the sub-district's field hearings, and managing the complexities of the sub-district office, Hohn squeezed in his wedding. But even that important personal event was eclipsed by Oahe politics. On 19 February, three days after the second sub-district hearing (the topic at that one was the James River), with Hohn's festive wedding reception under way at a restaurant in Mitchell, South Dakota, Hohn was paged to take a telephone call. On the line, interrupting the toasts being raised by best man George Piper and others, was not some well-wisher; it was Dean Rebuffoni, the environmental reporter for the *Minneapolis Tribune*.

Rebuffoni had covered Oahe for several years and was familiar with Hohn, George Piper, and John Sieh. Using his network of Oahe sources, he had tracked down Hohn and the gang of Oahe opponents on that Saturday to deliver big news. Rebuffoni had just learned that President Carter had completed the first phase of his water-projects analysis and was recommending a number of them be discontinued. Oahe, exclaimed the reporter, was on the list! Hohn quickly relayed the happy news to others at the party and a crowd hurriedly circled the new groom. Rebuffoni wanted someone to respond to the president's announcement. John Sieh was among the guests, and it was agreed that as chairman of the Oahe sub-district he was the appropriate person to comment. Surrounded by hushed partygoers, Sieh took the phone in his hand. "I feel the president, in deleting the funds for Oahe," he told Rebuffoni, "has come out on the side of the people in South Dakota."[16] Via the Associated Press, Sieh's reaction was spread nationwide. Oahe supporters groaned as they read about Carter's list and saw Sieh's quote in front-page stories the following day. But Sieh's was a rare voice supporting the president.

South Dakota Governor Richard Kneip was in Denver attending a meeting of western governors when Interior Secretary Cecil Andrus delivered the news in a speech to the group. The circumstances could not have been less auspicious. The governors' conference was focused on drought, and Kneip and other governors roared their outrage. Oahe was one of eighteen water projects on what became known as the "hit list." Calling the projects unsupportable, President Carter recommended that funding for the projects be withheld until each could be thoroughly examined. He said the country would save $289 million in 1978 alone by halting work on the projects.

Oahe was joined on the list by seven other Bureau of Reclamation projects, including Garrison, Colorado's Dolores and Fruitland Mesa projects, Savery Pot Hook in Wyoming and Colorado, Auburn-Folsom in California, the Central Utah Project (CUP), and the Central Arizona Project (CAP). Auburn-Folsom, Garrison, and Oahe were each projected to cost more than $500 million to complete; CUP and CAP would likely cost at least $2 billion apiece. The ten Corps of Engineers projects on the list included the $800-million Dickey-Lincoln dam in Maine, three projects in Kentucky, two in Louisiana, and projects in Kansas, Missouri, Arkansas, and Oklahoma. The Richard Russell project, proposed for South Carolina and Carter's own Georgia, completed the list. The president announced that further review of the listed projects and other questionable projects would be conducted. All the projects to be evaluated, said Carter, had been approved in the past "under different economic circumstances and at times of lower interest rates." These projects, he continued, "are of doubtful necessity now, in light of new economic and environmental policies."[17] Assigned to head the Oahe review team was Bob Lane.

President Carter was unprepared for the rapid and stormy backlash from Congress that followed the announcement. Feeling betrayed by a member of their own party, Democrats, especially those representing arid western states, were particularly bitter. Even those who agreed that federal water policy needed to be revamped were uneasy with the proposal's enormous scale. People inside Carter's administration, Guy Martin and Cecil Andrus among them, felt that the president's desire to slash projects that were already under construction did not make political sense. The Central Arizona Project, for example, was half completed, and more than $150 million had already been spent on Garrison. Reformers like Andrus and Martin favored change but worried that Carter's plan was not saleable to Congress or to the public. A more reasonable approach, they said, would be to improve policies that affected projects where construction was not already under way. Carter insisted that his proposal would succeed.

Furious at the president and determined to rebound from the setback, the Bureau of Reclamation marched into the Oahe sub-district's hearing on soils and drainage bristling with confidence. Although admitting that Oahe was a project with special problems, they were certain of their engineering prowess and soil classifications.

William Peters, a section chief with the bureau's Denver office, had flown in for the hearing. Sitting alongside Preston Funkhouser and four other agency officials, Peters boasted that Oahe would be one of the bureau's stars. "The testing that was done on this project," testified Peters, "is the latest and the best we can assemble, and there had been more testing done on it than any project that we have." Then he emphatically declared: "For this climatic and economic setting, I know of no other project in the world that would compare with [Oahe]."[18]

Indeed, there had been lots of tests. To determine soil irrigability and permeability, the bureau drilled more than 12,500 holes and extracted more than 63,000 soil samples at sites across the lake plain. Five classes of land were included in the project's irrigability descriptions. Classes 1, 2, and 3 were considered arable. The primary criteria in determining irrigability, however, was not the ability of the soils to sustain fertility during long-term, repeated watering; it was whether the land could produce yields high enough to offset irrigation's increased costs, including reimbursing the government's investment. Class 5s lands were originally viewed as nonarable, though the bureau later determined that deep plowing could make these lands irrigable. Deep plowing involved breaking soil to a depth greater than twenty-eight inches. This was not an authorized feature of the project; therefore, each farmer would be required to bear the considerable cost of purchasing or hiring special equipment to carry out such a program. Class 6 lands were not irrigable by any method.

The flat terrain of the lake plain and the permeability drawbacks of the soils there posed special problems. Not only would hundreds of pumps be required to deliver and circulate water to irrigation tracts, but hundreds more would be necessary to remove excess water from irrigation fields to prevent waterlogging and salinization. An engineer who served as a United Family Farmers consultant observed that this was the only irrigation project he had studied where the cost of pumping water to irrigate crops would be equaled by the cost of pumping it away from the crops.

Because Oahe's irrigation districts were located on what had once been the floor of a glacial lake, some soils contained high levels of salt. Oahe's irrigation water from the Missouri River would contain from five hundred to one thousand parts of salt per million. This was not a worrisome amount, but when combined with salts already in the soil to be irrigated, it increased the chances for soil destruction. Gambling on their soils surviving long-term irrigation was a risk that a growing number of farmers on the lake plain were unwilling to take.

Sub-district directors heard from a Wyoming rancher who cautioned that Oahe could repeat the disaster he had witnessed on a federal irrigation project in his area. Allen Talbott had struggled for fourteen years on a faltering reclamation project named Riverton. He had also served on his local irrigation district board of directors. Talbott described how accumulations of salt crusted over the soil, sealing it shut and killing the land. A plan to facilitate drainage had come too late to Riverton; not even tile drains could revive it. Talbott estimated that 80 to 90 percent of the land in his division of the project was ruined by alkali problems, forcing droves of farmers from their farms. "I agree with your suggestion," said John Sieh to Talbott, "that this Board look carefully at what [bureau] engineers tell us."[19] "Oh, yes," replied Talbott. "after Riverton I've become a skeptic. I don't take hardly anybody's word, sir, when it comes to things like this."[20]

In defense of the bureau, at Riverton the agency had inherited a project after it had gone awry. It proved impossible to control the project's drainage problems once salinization started to set in. Part of what ailed Riverton, said the bureau, were the farmers who had used Riverton's irrigation water. The bureau accused them of being lazy and inattentive to the intense management requirements of irrigation farming.

The drainage system mentioned by Peters, the bureau section chief from Denver, would be a critical factor in preventing waterlogging and salinization of the soil. The backbone of the drainage plan was to use tiles, buried 6 to 12 feet below the surface at intervals averaging 620 feet. These artificial drains—some 2,970 miles of them—were actually perforated tubes constructed of clay, concrete, or plastic. They would be placed within a narrow envelope of gravel. Ranging in size from four to fifteen inches in diameter, the closed pipe drains would divert used water, called return flows, away from irrigated fields to an expansive grid of large ditches or channelized streams. The destination for return flows within the project area was the James River.

Experts hired by United Family Farmers and many farmers claimed the artificial drains would not work because much of the land scheduled for irrigation lacked sufficient permeability in the first place. They warned that water would accumulate on the surface of the land, never reaching the artificial drains. There was also the fear that the mixture of soils and subsoils on the lake plain created a checkerboard of arable and nonarable land that would be difficult to manage. Farmers owning lands not scheduled for irrigation complained that they would be forced to withstand project impacts, including losing land to seepage from nearby irrigated fields. The Environmental Protection Agency backed up their fears, warning that not only were many of Oahe's 190,000 irrigated acres at risk if project drains failed or if soil classifications were mistaken, but at least 300,000, and possibly 500,000, acres were vulnerable to seepage and other damage.[21]

John Elsing brought his color-coded maps and modified glass jar to the soils and drainage hearing. Elsing showed how land classifications mysteriously changed at fence lines and roads, and he charged the bureau with upgrading lands from nonarable to arable to enhance the project's viability. His own land, he pointed out, had been upgraded to irrigable, even though he knew it was not sufficiently permeable to survive long-term watering. Other farmers described similar discrepancies. One farmer who was especially skeptical about the irrigability of Oahe soils was Ray Braun, whose farm straddled the James River in Spink County. Braun had closely examined Oahe documents, had attended numerous meetings, and had written an article detailing his doubts that was published in a national farm magazine.[22] Braun's main concerns were soil permeability and the spacing of the pipe drains beneath irrigated fields.

During United Family Farmers' lawsuit on Oahe (see chapter 8), Martin Weeks and John Davidson had discovered the drainage recommendations of three consultants hired by the bureau in 1954. The consultants advised bureau engineers to place the drains at a depth not greater than 9 feet and spaced at an average of 330 feet.[23] The agency's chief engineer applauded the calculations of the consultants and seemed convinced that their figures were reliable. "Further comments or suggestions [regarding the consultants' report]," wrote L. N. McClellan to the bureau's commissioner, Wilbur Dexheimer, "are not believed necessary at this time."[24] By the time the project underwent the scrutiny of congressional reauthorization hearings, in 1967, the bureau had refigured the drainage plan. The new plan proposed drains at depths ranging from 6 to 12 feet, and spacing distances were expanded to an average of 620 feet. These changes required fewer drains but threatened soil fertility with a higher water table.

Ray Braun recalled conversations with bureau officials in the late 1950s and early 1960s, a time when he had supported Oahe and helped circulate petitions to form the Spink County Irrigation District. Braun was told then that the decision to change drainage specifications had happened because of economics.[25] Apparently, the bureau discovered it could significantly reduce Oahe's overall cost by proposing a diminished drainage plan. The expense associated with installing project drains was very high—nearly identical to the cost of excavating the project's massive main canals, and by revamping the drainage plan the overall cost of the project could be lowered by as much as 10 percent. When total project cost is somewhere between $300 million and $500 million, 10 percent is serious money. By modifying its drainage plan, the bureau improved the project's cost-benefit ratio. When Congress approved the project in 1968, it appeared that no official explanation was given or requested regarding the engineering changes. At the sub-district hearing in 1977, the agency claimed that subsequent soil tests and advances in water-management techniques allowed the changes in drainage specifications.

Ray Braun's doubts about the bureau's classifications prompted him to perform his own tests on land he rented—land that was scheduled to be irrigated. He invited Dr. Larry Fine, a scientist associated with South Dakota State University, and John Elsing to view his experiment.

Dr. Fine led soil studies at the government's irrigation-experiment farm in Spink County and was considered one of Oahe's leading scientific supporters. He came to Braun's farm accompanied by Dr. Delwyn Dearborn, the dean of the College of Agriculture and Biological Sciences at South Dakota State University. To perform his experiment, Braun used a double-ring permeability test, a procedure he had learned from Dr. Fine. In this study, two concentric cylinders are driven into the soil and water is applied to the surface of soil. The larger, outer ring controls water in the test area. The inner ring measures true vertical movement of water through the soil. It was immediately evident that very little water had penetrated the soil. Most of it pooled on the surface. Braun explained that the soil had swelled shut after a small amount of water was applied. Dr. Fine stood nearby, listening to Braun warn about the dangers of irrigating this soil. Then Fine sat on the ground, his head bowed.

Braun knew Fine well, having often discussed Oahe with him. And he liked Fine personally. Both Braun and Elsing respected the agricultural accomplishments of Fine's institution, South Dakota State University. Braun proudly sent his children to study farming there, and Elsing had long been associated with the extension service and other agriculture programs at the school. But neither Braun nor Elsing approved of the school's strident support for Oahe. They felt Fine was part of the academic machine trying to push Oahe over farmers opposed to the project. When the four men went to Braun's home for coffee and lunch, Fine quietly took his place at the table, looking disturbed and dispirited. Braun's wife, Erlaine, worried about her guest, and asked Ray what had happened. "He knew he'd mislabeled the soil," explained her husband.[26] "Dr. Fine was absolutely crushed," remembered John Elsing. "We thought he was going to break down in tears."[27] Years later, when asked about the incident, Dr. Fine became agitated and described tests he had conducted on Braun's land, but claimed no recollection of being contradicted and embarrassed.[28]

At the soils and drainage hearing, George Piper introduced a transcript of a speech made by C. R. Maierhofer, formerly the bureau's chief of drainage and groundwater engineering. Though Maierhofer's remarks had been made in 1963, their worth to Oahe opponents was considerable. Speaking to bureau colleagues and irrigation supporters at a conference in Billings, Montana, Maierhofer addressed drainage problems plaguing bureau irrigation projects. A portion of the blame, explained Maierhofer, was due to "pressure from local boosters to build projects which are not very good ones." He mentioned chambers of commerce and politicians as examples of local boosters. "While these boosters may be sincere," he continued, "they will go to almost any length to make their pet project look good and have Congress appropriate money to build it. . . . Such local pressures can be tremendous, and sometimes people are blind to potential drainage problems that grew to be very serious after the project was built and irrigation started." Maierhofer cautioned: "Sooner or later, salts or groundwater, or both, will reach the surface zone of the [irrigated] soil. This may take 2 years or 20—sometimes longer."[29]

George Piper believed Oahe boosters were similarly blind. He felt there were too many uncertainties about Oahe's drainage plan, soil irrigability, and seepage threats to permit the project to be built. To construct the project, said Piper, meant risking a farming area that was already productive. Piper reminded sub-district directors that the bureau conceded that even its best irrigation projects could bankrupt or force from the land several generations of farmers before taking hold. If Oahe supporters performed an objective analysis of the bureau's history, suggested Piper later, they would have realized that the agency's reclamation program more closely resembled an ongoing experiment with uncertain results than a foolproof formula for agricultural prosperity.

Soil fertility was not the only aspect of the lake plain that was threatened. When city residents in Aberdeen, Huron, or Pierre described Oahe in glowing terms, they did not visualize the fate awaiting their rural neighbors. The impact of developing an irrigation project in country neighborhoods was not unlike rezoning an established residential neighborhood in the city to commercial status. Families in that part of the city would be overwhelmed by change. They would witness the widening of streets and the removal of trees from boulevards. Playgrounds would be replaced by parking lots and strip malls, billboards would be erected, traffic would increase, noise would escalate. Likewise, the impacts to the people, animals, and landscape in Oahe's irrigation areas would be severe. Some roads would be rerouted or closed. The James River valley would become laced with 1,000 miles of water-delivery laterals and 935 miles of drainage ditches. Winding streambeds and natural drainage ways would disappear, transformed into trenches and canals. The James River would also disappear, its corridor of trees and backwaters to be replaced by a neat ditch. Hundreds of pumps would produce a hum heard across the land. The style and pace of farming would also change. Dominating the lake plain would be the intense enterprise of irrigation agriculture, including the unrelenting requirement that irrigators produce yields sufficient to pay the high costs associated with water delivery, electricity, the increased use of agricultural chemicals, and other new expenses. It was no wonder that absentee landowners and corporate farms often invaded large federal irrigation projects. The historic goal of federal irrigation had been to settle the west with family farmers. That admirable objective had been subsumed by professional land managers, corporate accountants, and insurance companies diversifying into agriculture.

As the clock neared midnight, John Sieh finally adjourned the soils and drainage hearing. The hearing had lasted longer than the one in Blunt. For more than twelve hours, the bureau had endured criticism, tried to defend itself, and attempted to answer the confusing, redundant questions posed by the sub-district's directors. On the drive back to Huron, angry bureau officials complained about the treatment they had received. They had work to do, and the long hearings were diverting their energy. They looked forward to the next hearing about as much as an irrigator hopes for a cloudburst while center pivots pour water on his fields.

Relief for the bureau was not in the forecast. The next hearing lasted even longer than the preceding three. The topic for this thirteen-hour marathon—held on 17 March—was the project's cost-benefit ratio.

Ideally, federal irrigation projects attain economic benefits that exceed costs. In other words, for every dollar spent to build and maintain a project, there should be at least one dollar generated. How could anything else be acceptable? asked public-interest groups. But many federal water projects, and most irrigation projects in the West, could not make such a claim. As calculated by the Bureau of Reclamation, Oahe's cost-benefit ratio showed a gain of thirty cents for every dollar invested. That figure was dismissed by independent economists, including Dr. Thomas Power of the University of Montana. At the sub-district hearing, Dr. Power, who was serving as a witness for United Family Farmers, warned that the bureau's figure was self-serving.[30]

Several years earlier, an analysis of Oahe economics had been conducted by scholars from Johns Hopkins University. "The Bureau of Reclamation," stated the Johns Hopkins economists, "has developed the reputation of altering benefit-cost analysis to improve the appearance of the projects under its control." They concluded that Oahe's cost-to-benefit ratio was likely .50, or a fifty-cent loss for every dollar invested. The Johns Hopkins study was submitted to the Oahe sub-district board at the cost-benefit hearing.[31]

Farmers at the hearing accused the bureau of exaggerating crop-yield estimates to enhance the project's cost-benefit ratio. They also questioned how a project that required the destruction and/or acquisition of 110,000 acres to develop irrigation on 190,000 acres could be justified. Of the 110,000 acres, 42,000 were needed for wildlife mitigation. The other 70,000 acres would be flooded by reservoirs or ruined by ditches. It did not make sense, challenged the farmers, that the number of those able to irrigate would be about the same as the number who would feel the impacts of mitigation and condemnation.

The information presented at the cost-benefit hearing added compelling evidence to what had been presented at the three earlier hearings. Although three more sub-district's hearings remained, most of the sub-district's directors had already been convinced that the project was deficient in too many ways for construction to proceed. Two days after the cost-benefit hearing, a majority of the board adopted a resolution asking President Carter to enact a moratorium on the project.

Officials in the bureau felt as though they were being squeezed from two sides at once. While the sub-district was aggravating them in South Dakota, Bob Lane and his colleagues were pressuring them in Washington. As part of his project review, Lane conducted numerous briefings with the water agency. The relationship between the parties was predictably circumspect.

Bureau officials saw Lane as an environmental zealot prejudiced against their projects. Lane's earlier experiences with the bureau left him concerned about the reliability of the data supplied to him by the agency. He and others performing the administration's water-projects review judged at least some of the information given to them by the agency as inaccurate and dishonest. "We knew we'd have to push hard to get information and we knew we couldn't accept at face value everything they gave us," remembered Lane. According to Lane, Preston Funkhouser unwillingly cooperated with requests for information. "He manipulated the data and tried to stonewall the Oahe review," said Lane.[32]

Both Lane and Guy Martin identified a similar defect within the reclamation agency. "Manipulating the data to make their projects look good was standard operating procedure and probably unwritten policy [within the agency]," claimed Lane.[33] Lane discovered that internal pressures prevented some bureau staffers from being candid about agency problems. "The bureau was in many ways a closed shop, and its management structure was very militaristic," he explained. "If you worked for the Bureau of Reclamation and had an opinion that differed from the party line, you either kept it to yourself or you were out of work."[34]

Lane also met with another federal agency to gather information about Oahe. But his reception at the Fish and Wildlife Service was altogether different from his encounters with the Bureau of Reclamation. So was the message he heard. For years, the federal Fish and Wildlife Service had been nothing more than a rubber stamp for water-development projects, and in Oahe's early days the agency's wildlife biologists did what the Bureau of Reclamation told them to do. They may have winced when they realized that the project would destroy upland cover, prairie potholes, and the James River, but they felt impotent to thwart the superior political clout of the bureau. The power exerted by the bureau over the Fish and Wildlife Service was so great that bureau officials boldly demanded silence by wildlife biologists on critical issues and tried to alter the content of Fish and Wildlife Service comments or testimony.

That situation changed when strong conservation-minded men were appointed to lead the Fish and Wildlife Service. A key figure in the evolution of the wildlife agency was Nathaniel Reed, appointed by President Nixon as assistant interior secretary for Fish, Wildlife, and Parks. In the early 1970s, Reed led the first effective attack on river and stream channelization practices by federal construction agencies. He was determined that the Fish and Wildlife Service be a defender of wildlife and not an apologist for the Corps of Engineers and the

Bureau of Reclamation. "Reed stuck up for us," recalled Rolf Wallenstrom, the man who led the South Dakota–Nebraska regional office of the Fish and Wildlife Service from 1971 to 1979. "He made it possible for us to do our jobs."[35]

Reviewing notes and documentation in his office, Wallenstrom was shocked to discover the nonchalance of his predecessors about Oahe impacts to wildlife. Wallenstrom was convinced that Oahe development would intensify farming, increase the application of agricultural chemicals, and destroy valuable wildlife habitat, and he and his staff expressed those concerns. Despite relentless pressure by the bureau that he soften his positions, Wallenstrom persisted, confident he would not be undermined or compromised by weak superiors in Washington.

The information provided to Bob Lane by the Fish and Wildlife Service suggested Oahe would cause more environmental degradation than the Bureau of Reclamation was willing to admit. Lane's experience and skepticism about the bureau's self-serving data prepared him for that discrepancy.

To advance President Carter's plan to modify national water policy, the administration's project analysts conducted public hearings in those states impacted by the hit list. South Dakota's hearing on Oahe was held 21 March 1977.

Both sides in the Oahe fight understood the significance of the hearing. Carter's representatives would use information gathered at the hearing to help determine which projects would be omitted from the 1978 budget. Not only did Oahe stand to lose its anticipated appropriation of $17 million, a serious blow, but such an interruption in the project's yearly funding cycle could be a setback with permanent implications. Critical momentum during the project's early construction phase would be lost and might be unrecoverable.

Bob Lane was seated with four colleagues at a large table facing the house chamber of the South Dakota State Capitol. Some of Oahe's most intense debates had taken place beneath the soaring ceiling of that grand room. Lane looked out at a room so packed with people standing and sitting it seemed there was not a square foot of floor space to spare. Lane didn't know it, but members of United Family Farmers had arrived early, and most of the seats closest to him were occupied by project opponents.

Trailing in after the farmers had been hundreds of project supporters arriving on chamber of commerce buses from Aberdeen and Huron. Few of these people were able to enter the main floor and gallery of the house chambers. They joined others from the overflow to listen and watch the proceedings on closed-circuit televisions that had been installed in hallways and the rotunda area. As many as a thousand people were in the Capitol that day.

Law-enforcement authorities were prepared to separate bickering spectators and silence unruly outbursts. Ten highway patrolmen and at least one plain-clothes officer patrolled the building. But the belligerence that often erupted during highly emotional Oahe forums did not materialize. In front of the outsiders from Washington, South Dakotans were on their best behavior.

The morning's testimony was reserved for proponents; opponents made presentations in the afternoon. Governor Richard Kneip, Senator McGovern's aide George Cunningham, and Republican Representatives James Abdnor and Larry Pressler all spoke as proponents. Although Senator James Abourezk did not attend, his statement was read during the time slot reserved for those who wished to testify as neither supporters nor opponents. Abourezk requested the panel consider any recommendations made by the Oahe sub-district. "My position," explained Abourezk, "has always been that the people affected by [Oahe] deserve to make the final choice on its shape and future."[36]

The Oahe sub-district was allowed fifty minutes for its testimony, and nine board members presented statements. Sitting side by side were Bob Hipple and John Sieh, their testimony as different as drought and deluge. Hipple reminded the panel that the federal government owed Oahe to South Dakota as compensation for land lost beneath the Missouri River's mainstem dams. Sieh explained that the sub-district's series of seven hearings had not yet concluded—four of the seven had been held—but that the sub-district board had already heard such worrisome testimony that it had voted several days earlier for a moratorium on the project.

A total of fifty persons made presentations to Lane and the panel during the eight-hour hearing. Each witness deposited a copy of written testimony and supporting materials on a large table. As the day wore on, the pile of testimony, maps, charts, petitions, photographs, letters, and documents covered the table and spilled onto the floor. Reviewing these materials and the oral transcript would be a formidable task, but Bob Lane's assignment was to deliver a synopsis to Cecil Andrus within several weeks. Lane anticipated that President Carter would unveil his verdict on the future of Oahe and other water projects by mid-April.

14

A Flurry of Desperate Deeds

> I raised some money for Oahe, and I spent a lot of my own money. . . . I had
> the feeling that if we could make Oahe go, the benefits to myself and my
> business and the construction industry and the whole state justified that.
> Charles Kearns, interview

The 1977 South Dakota legislature had not nullified the authority of the new
sub-district majority as thoroughly as Oahe supporters would have liked. After
the sub-district's request that the Carter administration cancel Oahe's 1978
funding, it became more urgent to arrest John Sieh's power. With that in mind,
Friends of Oahe unveiled their next move.

At the behest of the pro-Oahe group, six sub-district residents filed a lawsuit
in the Circuit Court of Hughes County challenging the constitutionality of the
sub-district's board of directors. The system used to elect the sub-district's directors, said Friends of Oahe executive director Bill Riechers, was patently un-
fair to a majority of the voters residing in the sub-district. The suit, encouraged
and financed in part by Charles Kearns, argued that the board's two municipal
directors represented nearly 65 percent of the sub-district's population but
wielded only 18 percent of the votes on the board. Conversely, rural residents
elected nine directors though comprising just 35 percent of the electorate. To
remedy this alleged disparity, the plaintiffs sought a new apportionment of
power among sub-district directors.

The ramifications of the so-called "one man–one vote" lawsuit were considerable. If the plaintiffs prevailed, the directors representing municipalities—
Steve Thorson and Bob Hipple—would control the sub-district. John Sieh
would be ousted as chairman, Curt Hohn would lose his job as manager, and the
political advantages gained by United Family Farmers in the 1976 elections

would be wiped out. Filing such a lawsuit was a white-collar tactic perfectly suited to an organization like Friends Of Oahe. Lacking grassroots membership and strength, with little networking ability among citizens, especially farmers, in the sub-district, Friends of Oahe had devolved into a paper tiger. Most of the people whose names were on the complaint had little to do with the suit. One of the plaintiffs, a woman named Phyllis Huss, lived in Faulkton and owned a farm near an Oahe canal. She and her husband hoped to one day divert water from the ditch to irrigate their land. Over the telephone, she gave permission to be named on the lawsuit. She later said that when she agreed to join the suit, she did not know the other plaintiffs.[1]

If successful, the suit would overturn an arrangement that had been decided in 1960 by sub-district organizers, including Bob Hipple and Fred Holscher. During the campaign to form the sub-district, Hipple believed that it was not only politically expedient to distribute most of the directors among farmers, but it was also the fairest approach. Hipple realized that without the support of rural residents, the election to form the sub-district could fail. He and other sub-district organizers knew that city residents were more apt to be supportive and that farmers, because they would feel the brunt of the Oahe project's negative impacts, would be less receptive. They also understood that farmers would pay most of the sub-district's taxes—some 60 percent—and be responsible for most of the local costs associated with the project.

Sixteen years after that seminal decision had been implemented, John Sieh defended its appropriateness. "I don't think main street, occupied by chambers of commerce, will be mitigated for wildlife purposes. I don't think main street stores will have to be moved for canals."[2] Sieh and other majority directors retained one of South Dakota's leading trial lawyers, Larry Piersol, to join Tom May to defend the sub-district.

United Family Farmers wasn't watching passively as its hard-fought victories were challenged in the legislature and the courts. In Sully and Hughes Counties, Oahe opponents unhappy with Bud Yackley circulated a petition among farmers in the two counties that asked Yackley and other board members to seek deauthorization of the project. Confronted with the stack of petitions, Yackley admitted that his feelings differed from those held by most of his constituents, and he resigned from the board. Appointed to replace Yackley was Ken Marsh, a wealthy wheat farmer from Sully County who had been a leader in the effort to block formation of the Missouri Slope Irrigation District. He immediately joined ranks with the John Sieh faction on the board.

167

Meanwhile, the Bureau of Reclamation continued construction on the Pierre canal as if there were no political controversy. The agency had awarded contracts to begin digging twelve more miles (reach 1A) of the canal only weeks after United Family Farmers triumphed in the 1976 elections, and contractors started moving dirt the day after President Carter's review team concluded its Pierre hearing. Several days later, a majority of the sub-district's directors requested that no new canal construction be undertaken until the project's future was known. For the second time in four months, the bureau refused to listen. Not even the president, said Bob Hipple sarcastically, can stop the digging.

On 13 April, Bob Lane submitted his written review on Oahe. After forty-three years of planning by hundreds, perhaps thousands, of Bureau of Reclamation employees who had themselves written reports that totaled at least hundreds of thousands of pages, Oahe's fate was contained in a brief but concise twenty-five-page document. Lane's review identified several environmental concerns, including the probable worsening of water quality in the Oahe project area and the likely violation of water-quality standards on the James River. The review also mentioned the destruction of important wildlife habitat associated with prairie wetlands and the James River.

Although the bureau had long touted the recreation opportunities that would be created by the project's artificial lakes, the review dismissed the value of the new impoundments. Mudflats inhibiting access would ring the reservoirs, and water levels would greatly fluctuate. Overall, it appeared the Oahe project would degrade, not improve, outdoor opportunities in the project area.

Oahe's economics, according to the review, were not disastrous, but ample reasons for skepticism existed. The projected cost/benefit ratio suggested a break-even scenario, but even if this optimistic projection came true, the project would be an anomaly in the Missouri basin. The twenty-six irrigation projects already constructed under the Pick-Sloan Plan were generating a paltry thirty-three cents for every federal dollar invested. The review reported that the government's investment in Oahe would amount to a hefty $735,655 per irrigated farm unit, or $189,913 per resident of those farms. Economists in President Carter's budget office frowned when they saw those figures.

The recently passed Oahe sub-district resolution that requested a delay in Oahe funding was featured in the report. Lane's review did not ignore the support for Oahe that was found in the irrigation areas and in the state legislature, but it concluded, based on the composition and position of the sub-district, that local support for the project was uncertain.

The report also addressed the testimony that Bob Hipple had delivered at the federal hearing in Pierre. Hipple claimed that Oahe would serve as compensation owed South Dakota by the federal government for lands lost beneath the Pick-Sloan's Missouri River reservoirs. The federal review clarified the federal commitment to South Dakota because of the reservoir losses. "[South Dakota's] political leaders," explained the report, "believe that the Oahe Unit represents a commitment to South Dakota for lands taken for mainstream reservoirs . . . A review of the legislative history of the project reveals a political understanding between the Upper and Lower Missouri River Basin States and the Congress, but no evidence has been found to indicate that the United States made a formal legal commitment to a trade-off."[3] Oahe proponents didn't care that there was no "legal" commitment binding the federal government to build Oahe. The "political" commitment, as cited by the Oahe review, was, for them, sufficient to warrant the expectation that the federal government would one day build Oahe.

Ken Holum, in an interview, acknowledged that the federal obligation was based on a handshake. He suggested that South Dakota should have been more shrewd during negotiations with the federal government over details in the 1944 Flood Control Act that authorized the Pick-Sloan Plan; states in the Colorado River basin had negotiated a better, surer deal in the legislation authorizing a federal plan to develop their basin than had Missouri basin interests in theirs. Because the process to consolidate the Pick and Sloan plans was conducted in a hasty, somewhat panicked atmosphere, said Holum, Missouri basin interests negotiated for only a description of projects for eventual consideration. "People in the Colorado basin were smarter," he said. "They wrote it [project development] into the law."[4] Holum regretted that the Pick-Sloan Plan had not set aside funds from the outset to develop the projects it authorized. The many years that passed between passage of Pick-Sloan and the first meaningful appropriation of dollars for Oahe construction, in 1974, weakened the political incentive in Washington to build Oahe. And now Carter and his staff were convinced that the project lacked a sound economic and environmental rationale.

Guy Martin described the Oahe review as accurate and creditable. "It had to be," he explained, alluding to the intense scrutiny on the review process. "There's no way we could have gotten by if they [the reviews] were full of holes. By and large they held up."[5] Martin paid special attention to Oahe because it differed from other projects being considered. "In this case it was rare, one of the only cases, if not the only case," explained Martin, "where the [local water] board itself was part of the critical movement against the project."[6]

That fact also impressed Cecil Andrus, the secretary of the interior. Several days after the Oahe report landed on Andrus's desk, he issued a concise recommendation on the project: "I recommend that funding [for Oahe] be withheld until assurances of local support are given." Andrus also suggested that funding should not be resurrected unless the sub-district board reversed its position.[7] At the time of Andrus's recommendation, about $45 million had been spent on Oahe. Andrus and his staff concluded that Oahe's problems were so excessive that the best strategy was to acknowledge that the monies already expended had been a bad investment, and the appropriate course for the federal government was to walk away from the project.

On 18 April 1977, the day Congress returned from its Easter recess, President Carter announced his decision. "I have tried to be fair and to give the benefit of the doubt on some projects which would certainly not be justified if they were proposed today," he said.[8] Citing the need to protect natural resources and safeguard the treasury, the president identified eighteen water projects he wanted to slice from the federal budget completely. With several notable exceptions, the group was mostly a duplicate of the list Carter proposed two months earlier. At number seventeen was Oahe.

Not only did President Carter recommend that Oahe lose its 1978 funding of $17 million, he suggested that the project be permanently halted. Oahe supporters were shocked. If President Carter could convince Congress to agree with him, at least $400 million, perhaps more than $900 million, in federal subsidies would be erased from South Dakota's future. Oahe was the second most expensive project on Carter's sweeping list. Taking top honors was California's Auburn dam, slated to lose more than $37 million in 1978 and $900 million overall.[9]

In spite of Lane's report, many South Dakotans remained enamored with Oahe. After all, it was the Bureau of Reclamation, an agency they trusted, that had constantly reminded them that the federal obligation to South Dakota would be fulfilled by the mighty Oahe project. In fact, Lane had been less hostile to the bureau than the bureau itself realized. Lane persuaded Andrus to allow the Garrison project to survive, although the project (and several other Bureau of Reclamation monsters, including the Central Utah and Central Arizona projects) would be subject to drastic modifications. Regarding Oahe's fate, however, the two men wholeheartedly agreed.

Senator George McGovern and other Oahe supporters immediately blamed the president, the Oahe sub-district, and the state's divided delegation for the Oahe project's predicament. They contrasted their state with North Dakota, where Garrison's local water board and the entire delegation were united in their support for Garrison. Jimmy Carter, Jim Abourezk, and John Sieh became the scapegoats. The South Dakota Water Development Association purchased full-page ads in South Dakota daily newspapers condemning Sieh and Abourezk. Charles Kearns bought an entire page in the *Washington Post* to criticize President Carter.[10]

The real moment of truth for President Carter would come during the summer of 1977, when Congress would take up his proposal. Congress could affirm or reject the measure, or counter the president with a compromise. Guy Martin. who was often sent to Capitol Hill to defend the president's position, discovered that Congress had dug in its heels. The public works bill that emerged from the House Appropriations Committee restored 1978 funding for all the projects Carter proposed, deleting but one, the small Grove Lake project in Kansas. Adding to its brazen defiance of the president, the committee suggested expenditures for a dozen new water projects. On the Senate side, there was similar hostility, and Guy Martin sensed the president's plan would sink. Carter's proposal may have been overly ambitious, thought Martin, but many of the projects targeted by the president were fraught with problems. A vengeful Congress, Martin learned, was unwilling to impartially analyze both the merits and liabilities of the projects. They seemed more intent on dishing out retaliation.

Back in South Dakota, Oahe supporters continued their efforts to undermine the sub-district and to disprove the federal belief that local support for the project was uncertain. Governor Richard Kneip and the newly formed Oahe Task Force urged the Carter administration to consider the position of the entire state, not just the sub-district, when determining the future of the Oahe project. Kneip and Congressman James Abdnor suggested that a referendum be held to demonstrate the project's local commitment and to guide the Carter administration's position. Two years earlier, Kneip and Abdnor had played important roles in defeating a similar legislative proposal that was sponsored by United Family Farmers.

The sub-district was dealt a setback when a circuit court judge, Robert Miller, ordered that director votes be weighted according to the number of people a director represented. Miller's prescription for fairness was that each municipal director cast the equivalent of 32.5 votes. Directors representing rural areas would possess from 2 to 6 votes, depending on the population of the area they represented. The total number of votes to be cast by the nine rural directors was 35. The consequence of Judge Miller's decision was starkly evident: if the two municipal directors worked together, they could outvote the nine rural directors. John Sieh, acting in his capacity as chairman of the sub-district and on the advice of sub-district counsel, refused to implement the ruling until an appeal was resolved in the state supreme court.

The showdown over Oahe on the U.S. Senate floor featured old friends George McGovern and James Abourezk. Abourezk referred to the debate as painful for both men. "It was probably the toughest thing I ever had to do in my political life," said Abourezk.[11] South Dakota's Democratic senators squared off over a public-works spending bill sent by the Senate Appropriations Committee to the full Senate that culled Carter's list of defunded projects to eight. Oahe was one of the projects that remained on the chopping block, and Abourezk was determined that it stay there. He had already written each of his Senate colleagues, informing them that he supported the president's decision to suspend funding for Oahe. The people most affected by the project, Abourezk wrote, did not want it. "It would be a travesty," he asserted, "to impose it on them."[12] McGovern argued that if Oahe funds were not reinstated, they would be lost forever. The Senate rejected McGovern's request.

President Carter was not pleased with the reception his proposal had gotten in either legislative body, but the Senate version was better than the House version. After some complex political deal making, the House agreed to an equivalent of the Senate's 1978 spending bill, and the president had a difficult decision to make. If he signed the bill into law, the 1978 budget would contain funding for nine of the projects he wanted to delete. Only eight of the projects on his hit list would be defunded. Cecil Andrus and Guy Martin urged their boss to veto the bill. They wanted him to fight for more of his original measure. Though Martin had initially been skeptical of the president's vast plan, he hoped that political expedience would not enter into the decision. Most of the president's staff expected their boss to reject the bill. They were stunned and disappointed when he signed the compromise into law.

Despite the reprieve for some water projects, Oahe was not spared. For 1978 funding, the debate was over. Oahe had been wounded, perhaps fatally.

The South Dakota Water Development Association scheduled a grand rally for Pierre, describing it in full-page newspaper advertisements as a last-ditch effort to save Oahe. On 16 August, the state's Oahe elite would gather in an effort to offset the momentum raging against them. The public was invited to attend, but special invitations were issued to certain businessmen, farmers, bureaucrats, and politicians from across South Dakota. John Elsing sent an inquiry to the address listed on the advertisement, and several days later the mail brought a small yellow card with instructions that read: "This Is Your Reserved Seat Reservation For The Pro-Oahe Meeting. . . . Bring This Card And Present [It] At The Door." Elsing immediately drove to Aberdeen and presented the ticket to Curt Hohn. Hohn, already upset because the Oahe sub-district had not been invited to participate in the meeting, took the ticket to a printshop, ordered five hundred replicas, and began distributing them to members of United Family Farmers. John Elsing kept some tickets on hand and took them to the rally, where he presented them to farmers who, by arrangement, had arrived at least an hour before the meeting was to start. The farmers had also been instructed to occupy the front rows in the reserved-seat section.

As Elsing stood by the entrance to the Kings Inn Convention Center, disbursing the counterfeit tickets, he watched Preston Funkhouser step to the registration table. Apparently, Funkhouser did not have a ticket and had difficulty convincing anyone that he should be allowed to sit in a reserved seat. Elsing admitted to a twinge of guilt as a group of farmers bearing fake tickets signed the registration book and entered the hall while Funkhouser stood nearby pleading his case. By the time the bureau's top man in South Dakota was granted permission to enter, the best seats in the reserved section were occupied.

The meeting itself had been planned as nothing more than a grandstanding event for Oahe diehards. Though it was billed as a forum to discuss the project's future, including possible alternatives to the project, no panel discussions were scheduled and no time was allotted for organized, meaningful interaction for those who attended; there would be no attempt to resolve by consensus or otherwise the difficult realities facing water development in South Dakota.

At the rally, as the first speech started, theee hundred members of United Family Farmers simultaneously slapped large anti-Oahe stickers on their shirts and jackets. "It changed the tone of the meeting," recalled Curt Hohn.[13] Speaker after speaker stepped to the podium and faced at close quarters a sea of grim-faced adversaries. John Elsing remembered all of the speakers in this strained environment struggling to soften and hurry their pro-Oahe presentations. By the time Congressman Larry Pressler arrived, fifteen minutes before his slot on the agenda, the sabotaged meeting had ground to a premature halt.

But this was not before Curt Hohn had risen from his chair and walked toward the stage. Hohn had been quietly stewing as representatives of the state's other sub-districts made speeches. How preposterous, he thought, that the sub-district holding Oahe's main contract with the federal government was not asked to participate in the dialogue. As the program moderator began to adjourn the meeting, Hohn made his way to the podium. After introducing himself, Hohn announced that he would like to describe alternatives to Oahe that South Dakota could pursue. Midsentence, the microphone was disengaged. From his onstage vantage point, Hohn could see Charles Kearns speaking with a Pierre policeman. Television cameras and newspaper photographers and reporters recorded the moment as the uniformed officer bounded up beside Hohn and instructed the sub-district manager to leave the stage. "The tension in that room was so thick," Hohn recalled, "that if I had resisted there would have been a huge fight."[14] Media accounts of the meeting left the impression that autocratic Oahe supporters had treated Hohn unfairly. "After a dozen speakers said South Dakota must work together for water development," read the Associated Press story, "the manager of the Oahe Conservancy Sub-district Board was refused a chance to speak at a public hearing."[15]

News about Curt Hohn's eviction reached Washington, and Interior Secretary Cecil Andrus wrote Douglas Haeder, executive director of the Oahe Task Force: "We are disturbed that opposing points of view were not dealt with in a more constructive manner."[16] Had they let Curt Hohn speak that day, Oahe zealots might have learned that although the irrigation project lacked local support, there were other projects that enjoyed favor in local areas of the Oahe sub-district. Hohn might have told them about being on the campaign trail the previous summer in Edmunds County with Arnold Schurr. A Schurr supporter invited the candidate and campaign manager out of the blazing sun and into his farm home for cool refreshments. Hohn never forgot his own dismay and the matter-of-fact indifference of his host when glasses of cola-colored tap water were presented. With that one incident, Hohn understood the need for better drinking water in rural areas of the Oahe sub-district.

Several years before Curt Hohn held up that glass of dark water and reluctantly drank it, a small group of people from Aberdeen and small communities west of Aberdeen began meeting to discuss water quality and supply problems. They decided to resurrect an idea dismissed years earlier by Aberdeen officials that proposed piping filtered Missouri River water from Mobridge to Aberdeen and possibly to points east of Aberdeen. After several preliminary meetings in 1974 and early 1975, the organization expanded to six counties, adopted a name, and elected a board of directors. By late 1975, the WEB Water Development Association had hired engineers to study a service area consisting of thirty-six cities and towns and providing domestic water to thousands of townspeople and farmers in north-central South Dakota.[17]

The feasibility study confirmed what many residents already suspected: the water used in thirty-four of the thirty-six communities did not satisfy federal guidelines for safe drinking water. The study also revealed that nearly one-third of the communities had already experienced or expected to experience supply deficiencies and that many farmers in the area used poor water from unreliable wells. Eighty percent of the farmers in the proposed service area responded favorably when asked if they would participate in a pipeline program. A South Dakota official later said that the state may have the most mineralized water in the country. Heavy mineralization translates into foul-tasting water, corrosion of plumbing and appliances, stunted livestock growth, higher calf mortality, diminished dairy-herd production, and possible human health problems. The WEB engineers suggested a water intake be built on Lake Oahe south of Mobridge. The raw water would be pumped eastward for thirteen miles, through a pipe to a treatment plant. After purification, the water would enter a vast pipeline distribution system. Estimated cost: $70 million.

Domestic water pipelines were not unusual in farm country, and other states had already established rural water organizations to facilitate their development. What distinguished WEB from previously developed systems was its immense size. If constructed to a scale desired by WEB's board of directors, WEB would be the largest pipeline of its kind in the nation, serving an area nearly as large as the state of Connecticut.

15

The Sub-district Is Defended

Now that funding has run out on the Oahe Irrigation Project, is it dead—
forever?

John Wooley, editor, *Pierre Times*

On 3 January 1978, a front-page headline in the *Aberdeen American News* declared: OAHE VOTE RULING REVERSED.

United Family Farmers were overjoyed. The state supreme court had over-
turned the temporary injunction issued in circuit court that stipulated an ad-
justed voting system among sub-district directors that favored municipal directors. The ruling in the high court preserved the power held by rural interests in
the sub-district. It also freed the Oahe board to take action on the Oahe project,
negating a condition imposed by Judge Robert Miller as part of his earlier ruling.

On 17 January 1978, another front-page headline in the *Aberdeen American
News* announced additional, important information about the Oahe project:
OAHE BOARD ASKS DE-AUTHORIZATION.

Introducing the resolution asking President Carter and Congress to deauthorize Oahe, Arnold Schurr had told the board the time had come to settle Oahe's
future and open the way for other water projects that were more acceptable to
local citizens (WEB was one of the projects that Schurr hoped would benefit).
Congressional deauthorization of Oahe would be the ultimate victory for Oahe
opponents. Such an action would erase Oahe from the roster of federal projects.
The project would die and be buried.[1]

In the audience at the sub-district meeting were seventy people. Not one of
them spoke against Schurr's resolution, and seven board members endorsed the
measure making deauthorization the sub-district's official position.

Publisher Bud Maher's reaction to the board's deauthorization position was more thoughtful than hostile. In an editorial he wrote: "If this action does not trigger a positive response by the irrigation districts, the municipalities and the state itself, we doubt that anything ever will."[2]

A response did in fact materialize, and only one day after Schurr's momentous proposal was approved. But it did not emanate from within South Dakota. In the basement of the South Dakota capitol, a memorandum from Washington DC arrived via an electronic message-receiving machine. Addressed to Governor Richard Kneip, according to its letterhead the communication originated within the White House and was attributed to an organization called the White House Water Study Group. At the top of the memorandum were the initials JC, and Governor Kneip surmised that they were written by President Carter. The message informed Kneip that "if the State Legislature adjusts the legal standing of the Oahe Board in relation to the Oahe Master Contract, the [Carter] Administration will deal with whatever legal entity is established by the [South Dakota] Legislature as the successor in interest to the Oahe Board on the contract for the state of South Dakota."[3] Kneip was ecstatic.

News about the White House memorandum spread quickly. Oahe supporters in Pierre and around the state excitedly discussed the new direction the memo portended for the Oahe project. Governor Kneip's desire to circumvent or supplant the Oahe board suddenly seemed possible. Kneip promptly dispatched his top aide and his allies on the Oahe Task Force to Washington for a high-level meeting with Interior Secretary Cecil Andrus—a meeting hurriedly arranged by Senator George McGovern. Though the agenda topic was ostensibly the Oahe project, Kneip was most interested in Andrus's feelings about the memo.

The sub-district's representatives to the task force, John Sieh and Glenn Overby, were not told about the trip. Many legislators learned the next day that their colleagues were en route to Washington when task-force member Senator George Shannard failed to testify before the Senate Appropriations Committee on a bill that he had sponsored. By the time Sieh and Overby discovered that their task-force colleagues were traveling to meet with Andrus, a blizzard prevented air travel out of South Dakota. Sieh was livid about being snubbed, but the same nasty weather that blocked him and Overby also stranded Shannard and his collaborators in Minneapolis. The meeting with Andrus was postponed until 23 January, and this time Sieh and Overby accompanied the group.

Task-force members were barely through Andrus's office door when they inquired about the memorandum. Andrus and his staff looked at each other, shrugged their shoulders, and asked their visitors to elaborate. "So far as we can tell," said Dan Beard, an Andrus assistant, "the memo is a complete fabrication."[4] Beard also said there was no such thing as a White House Water Study Group. John Sieh suspected that the phony memo had originated in Senator McGovern's office, but McGovern and his staff denied having anything to do with the communication. George Piper claimed the memo was "an effort to stampede the South Dakota Legislature into taking punitive action against the Oahe sub-district."[5] An investigation launched by the federal Justice Department uncovered nothing. Though the culprit—or culprits—was never apprehended, Oahe boosters were back at square one. The mysterious memo cast a dark, unsavory shadow across the movement to promote the Oahe project, and efforts to expand the powers of the state conservancy office and weaken the sub-district failed in both houses of the state legislature.

Oahe advocates had always counted on the support of the commissioner of the Bureau of Reclamation. That support had been useful because the commissioner traditionally occupied an imposing throne of authority in Washington. By dispensing construction favors, the commissioner had been able to hoard power and retain powerful allies in key congressional posts.

Before his appointment as bureau commissioner in 1977, Keith Higginson had distinguished himself directing the Idaho Department of Water Resources under four governors, including Cecil Andrus. It was at Andrus's behest that Higginson joined the Interior Department, though Higginson was reluctant to take the bureau post. With a billion-dollar budget and about nine thousand employees, the bureau was difficult to direct even when things were going smoothly. And in 1977, things were not well at the agency: the first version of President Carter's hit list had just been released, and the agency was also still reeling from a catastrophe it caused the previous year when one of its dams ruptured.

Teton dam was an engineering debacle, hastily erected on an unstable site for political reasons. The wall of water unleashed by the dam's failure killed eleven people and demolished several communities. But the bureau had been lucky. Fatalities could have been much greater had the dam, 305 feet high, collapsed at night. Fortunately, the looming disaster presented itself in the form of several gushing leaks at midmorning on 5 June, and twelve thousand people living below the dam were evacuated. By the time the dam gave way just before noon, most of the eight thousand residents in the small city of Rexburg had reached the safety of high ground. From that vantage point, they watched in disbelief as a powerful tide of water churned, like a line of tornadoes in formation, a dozen miles down the valley before battering their small city. Rexburg recovered, but Wilford, a town closer to the dam, forever ceased to exist, swamped by a twenty-foot wave that arrived only twenty-five minutes after the dam went down.

Keith Higginson was intimately familiar with the Teton disaster, having served on a federal commission that concluded Teton's failure was due to Bureau of Reclamation errors. Higginson's predecessors at the bureau, men like Gil Stamm and Floyd Dominy, had functioned nearly autonomously within various presidential administrations and had enjoyed immense, independent political power. Dominy in particular had been a master at getting his way and bulldozing a wide swath through Congress. By virtue of protocol, Ken Holum may have been Dominy's supervisor, but Holum never could rein in the irrepressible, swashbuckling commissioner. Dominy, it seemed, was accountable to no one.

Higginson, on the other hand, owed his appointment to his friend Cecil Andrus, respected the loyalty expected of him by the Carter administration, and tried to follow the orders of his immediate supervisor, Guy Martin. Beneath Higginson were layers of the bureau's old guard. In the agency's Washington headquarters and out in the far-flung project and regional offices were bureau officials who felt disdain for President Carter and his intention to reform water policy. Their loyalty was to their agency, not to the Carter administration. These were career professionals accustomed to planning and building projects for a commissioner who vigorously promoted that mission.

Not long after President Carter's hit list had been made public, the Oahe sub-district chairman, John Sieh, wrote Commissioner Higginson and asked about the bureau's position regarding Carter's plan. While it was not unusual for such correspondence to be circulated through the bureau's offices, it was unusual that bureau underlings would find severe fault with their commissioner's words. In the margin of Higginson's response to Sieh, someone angrily scribbled a question mark and an arrow that pointed straight to a sentence containing the words "I fully support the President's actions."[6] Higginson later admitted that he had grave reservations about Carter's plan. "It was a slap in the face to members of Congress who had gotten the projects authorized and [gotten] funding to start them," he said.[7] Despite his misgivings, the public position Higginson maintained was supportive of the president.

Bob Lane and Guy Martin later described Higginson as an honest, intelligent man trying to control an agency that was hostile to him and was working to undermine him. Martin sympathetically described Higginson's dilemma: "He

179

was torn between defending the projects which had been developed by his bureau and his loyalty to the administration that had appointed him."[8] "What did they expect from a presidential appointee?" asked Higginson, sounding exasperated when describing the tension and disagreements between him and others in the agency. "[I had] to either support the position of the administration or resign."[9]

During 1977, while mutterings of mutiny swirled about the agency, a confusing, contradictory series of communications was issued by bureau officials regarding the Oahe project and the role of the Oahe sub-district and the Oahe Task Force. Commissioner Higginson acknowledged that it was solely the sub-district that had the power to alter or enact contracts with the federal government regarding Oahe. But he offered up hope to Oahe supporters when he wrote: "We understand that the [Oahe] task force has the authority to speak in behalf of the State of South Dakota in conformance with the public policy of South Dakota."[10]

John Sieh was not pleased with this interpretation. It appeared that the bureau was receptive to the task force formulating policy for South Dakota on Oahe matters. Guy Martin stepped in to clarify the administration's position on who it recognized as speaking for South Dakota. In a succinct memorandum to Higginson, Martin stated that no further misunderstanding should exist regarding which organization represented the local interests in South Dakota: "Local support . . . means primarily the Oahe Sub-district," he instructed. "It is to this entity the Bureau should turn primarily and directly for recommendations."[11] Dan Beard, the Andrus assistant who was later appointed to be commissioner of the Bureau of Reclamation during the first term of President Bill Clinton, reiterated Martin's position when he addressed a meeting of the South Dakota Natural Resources Development Council in late October 1977. "It has been long-standing policy [of the Interior Department] that the contracting entity [the Oahe sub-district] represents the desires of those who expect to be served by the project," he said. "Just because the Conservancy Sub-district has expressed opposition to the authorized project does not require that they be treated any different from those conservancy districts throughout the West who support their projects."[12]

For the time being, the authority of the Oahe sub-district board appeared to be secure. If John Sieh and his allies on the sub-district board were to be overthrown, it would have to be through the election process, and the next sub-district director elections would take place in November 1978.

By 1978, Friends of Oahe had deteriorated to practically nothing. The organization created at the urging of Senator George McGovern possessed neither sufficient presence in the agricultural countryside nor the zeal needed to survive the setbacks inflicted by President Carter and United Family Farmers. Other organizations designed to promote the project had also come and gone. This lack of continuity hurt project supporters but did not stop them from organizing new groups.

Charles Kearns led fund-raising for the freshly organized Save Our Water Political Action Committee. The organization's acronym SOWPAC invited humorous criticism from United Family Farmers, and one cartoonist capitalized on a deadly and inviting metaphor by depicting the SOWPAC leadership as hogs crowded around the federal money trough. SOWPAC was organized by bankers, businessmen, and others specifically to win back the Oahe sub-district board. Its chairman was C. H. "Jumbo" Peterson, a former Huron mayor and one of the people who had lent their names to the one man–one vote lawsuit. Another leader of the group was Huron banker Ronald Campbell, who managed the Huron branch of the National Bank of South Dakota. On National Bank's board of directors sat Charles Kearns. Campbell and others, with the help of the powerful East River Electric Cooperative, helped found the South Dakota Water Congress earlier in 1978. The water congress announced that its primary goal was to pursue completion of the Oahe project, and it retained Jeremiah Murphy, a Sioux Falls lawyer and arguably the most influential lobbyist in South Dakota, to promote its agenda in Pierre. Murphy had previously assisted Friends of Oahe. SOWPAC then hired a man named Gerald Andrews to coordinate the campaigns of pro-Oahe candidates in the sub-district elections. Andrews, owner of a consulting business in Sioux Falls, had formerly served as executive director of the South Dakota Democratic Party and had been one of Richard Kneip's top advisers from 1971 to 1977.

In Brown County, Oahe supporters offered a formidable candidate in their attempt to depose John Sieh. Jim Sperry was a soft-spoken man with a reputation for public service. His devotion to Oahe was fervent and inherited. Sperry's father, Allen, a former state senator, helped organize the West Brown Irrigation District and had been honored by the Upper Missouri River Water Users group for his work promoting the Oahe project. The area where Jim Sperry lived—near the James River, just east of Aberdeen—was classified as rural, but its proximity to Aberdeen influenced its politics. Sperry's farm was in the Aberdeen school district, and Sperry served as chairman of the Aberdeen school board. Correspondingly, Sperry's views on Oahe had more in common with Aberdeen businessmen than with farmers in the rest of Brown County. During the campaign, he said that he would not object if the outcome of the one man–one vote lawsuit determined that Aberdeen and other cities in the sub-district should exercise more voting power over sub-district matters than farmers in the sub-district.[13] John Sieh viewed this position as a betrayal of the farmers Sperry hoped to represent.

Sperry's neighborhood was one of the few places in the entire Oahe sub-district where there was a concentration of farmers ardently supporting the Oahe project. This area had produced Ned Hundstad, the man defeated by John Sieh four years earlier, and Ken Holum, who was Ned Hundstad's first cousin and a close friend of Allen Sperry.

Sieh and Sperry waged effective advertising campaigns in newspapers and on the radio, but the real battle for the hearts and minds of Brown County farmers was of the hand-to-hand variety. When farmers left their fields and mingled at the local elevator or implement dealer, it was likely they would discuss Oahe. Who should represent Brown County on the Oahe board? Should the project be killed or brought back to life? In line, waiting for a cashier to ring up their purchases, farmers on opposite sides of the issue often stood silently, averting their eyes, boiling inside. Either that or they argued, starting from inside the store right up until they slammed shut the doors on their trucks in the parking lot. "In the trenches" is how United Family Farmers referred to the proposed irrigation areas of Brown and Spink Counties. This was where the most bitter, contentious competition for Oahe votes took place.

Bud Seaton and his sons ran a diversified farm on the banks of Moccasin Creek, just south of Aberdeen and in the center of the trenches. Seaton's farm contained one thousand acres identified as irrigable by the Oahe plan, and the land was part of the irrigation district. Seaton had been born on the place in 1923, forty-three years after his grandfather had homesteaded there. Jim Sperry's neighborhood lay a short distance to the north and east, and a hotbed of United Family Farmers was situated not far to the south. Seaton's farm was where two tense and adversarial parts of Brown County collided.

At one time Seaton had supported Oahe, but he had been converted to United Family Farmers after meeting George Piper and viewing the film *Oahe: A Question of Values*. He quickly became a friend and supporter whom John Sieh relied on for help and advice. He was also a pilot, and in a pinch United Family Farmers could count on him to supply rapid transportation to important meetings around the state.

Seaton drew the ire of Oahe supporters when he initiated an investigation regarding election irregularities during the 1976 election for a director of the West Brown Irrigation District. Like sub-district elections, the campaigns for director positions on both irrigation district boards were rancorously contested. United Family Farmers was at a distinct disadvantage in the irrigation districts because many project opponents had withdrawn their land from the districts and relinquished their voting privileges in irrigation district elections. But there were some like Bud Seaton who had not removed their land.

Seaton remembered the 1976 West Brown Irrigation District election as being particularly nasty. Oahe supporters and opponents fought it out for a single seat in an area of the district where fewer than one hundred votes could bring victory. Longtime Oahe supporter and irrigation-board incumbent Virgil Locken faced a stiff challenge from a member of United Family Farmers named Keith Larson. Seaton, who had aided Larson, nevertheless wanted to remain on civilized terms with Locken, so on the eve of the election he phoned the incumbent. Locken's son told Seaton his dad was at a neighbor's home, and Seaton decided to drive over. When he arrived, the farm's driveway was lined with parked pickup trucks. Standing in the doorway to the home, Seaton could see Frank Dixon, an Aberdeen businessman and one of the plaintiffs in the one man–one vote lawsuit, providing notary-public services as farmers cast absentee ballots in the irrigation district election. Locken sat nearby, talking with the voters. "They were running people through there," remembered Seaton, "like sheep through a chute."[14] The next day, after the local polling place closed, the votes were officially tallied. Buoyed by a generous batch of absentee ballots, Locken retained his seat by a slender margin of fifty-four to fifty-one.

At the urging of Martin Weeks, Keith Larson filed a lawsuit in circuit court charging his opponent with absentee-voting violations. A local judge concurred with Larson, canceled the election, and ruled that a new one must be held. Locken appealed that ruling to the state supreme court, but in early 1978 the lower court was upheld and another election was scheduled. With Bud Seaton flying several missions collecting absentee ballots from irrigation-district landowners who lived far from Brown County, Larson posted a hard-fought victory, ousting Locken by a margin of sixty-nine to fifty-three.

Larson joined fellow United Family Farmer Bill Oliver on the board. Several years later, United Family Farmers actually gained control of the West Brown Irrigation District board. At one time it seemed improbable, even impossible, that Oahe opponents would ever rule an irrigation district. But by the time they had accomplished their takeover of Brown County's irrigation district, they were already in control of the Spink County district.

On the shoulder of Brown County Highway 14, and adjacent to the quarter-mile gravel driveway leading to his farm, was Bud Seaton's mailbox. It was a typical rural box: tin, barn-shaped, fastened to the top of a fence post. One morning, Seaton discovered his bent, bashed mailbox lying in a nearby field. Several weeks later, a new mailbox met a similar fate. Again, Seaton promptly installed another one. But the late-night marauders didn't let up. Over the course of twelve months, eight mailboxes were run over, shot at, or clubbed. Fed up, Seaton paid an Aberdeen welding shop $300 to create a special mailbox built from thick steel and securely mounted to a fat wooden post girded by metal bars and wrapped with wire. The post and its armor were planted deep into the ground, and one of Seaton's sons painted a brightly colored target on the wide side of the mailbox, which was slightly and invitingly turned to face the road, as if to dare vandals. Never again was the mailbox attacked.

Bud Seaton's mailboxes were not the only property damaged in the irrigation district during the Oahe controversy. Oahe proponents reported slashed tires on trucks, shattered headlights, and tractor engines disabled by sugar being poured into fuel tanks. Seaton feared his airplane would be sabotaged. A favorite way to harass adversaries in those days, pre–Caller ID, was to make late-night phone calls, and threatening, anonymous phone messages came regularly for prominent Oahe combatants like Virgil Locken, Jim Sperry, and John Sieh. Seaton admitted to phoning Oahe supporters during the wee hours to gloat about election victories. Many of the farmers lived a mile or more from their nearest neighbor, which made them feel especially vulnerable when menacing phone calls or trespassing occurred. An unsigned death threat mailed to John Sieh was reported to the local sheriff. Sieh thought about the danger when returning home on dark roads after yet another late meeting in a distant corner of the sub-district. Walking alone through the still night from his garage to the back door of his home, he thought about it then, too.

Like John Sieh, Bill Piper faced a critical reelection challenge. Piper and Sieh had become close friends and political partners through their association on the board. For two years following the 1974 election, they had effectively conspired and collaborated as a minority faction. Now that United Family Farmers had taken over the board, both men played important roles in directing sub-district policy. Project opponents needed them on the board not only to retain their majority but also for their leadership and character. Oahe supporters in the Huron area had so much difficulty finding someone to oppose Piper that they advertised for a candidate in the *Daily Plainsman* classified ads. By summer, a farmer had been recruited.

Another board member up for election was Ken Marsh, who had been appointed to the board after Bud Yackley's resignation. Marsh now faced an election to represent rural voters in Sully and Hughes Counties. Oahe supporters lost a friend on the board when Mike Madden decided not to seek reelection. Two newcomers to Oahe politics, Leslie Heisler and Leslie Knudson, sought the seat representing rural areas in Campbell and McPherson Counties. Neither candidate was supported by United Family Farmers or by SOWPAC. Knudson indicated his support for deauthorization; Heisler opposed deauthorization. Steve Thorson campaigned for reelection as one of the sub-district's at-large municipal directors. Curt Johnson, who had nearly toppled Bob Hipple two years earlier, decided to make another run for a sub-district seat.

How important was the 1978 sub-district election? Cecil Andrus had already suggested the possibility of his department pursuing deauthorization legislation. According to Andrus, that decision would be based on the outcome of the election.[15]

Richard Kneip resigned as governor as the critical 1978 sub-district campaign began. Kneip was leaving South Dakota to accept appointment as United States ambassador to Singapore. His replacement, Lieutenant Governor Harvey Wollman, would come up for election in the state's Democratic gubernatorial primary almost immediately.

Wollman, a former Spink County legislator, was a landowner in the Spink County Irrigation District and a devoted Oahe backer. That earned him special attention from United Family Farmers. The group canvassed rural areas and encouraged farmers to vote for Wollman's opponent, a banker from southeastern South Dakota. They also urged Republicans to switch parties in order to vote against Wollman. In Brown County, Wollman's backyard, Wollman should have attracted a sizeable majority. Instead, he won only narrowly. It was a bad omen for Wollman. His reign as governor would last only until the next general election.

Jim Sperry and other proponents claimed the 1978 sub-district elections would serve as a referendum on the project. They declared that voters were presented with a clear choice: candidates supporting deauthorization versus candidates opposed to it.

Three weeks before the election, the *Aberdeen American News* championed pro-Oahe candidates in an editorial that concluded: "It is economic suicide to encourage deauthorization of the Oahe project."[16] Two days later, the newspaper reported that all eight candidates for major political office in South Dakota, including both candidates for governor, both candidates seeking the U.S. Senate seat vacated by a retiring James Abourezk, and all four running for the state's two House seats, opposed deauthorization.

Defending his support for deauthorization, John Sieh offered the following analysis: "Deauthorization would remove an unacceptable plan of open ditches, mitigation, land loss and taxes from the books and make possible acceptable alternatives like riverside [Missouri River] irrigation, domestic water pipelines, rural water and others." The present Oahe plan was established as law by congressional authorization, explained Sieh. "Meaningful alternatives cannot be obtained until the law is changed."[17] Jim Sperry responded: "We do not have time to start over with a new design and authorization." The urgency, according to Sperry, sprang from the ongoing threat by states outside the Missouri basin to pirate away Missouri River water before South Dakota could use it. "Use it or lose it" was integral in Sperry's rationale to build Oahe.[18] That notion was also incorporated into the campaign themes of other SOWPAC candidates.

The SOWPAC plan to salvage the Oahe authorization hinged on the so-called Build to Blunt proposal. Advanced by Oahe promoters as a reasonable alternative to deauthorizing the entire project, the Build to Blunt concept would allow the Bureau of Reclamation to develop the westernmost features of the Oahe project, including the pumping plant, the Pierre canal, and the Blunt dam and its associated reservoir. Oahe supporters claimed that by building the Oahe blueprint as far as Blunt, the opportunities to distribute water to many locations in eastern South Dakota would remain available. "The[se] facilities," said the *Sioux Falls Argus Leader*, referring to Oahe's western features, "are basic to South Dakota's beneficial use of water in areas east of the Missouri, other than the Oahe subdistrict."[19] John Sieh dismissed the idea as a ruse to procure new funding to construct Oahe irrigation features without offending the Carter administration's opposition to irrigation in the lake plain.

By the time the bitter campaign ended on election day, 8 November, both sides had spent an equal amount of money—roughly $35,000 each. Both were confident they would be victorious. When the results were published, if there was any truth to Jim Sperry's claim that the election represented a referendum on the

Oahe project, Oahe supporters should have prepared to hoist a white flag. Among candidates opposed to deauthorization, only Steve Thorson was a winner. Although Bill Piper's margin of victory was narrow, John Sieh and Ken Marsh won handily. So did Leslie Knudson. The United Family Farmers position on the Oahe sub-district board was strengthened, not diminished.[20]

Gerald Andrews was satisfied with SOWPAC's effort. "We did about as good as we could have under the circumstances," remembered Andrews, citing SOWPAC's lack of grassroots machinery as a chief reason for the losses.[21] The intensity and effectiveness of United Family Farmers left a lasting impression on Andrews, and he became convinced that as long as the farm organization existed, Oahe was doomed.

Also in 1978, William Janklow defeated Democrat Roger McKellips in the race for governor. During the campaign, both candidates pledged to pursue the development of large water projects. Gerald Andrews had known William Janklow during the Kneip administration when Janklow served first as an assistant attorney general and later as attorney general. In the aftermath of the sub-district elections, Andrews wrote the governor-elect to advise him that the Oahe fight could not be won. But William Janklow was accustomed to getting what he wanted.

16

Not Quite Deauthorization

> There was no place in the country that was as well organized to fight the Bureau of Reclamation.
>
> David Weiman, speaking of South Dakota in an interview

Governor William Janklow was determined to do what no South Dakota politician before him had been able to do: force the federal government to live up to the Pick-Sloan Plan's political obligations to South Dakota. Complaints by Missouri River states, particularly those in the upper basin, about the unequal distribution of Pick-Sloan benefits were not unusual. But no one matched Janklow's fervor to remedy those inequities.

South Dakotans soon learned that their new governor brought other notable characteristics to the office. Foes and allies alike described him as brash, brilliant, reckless, bold, egotistical. In discussion or debate, he was as reticent as a cornered wolverine. He had that rare ability to seemingly lose his temper but remain in control. His combativeness, coupled with an articulate, rat-a-tat-tat, coming-right-at-you style of speechmaking, propelled Janklow's reputation among South Dakotans as a fearless defender and promoter of their small, deprived rural state.

Curt Hohn and John Sieh were convinced that Governor Janklow's agenda for water development included subduing Oahe opponents. Just days after Janklow won the governor's race, John Sieh drove to Pierre to talk Oahe politics with the state's new top executive. The outcome was predictable. Strong-willed men debating a topic on which they had opposite viewpoints was a certain recipe for a noisy impasse. Even Sieh, known for his fist pounding and his jutting jaw, was startled by Janklow's confrontational ranting. "Janklow," explained

Curt Hohn, "was going to beat United Family Farmers and the sub-district into submission and get the project built."[1]

Guy Martin had grown accustomed to spirited disagreements over water projects with politicians from western states, but Bill Janklow's contentious outburst stood apart. Janklow gestured wildly as he insisted that the Carter administration was denying South Dakota its best opportunity to recoup the agricultural productivity that had been lost when the Missouri River's mainstem dams were built. You owe us, Janklow lectured.

Martin had a more civil but equally difficult meeting with Senator George McGovern. Martin admired the veteran senator but held his ground as McGovern appealed to the young official that Oahe be spared. "He made a personal plea," said Martin, sounding sorry, "but I had to say no."[2] Martin later admitted he sympathized with South Dakota and agreed with some of Bill Janklow's rationale. "We didn't acknowledge a legal debt [to South Dakota], and to whatever extent there was a debt it was undefined," explained Martin, before adding, "but there were water needs there."[3]

Based on Interior Department reports, Martin believed the Oahe plan was riddled with irreparable mistakes and that the plan was not the solution to South Dakota's needs. He encouraged Governor Janklow and other South Dakotans, including both Oahe proponents and opponents, to determine just what sort of water projects would be appropriate in terms of public support and genuine need.

As early as February 1978, discussion was under way in Guy Martin's office regarding the dispensation of carryover funds in the Oahe account. Martin felt that the money should be spent to commence a study related to termination of the project. Keith Higginson and his agency grumbled. Termination, that dreaded word, meant performing an inventory of project features fully or partially built. It meant a plan would be developed discussing how to dismantle, dispose, or secure those features for safety purposes. The bureau preferred using carryover funds to continue building toward Blunt and to study alternative applications of Oahe's westernmost features. Talk of developing a new irrigation project in the southern tier of the sub-district continued to gain momentum, and the bureau hoped its services could be plugged in there.

More than $46 million had already been spent on Oahe. But whatever impetus the bureau hoped this statistic might provoke deflated when it was determined that another $51 million was required to complete the project up to and including the Blunt reservoir. Instead of approving the bureau's request to continue building toward Blunt and planning for substitute development, Guy Martin issued rigid, unalterable orders for the termination study to begin.[4]

Morale at the bureau's Oahe office in Huron hit rock bottom. Construction funding had been exhausted in September 1977. Positions with the Oahe Unit office in Huron were being steadily eliminated, and hope by the bureau's staff that Oahe would experience political recovery depended on Congress foiling President Carter. Carter recommended that the 1979 federal budget provide only $150,000 for Oahe. Congress countered by proposing $16 million for the project. But restoring generous funds for Oahe was minor insolence compared with the overall water-development budget proposed by federal lawmakers. Their public-works appropriations bill replenished funding for all nine of the water projects that had been defunded in the compromise package reluctantly agreed to by Carter the previous year. This time the president did not back down, and his veto withstood an override attempt. Oahe's meager 1979 appropriation would barely keep a skeleton staff in Huron. A couple of years earlier, there had been 150 Bureau of Reclamation personnel working on Oahe out of the project's Huron headquarters.

Guy Martin was not sure if he should oblige the invitations extended to him by United Family Farmers and the WEB Water Development Association to provide keynote speeches at the groups' two 1980 annual meetings. His schedule was jammed up tight, but David Weiman, the former United Family Farmers consultant with a growing business as a Washington-based lobbyist and political organizer, convinced him to make the trip.

As Martin entered the crowded gymnasium at Aberdeen's Sacred Heart School, escorted by Curt Hohn and Roger Schuller, hundreds of United Family Farmers stood and began applauding. Martin had traveled across the country to dozens of places defending President Carter's hit list, but he had never been welcomed like this. His hosts invited him to officially begin the banquet's supper and pointed him toward the largest potluck Martin had ever seen. "It seemed like the tables piled with wonderful food were a mile long," he remembered gleefully, "and I got to be first in line."[5]

According to Martin, his speech that night was "duck soup." Often interrupted by cheers, Martin praised United Family Farmers for encouraging the Carter administration to keep fighting for water-policy reforms. "This group, more than any other I know in the country," declared Martin, "has had the right answers . . . and the staying power to continue to make a difference."[6] The gymnasium shook when Martin announced that "Oahe is dead, even if the undertaker hasn't arrived to take it away."[7] There was more cheering when Martin was presented with a plaque honoring him for his help.

Afterward, en route to Aberdeen's airport with Hohn and Schuller, Guy Martin probed for some advice. Perhaps, Martin observed, the process of deauthorizing Oahe would be more agreeable to South Dakota if other water projects were offered as replacements. Hohn and Schuller looked first at their visitor and then at one another as Martin asked what they thought about trading Oahe's deauthorization for WEB's authorization.

For several years, United Family Farmers and the Oahe sub-district had been suggesting that substituting Oahe's deauthorization for authorizations and appropriations creating other South Dakota water projects was a reasonable solution to the Oahe controversy. Never before had they heard a high-ranking federal official endorse the idea.

Promoters of WEB had been diligently building interest in their project and expanding the proposed service area. With Guy Martin's help, preliminary engineering studies for the pipeline were under way. The Oahe sub-district demonstrated its commitment to WEB by approving a $3.1 million construction grant, creating a special planning fund for drinking-water projects, and hiring a domestic-water coordinator to help sub-district citizens develop pipeline systems.

Ten days after Martin broached the subject of the WEB-for-Oahe trade during that car ride to the Aberdeen airport, the White House informed South Dakota's congressional delegation that its continued support for WEB hinged on Oahe deauthorization. The notion of a swap was now official.

The backlash from Oahe supporters was immediate and harsh. Congressman James Abdnor described it as "blackmail."[8] South Dakota State Senator George Shannard, chairman of the Oahe Task Force, advised the state's federal delegation to reject the offer. Shannard had authored legislation approved by the state legislature calling for the federal government to pay South Dakota $25 million per year for twenty years in return for Oahe deauthorization. Aberdeen's leaders ridiculed the proposal. "To give us a bag of peanuts [WEB] in exchange for [Oahe]," complained Jeff Solem, the city's mayor, "I just can't accept that."[9] Solem and Aberdeen's city commission joined city officials from Huron and Mitchell to adopt resolutions that opposed Oahe deauthorization.

United Family Farmers president Tom Fischbach, a Brown County farmer, was disappointed but not surprised that Aberdeen remained committed to Oahe at the same time many farmers in the city's trade area opposed the project and supported WEB. "They fought us [United Family Farmers] hard and weren't about to give up," said Fischbach, years later. "Yes, we wanted to get rid of Oahe. But we felt WEB was a good project, with or without its connection to Oahe. Aberdeen was just plain stubborn."[10]

Governor Janklow also urged the delegation to ignore the proposal. Anticipating President Carter's defeat by Republican Ronald Reagan in 1980, Janklow suggested that South Dakota could expect better treatment from a Republican administration regarding water development. "We should hang tough," said the *Aberdeen American News*, agreeing with the governor, "and see what develops in the fall election."[11]

A trading of WEB for Oahe, observed Senator George McGovern, was a disproportionate exchange. An $80 million project, he explained, was an inadequate substitute for a project worth at least half a billion dollars. But McGovern had another pressing worry: his 1980 reelection. An early sign that McGovern's reelection would be anything but routine was evidenced in the primary. For the first time since being elected to the Senate—three consecutive elections—George McGovern faced a primary challenge. South Dakota's leading Democrat and most famous politician was opposed by Larry Schumaker, an unknown native of Britton, South Dakota, who returned from Texas to be a candidate. Schumaker, a forty-year-old mathematics professor at Texas A&M University, came back to South Dakota armed with encouragement from conservative interests, including abortion opponents, who hungered to rid Congress of liberals like George McGovern.

United Family Farmers took no official position in the primary, but some members offered to help the Texan financially or with tactical and briefing assistance. They were eager to render McGovern more vulnerable against the Republicans and their likely candidate, Congressman James Abdnor. That McGovern triumphed in the primary was not surprising. But the number of votes his opponent attracted portended difficulties for the incumbent. Larry Schumaker had almost no name recognition, and despite being outspent $590,000 to $35,000, he received nearly 40 percent of the vote. Many Republican members of United Family Farmers actually switched parties in order to vote against McGovern. Schumaker in fact carried Sully County—the only county he did carry east of the Missouri—and Sully, significantly, was a United Family Farmers stronghold.

In the general election, McGovern faced the weighty trend of conservatism that was sweeping the nation. Right-wingers in his own party and in the Republican party toiled to oust him. Abortion was a significant issue. So was

McGovern's image as a globe-trotting statesman who had lost touch with the ordinary people in his own state.

McGovern's advocacy for Oahe, as robust as it had been, became a nonfactor among South Dakota's Oahe supporters. Although he had long been Oahe's principal champion, McGovern had not been able to save Oahe during the presidential administration of a Democrat. His opponent, James Abdnor, had a comfortable relationship with water-development interests in South Dakota. Abdnor's election team was aware of the rift between United Family Farmers and McGovern, and they actively courted the farm group and WEB backers.

United Family Farmers decided that opposing McGovern should be part of their agenda. They canvassed for Abdnor, bought newspaper ads, and blasted McGovern in their newsletter. They worked especially hard in the traditionally Democratic James River valley, where McGovern needed to do well to be reelected.

On 4 November 1980, McGovern's congressional career came to a crashing halt. The vote totals were striking: James Abdnor, 190,726; George McGovern, 128,956. From coast to coast, liberals and Democrats took a beating, including Jimmy Carter, but McGovern suffered the most lopsided loss of any congressional incumbent. Political observers gave ample credit for McGovern's demise to United Family Farmers. Although it is likely McGovern would have lost had United Family Farmers steered clear of the campaign, the involvement by the farmers and his own history regarding Oahe certainly cost McGovern a sizeable block of votes. In Brown County, Democratic in most elections but where United Family Farmers had a very strong presence, McGovern was clobbered.

Curt Hohn and George Piper were probably correct in describing McGovern as a politician who had lost his connection to his constituents as his career escalated. For all his enthusiasm about Oahe, for all the supportive votes he had cast, and all the money he had helped secure for the project, George McGovern later admitted he did not know the project's details—that he had relied on others for advice about Oahe. "I wasn't a water development expert," he explained, before remarking, and unknowingly confirming the contention of Hohn and Piper, "but ask me anything about Vietnam. . . ."[12]

The 1980 Oahe Conservancy Sub-district elections confirmed that irrigation's new constituency in the sub-district was in the southernmost tier of counties. It was in these counties—Hughes, Hyde, and Hand—that the Oahe project's westernmost features would be located. This was also where severe drought was pushing many young farmers and ranchers toward bankruptcy. Under those circumstances, discussions about redirecting and renaming the Oahe project found widespread favor. Assisting the 1980 campaigns of pro-Oahe candidates was yet another group established to promote large-scale water development—the James Basin Water Development Association. The association consisted of many familiar names from the water-development community, but the group was not as well organized or staffed as its predecessors, Friends of Oahe and SOWPAC. Nevertheless, the 1980 election was fruitful for irrigation advocates.

Glenn Overby lost his bid for reelection in a close race with an irrigator named Ron Frankenstein. Sieg Swanhorst, too, was unseated. His narrow loss came in a recount. Doug Beckett did not seek reelection, and his seat was won by Dale Hargens, a proponent of irrigation for his district of Hyde and Hand Counties. However, United Family Farmers stalwarts Arnold Schurr and Leonard Naessig were victorious by huge margins.

All three new rural directors resided in the southern half of the sub-district. Each opposed trading WEB for Oahe and advocated modifying the Oahe project to serve new irrigation areas. This notion had been given a catchy name, CEN-DAK, and enjoyed increasing credibility thanks to Governor Janklow.

The 1980 sub-district election marked the retirement of sub-district founder and twenty-year board member Bob Hipple. Hipple had broken dirt at Oahe dam's groundbreaking, introduced Pick to Sloan, and at one time was on a first-name basis with twenty U.S. senators. Water-development organizations from across the Missouri basin would honor this veteran of water development many times. But he had grown weary of sparring with John Sieh and United Family Farmers and was frustrated by the political obstacles that threatened to destroy a water project he had spent half his life promoting. Winning Hipple's vacated seat was Huron resident Ted Spaulding, a booster of big water projects who employed the "use it or lose it" theme in his campaign. Although replacing Hipple was impossible, Spaulding proved to be a capable and forceful advocate for irrigation.

By winning four of six races, pro-Oahe forces had rebounded to within one vote of controlling the sub-district. The tenuousness of United Family Farmers' hold on the board was evident considering that two directors sympathetic to the farm group had been appointed, not elected. A man named Roger Hanson had been appointed to replace the ailing Les Knudson, and Beadle County farmer Irving Wessell had replaced Bill Piper. It was serious illness that also forced Piper to give up his seat. His deteriorating health—he was diagnosed with Lou Gehrig's disease—was an emotional blow to his brother and to many United Family Farmers.

Although Oahe proponents made progress in their effort to win back the Oahe board, local pressure against Oahe advanced at a relentless pace. Six county commissions within the sub-district passed resolutions supporting deauthorization. Three other county commissions requested congressional deauthorization hearings.[13] The Spink County Irrigation District asked Congress to deauthorize the project and began researching how to terminate its Oahe contracts and obligations. Additional support for deauthorization would soon come from the West Brown Irrigation District.

In addition to coordinating and encouraging these political actions, United Family Farmers found someone to replace retired Senator James Abourezk as their most reliable ally in the Congress. Senator Abourezk had introduced legislation to deauthorize Oahe, but the measure lacked support from his South Dakota colleagues and was never acted upon. Iowa Democrat Berkley Bedell had cosponsored Abourezk's bill, and United Family Farmers asked Bedell to lead a new deathorization effort. Congressman Bedell invited representatives of the farm group to his lake cabin in northwest Iowa to discuss strategy. "Our Congressmen would hardly meet with us in their offices," remembered Curt Hohn, one of several who met with Bedell, "and this guy was having us to his house."[14] When Bedell reintroduced deauthorization legislation, in South Dakota he instantly became a hero to some, a pariah to others.

Helping to feed the animosity was Governor Bill Janklow. Bedell made an ideal target for Janklow. The congressman's district in the northwestern part of Iowa, including Sioux City, benefited from flood control and river navigation because of the Missouri River's mainstem dams. Bedell's district was also the recipient of low-cost hydropower from mainstem generating facilities. If Oahe were developed, explained Janklow, some of that cheap power would be used for Oahe in South Dakota and would not be available to Iowa. "It was in his interest," Janklow snarled, "to stop water development in South Dakota. . . . He [Bedell] was looking for any argument he could use to prevent his neighbors from taking that juice away from Iowa."[15] Janklow pointed out that Iowa, Minnesota, and Nebraska received more power from the Missouri's mainstem dams than did South Dakota. It was just another example, he fumed, of how South Dakota got shortchanged from Pick-Sloan's benefits.

Bedell's immediate objective for cooperating with United Family Farmers may have been to look after the best interests of his constituents, but in a broader sense his motives were more sophisticated. Bedell's fishing-tackle business—Berkley—had made him a wealthy man. As an angler and an outdoorsman, he was sensitive to conservation issues. "Berkley Bedell was a committed environmentalist and a progressive on water policy," said Guy Martin, before describing how Bedell helped the Carter administration pursue its program to reform federal water policy.[16]

Bill Janklow's wrath toward Bedell was rooted in his belief that Missouri River states downstream of South Dakota were aligned against his state to prevent water development. Berkley Bedell's behavior reinforced that belief. Before his activities against Oahe, Bedell had worked to undermine another Missouri River water project that Janklow craved: the ETSI (Energy Transportation Systems, Inc.) coal-slurry pipeline.[17]

Janklow became the most vehement and confrontational water project promoter in the history of South Dakota. Not only did he sue and harangue states in the Missouri's lower basin over the allocation and use of Missouri River flows, he waged bitter war against his own constituents who opposed his water-development proposals.

The same conservative movement that helped oust George McGovern from public office caused Jimmy Carter's eviction from the White House. But Carter's war on pork-barrel water projects also cost him dearly. In the months preceding Carter's loss to Ronald Reagan, a deal with the South Dakota delegation on the WEB for Oahe trade was brokered. Carter bestowed WEB authorization when the South Dakotans agreed to introduce legislation to deauthorize Oahe. In addition, South Dakota would be able to develop a list of other water projects needing federal support. The bill's "sunset" provision was set at one year: WEB's authorization would expire on 30 September 1981 if an Oahe deauthorization measure had not passed by then.

In early 1981, the new president, Ronald Reagan, began to install his own Interior Department crew. Succeeding Cecil Andrus was James Watt, who would soon become a leading enemy of the nation's environmentalists. United Family Farmers lost their friend Guy Martin. His replacement was Garry Carruthers, who became friendly with Bill Janklow. Keith Higginson was willing to continue as commissioner of the Bureau of Reclamation and for two months was recruited by Reagan's transition team to stay on the job. Then, without warning, James Watt coldly dismissed Higginson.

Higginson, an engineer with many decades of water-management experience, was angry about the double-talk and the unexpected dismissal, but even angrier when he learned that a man named Robert Broadbent would be taking over the bureau. His replacement, Higginson griped, seemed ill-prepared for such an important position. The man who would be in charge of the Bureau of Reclamation was a registered pharmacist.

Though Reagan and his new water team were more supportive of business interests than environmental interests, their emphasis on budget cutting and cost sharing between the federal government and the states shifted a significant share of the economic burden associated with developing water projects to local beneficiaries. Water project promoters discovered that instead of providing relief from Jimmy Carter's war on water pork barrel, the Reagan presidency presented a new set of barriers. It would be difficult for South Dakotans to convince the new administration to support projects like WEB and CENDAK.

Curt Hohn and the Oahe sub-district had their eyes on the calendar. In the summer of 1981, nursing a closely divided board and nervously cognizant that another set of director elections was coming up in 1982, Hohn and John Sieh pushed the settlement process hard. Newly elected Senator Jim Abdnor and Congressman Tom Daschle were willing to work constructively with them. Soon there was yet another bill, S.B. 1553, crafted primarily by Senator Abdnor's staffer Owen Ambur and aimed at amicably ending Oahe and initiating WEB. Abdnor was particularly sensitive to the obligation of the federal government to provide water development to South Dakota because his own family had lost land beneath the Missouri River reservoirs. During his campaign against George McGovern, Abdnor had courted Oahe opponents and WEB supporters and appreciated the help he had received. Tom Daschle appreciated what WEB meant because he was an Aberdeen native and his family and relatives, some of them farmers, lived in WEB's proposed service area.

At the congressional field hearing on S.B. 1553, held in Pierre on 12 September 1981, Leonard Naessig presented the Oahe sub-district's testimony. The sub-district, said Naessig, was pleased that a bill was introduced but was concerned that the bill's language inadequately addressed Oahe's fate by merely canceling the federal government's Oahe's contracts with the sub-district and irrigation districts. "Cancellation of the contracts," advised Naessig, "will not in itself assure that the old Oahe plan will not be constructed."[18] The sub-district preferred that the bill include a list of fourteen Oahe features that "shall no longer be authorized."[19] The list included the Blunt dam and reservoir and every feature east of there, including the irrigation areas in Brown and Spink Counties.

When 30 September 1981 came and went without a consensus by South Dakota on the bill, WEB's authorization died and South Dakota's delegation began scrambling. Congressmen Daschle and Clint Roberts, the state's two representatives, would be facing off in 1982 for a consolidated House seat. The WEB constituency was already large and growing: it represented a collection of voters that could make or break the election.

Over the next year, there was considerable jockeying regarding language in S.B. 1553 that dealt with the various features of the Oahe design. Two critical items required resolution. The first issue was to determine which project features, if any, would be allowed to survive. The second matter concerned semantics. What language would end Oahe and begin WEB to the mutual satisfaction of both the delegation and the sub-district?

United Family Farmers and the sub-district preferred *deauthorizing* Oahe features. Project proponents wanted words such as *deleted* or *shall not be constructed* instead of *deauthorization*.

Senator Abdnor reminded all parties that a significant share of the cost associated with constructing the Missouri's mainstem dams was allocated to irrigation water storage. Under federal reclamation law, Abdnor explained, that portion of the dams allocated to irrigation storage did not have to be paid for until it was used for irrigation, and when that time arrived, there would be no interest connected to repayment. Deauthorization of the Oahe project, said the senator, would cause water storage in the mainstem system to be reallocated. At that point, it would become reimbursable and interest bearing, and power rates would increase significantly. "That was another reason," said Abdnor aide Owen Ambur, "why we would never have agreed to the deauthorization of Oahe."[20]

Another hurdle was the Reagan administration, where budget officials were reluctant to support an expensive rural pipeline system like WEB and massive irrigation projects like Oahe or CENDAK.

James Watt tersely advised Bill Janklow that he would be the last secretary of the interior to understand the Pick-Sloan obligation to South Dakota. "You're either gonna get it done with me," warned Watt, "or you won't get it done."[21]

Janklow, the quintessential wheeler-dealer, conceived a plan that melded political partisanship with water development. Janklow and Garry Carruthers decided to use WEB's predicament to bolster Republican Clint Roberts's election bid against Democrat Tom Daschle. They planned a meeting where it would be announced that Roberts had persuaded the Reagan administration to support WEB's reauthorization. South Dakota voters would be told that Roberts's political skills and connections to the Reagan administration had cinched this important commitment.

Joining Janklow at the meeting in the Capitol in Washington were James

Watt, Carruthers, Robert Broadbent, and all four members of the South Dakota delegation with staff members in tow. Senators Abdnor and Pressler and Congressman Daschle were in the dark regarding the meeting's real political agenda. After the group gathered around a table, Secretary Watt informed them about Roberts's accomplishment. "Everybody's jaws dropped," remembered Janklow, pleased that the element of surprise had survived.[22] Not long after that, according to Janklow, Larry Pressler excused himself from the meeting.

James Watt explained why the administration supported WEB, then he turned to Tom Daschle and challenged the young congressman. Because this reauthorization involves an appropriation, stated Watt, it must originate in the House. It's up to you, he asserted, narrowing his eyes and staring at Daschle, to persuade the Democrats to move WEB through the House. Tom Daschle can't forget Watt's icy glare as the command was delivered. He'd seen that look before. He and Watt lived in the same townhouse complex and occasionally crossed paths in the parking lot. Watt would either glower at the congressman or simply ignore him. "He made it clear," remembered Daschle, "that he disliked me."[23]

Everyone in the room was aware that important Democrats in the Democrat-controlled House were reluctant to endorse WEB. Daschle suddenly realized that Watt, Janklow, and the other Republicans hoped he would fail. Their plan was now obvious to Tom Daschle: Roberts would appear successful to South Dakotans; Daschle would not. "[Watt] made it clear to everyone sitting in that room," said Tom Daschle of the meeting and the pressure he felt, "that if [WEB] fails it will be Daschle's failure, and it's not going to be [the Republicans]."[24]

Arriving back in South Dakota that evening, Bill Janklow discovered where Larry Pressler had gone when he left the meeting: South Dakota's senior senator had gotten a head start on the others. "Before I'd even boarded my flight in Washington to come home after the meeting," explained a peeved Janklow, "Larry Pressler was standing at the Sioux Falls airport holding a press conference announcing how he had persuaded the administration to support WEB."[25] Janklow's carefully planned sleight of hand had itself fallen victim to sleight of hand. "Pressler got the credit," Janklow groused, "and he didn't even know what we were doing when he went into the meeting."[26]

Tom Daschle surprised Janklow and Watt when he quickly convinced Democratic leaders in the House to support WEB. Behind the scenes, Daschle discovered several Watt staffers willing to help WEB. "They pleaded with me not to let Watt know they were doing as much as they were doing," recalled Daschle.

"They thought [WEB] was a good project and deserved to be built in spite of the fact that they knew Watt was involved for nothing more than political cosmetics."[27]

Garry Carruthers insisted that WEB's reauthorization be part of the Oahe settlement bill. Study money for CENDAK was also to be part of the settlement package. So was study money for another Janklow-inspired concept called the Garrison Extension Project. As proposed by Janklow, the Garrison extension would deliver return flows from North Dakota's Garrison Project down the James River to South Dakota. Janklow hoped the water could be used for irrigation and municipal and industrial purposes.[28] Neither CENDAK nor the Garrison extension made much sense from an economic or an environmental standpoint. Even the Bureau of Reclamation acknowledged CENDAK's glaring deficiencies, including soils that were not irrigable and a cost-benefit projection that looked disastrous. To build CENDAK's blueprint necessitated using the Oahe pump facility and the Pierre canal and Blunt dam and reservoir. But as the political support for CENDAK increased, so too did the interest in preserving the Oahe authorization for those features.

The Garrison extension meant dirtier water and exacerbated flooding on the James River, and local interest was sketchy at best. Including these projects in the settlement package satisfied those South Dakotans—Janklow included—who remained attached to big irrigation projects. Their hopes were at least being considered as their Oahe dream was dashed.

Another component of the proposed settlement package was low-cost electrical power for irrigation projects on Indian reservations. This would help correct the injustices suffered by tribes when the Pick-Sloan Plan was enacted.

By summer 1982, the Oahe sub-district and all four members of South Dakota's congressional delegation were narrowing down their disagreements over the settlement bill. Curt Hohn was on the telephone from morning to night and made numerous trips to Washington to facilitate negotiations. Hohn was growing increasingly nervous about the upcoming sub-district elections. John Sieh faced a stiff test from a young relative in his bid for reelection. Four other seats, all seemingly up for grabs, were also at stake. If Sieh and project opponents were to lose their majority, the settlement process would disintegrate, WEB would suffer, and attempts to resurrect Oahe would begin in earnest.

United Family Farmers and the sub-district leveraged all the political power they had accumulated. "We pushed like crazy to get it passed before the election," remembered Curt Hohn. That included reminding Tom Daschle and Clint Roberts that the large roster of United Family Farmers could be activated against them as it had been activated against other candidates. "We warned public officials that if it didn't pass we would encourage people to vote against them."[29] Hohn, Sieh, and the sub-district agreed to drop their insistence that the word *deauthorization* be used, and they reluctantly allowed the pump plant, the unfinished Pierre canal, and the yet-to-be-built Blunt dam and reservoir to survive in the bill's language.

In exchange for that concession, Oahe's features east of Blunt, according to the bill, "[would] not be constructed . . . without further action by Congress."[30] Oahe proponents also allowed that the project's master contract and security contracts would be canceled, subject to the wishes of the Oahe sub-district and the irrigation districts. This wording protected the James River valley from irrigation development but allowed water developers to use Oahe's surviving features for CENDAK or some other proposal. It was a hard-fought agreement, and both sides had lost something of value.

John Sieh, Curt Hohn, George Piper, and United Family Farmers wanted the entire project deauthorized. They felt they had earned a complete killing. John Sieh undertook the difficult task of explaining to loyal United Family Farmers in the Blunt area that the Blunt dam and reservoir would remain authorized. He had to tell Roy Runge, Ted Albright, and others along the Pierre canal the same thing. But he assured them that CENDAK was a defective proposal and would advance no further than the planning process.

Senator James Abdnor would have preferred not giving up the Oahe contracts and so many Oahe features. "For the sake of unanimity," he told George Piper, " . . . I have compromised."[31] Governor Janklow hated to see Oahe lost. "If only I'd been governor ten years earlier," lamented Janklow, implying that Oahe would have been built had he been in office.[32]

On 23 September 1982, the Oahe settlement bill passed out of Congress and was sent to the White House for President Reagan's approval. One week later, Reagan signed the measure and Oahe was past tense. Just thirty-three days later, John Sieh narrowly lost his sub-district seat, and United Family Farmers lost their majority on the sub-district board.

Regaining control of the sub-district was a hollow victory for supporters of large-scale irrigation. "We'd fought long and hard and won," said Ron Frankenstein, the man who replaced Sieh as chairman of the sub-district, "yet we didn't have anything."[33]

Tom Daschle, the young Democratic comngressman from Aberdeen, had surprised Republicans conspiring against him when he convinced the Democratic leadership in the House to support WEB. Daschle surprised them again when he prevailed over Clint Roberts to claim the state's consolidated, sole seat in the House. Had Bill Janklow's plan to heap credit for WEB on Clint Roberts not backfired, or if Daschle had not been successful convincing Democrats in the Congress to support WEB, the results might have been different. Losing to Clint Roberts would not have precluded Tom Daschle from again seeking elected office. But it is likely that a loss to Roberts would have ended his promising career in Congress.

Frustrated CENDAK supporters wanted to withdraw their counties from the Oahe sub-district in order to promote their project. Two years after Oahe's demise, Governor Janklow dismantled the state's sub-districts and created a new system of water-development districts, including one tailored around CEN-DAK's area. Studies for CENDAK consumed an inordinate amount of public money—hundreds of thousands of dollars—and embarrassed the state's water-development cheerleaders before finally dying. John Sieh had been right when he had calmed Roy Runge's fears about the boondoggle. Several years after CENDAK expired, farmers and towns in the CENDAK area rallied behind a rural water pipeline similar to WEB.

The Garrison extension also floundered after wasting study monies and generating its own controversy. Many South Dakotans did not like the idea of welcoming Garrison's polluted flows down the James River and into their state. James River issues were never the same after Kay Cool's intrepid political adventure.

Curt Hohn resigned his position at the Oahe sub-district in late 1982 before the new board could fire him. Oahe's loss was WEB's gain, for Hohn was immediately hired to serve as the first manager of the WEB system. Hohn guided the project through its important early years of construction, watchdogging contractors, negotiating advantageous contracts, and protecting WEB's authorization, appropriations, and the interest rate on federal loans.

The WEB project was unusual in that it was the first rural drinking-water project to derive its federal grants through the Bureau of Reclamation. The irony of that relationship certainly involved Curt Hohn. "Not long before I started working with the bureau on funding and building WEB," Hohn recalled, "I was working against them to stop Oahe."[34] Hohn discovered a more productive side to the bureau as he worked with them on WEB. "There was tension in the beginning," he recalled, "but they showed great professionalism and ended up helping a great deal."[35]

WEB's service area eventually stretched from the Missouri River east into Day County, an area exceeding 5,200 square miles. The system provided safe water to more than half a million livestock and thirty thousand people living on four thousand farms and in sixty-six towns and cities. The WEB project cost $110 million, a far cry from Oahe's probable completion cost. But it was hard to find a single soul who opposed WEB.

WEB leaders pleaded with Aberdeen's mayor, Jeff Solem, and the city commission to join WEB. Adding Aberdeen to the pipeline system would have strengthened the project's already promising viability. But Aberdeen's historic support for the Oahe project and the feud city leaders had carried on with Oahe opponents influenced, at least in part, their decision to reject joining WEB. It was a dazzlingly shortsighted decision. WEB engineers consequently sized the project's delivery system without considering Aberdeen's needs, and the city was bypassed in the pipeline's blueprint. Instead of abundant, clean Missouri River reservoir water delivered to its doorstep, Aberdeen would continue to derive most of its water from a small, unpredictable, and often turbid tributary of the James River.

Two years after Oahe was officially ended, and with WEB construction under way, water samples from Aberdeen's drinking water system were found to contain trihalomethane contaminants, a suspected carcinogen, in excess of federal standards. Although the condition that caused the problem was corrected, Aberdeen will battle water turbidity problems and tricky chemical adjustments in its water treatment process as long as it relies on traditional sources.

At the dawn of the 1980s and during the height of Ronald Reagan's influence, a period that coincided with rising awareness and concern about the massive federal budget deficit, the Bureau of Reclamation was in the beginning stages of a dramatic transformation. Shrinking federal contributions to local water projects tightened the noose already placed by burgeoning environmental interests. Staring the concept called cost-sharing in the face, the Bureau of Reclamation at first resisted financial constraints, and finally, reluctantly, the agency sought to reposition itself. There was no bulldozing the Reagan administration and its stalwart allies in Congress, at least not in the sense that the Bureau of Reclamation wrangled with environmentalists.

Without free-flowing federal money, the bureau could do little more than tread water. But there were new areas of public need that could benefit from the agency. Slowly, the bureau began to shift its focus from developing large irrigation or river-modification projects to maintaining projects it had already built, fixing problems its projects had created, and embarking on entirely different endeavors, such as helping WEB. During 1984, for the first time in the bureau's history, more money was spent on operations and maintenance than on construction. Despite the bureau's new direction, there was little solace for environmentalists. Nearly as influential on the bureau's dwindling construction program as restrictions occasioned by the federal deficit was the fact that the agency had run out of places to play. The pursuit of federal reclamation had already caused colossal damage to rivers and valleys and other western ecosystems. Suitable project sites, except for those with excessively lenient eligibility requirements, were rare by the 1980s.

The bureau's shift in responsibilities away from Oahe and toward the WEB project was a harbinger for a new era in water development. Water giveaways were scrutinized. Endangered species gained stature. The values of instream flows were recognized. Preserving and providing clean, ample drinking water became a national priority. The days of developing large federal irrigation projects were, for the most part, over. Oahe was a goner for good; its unfinished, unused canals and pump house became symbols of a time when pork barrel and boondoggles meant progress.

Oahe's funeral was noted by environmentalists and others across the country. David Weiman, who came to understand the history of federal reclamation in the United States as few others did, praised the work of United Family Farmers. "There was no place in the country," said Weiman, "that was as well organized to fight the Bureau of Reclamation."[36] According to Weiman, Oahe is the only federal reclamation project that was halted while under construction.

United Family Farmers functioned for nearly a decade following Oahe's demise in 1982. The organization helped derail CENDAK and led a successful campaign against Bill Janklow's plan to dredge and straighten the James River as part of the Garrison extension proposal. At the organization's final annual meeting, a traditional potluck feast fed some fifty loyal members. Afterward, the evening was devoted to storytelling. Nearly every man and woman at the banquet stood and recalled an incident or an event from the Oahe controversy. The fight over Oahe connected them all, but the influence of United Family Farmers extended far beyond changing the face of water development in South Dakota. Each storyteller had been changed by the Oahe experience.

United Family Farmers was an incubator for countless new leaders in South Dakota's rural communities. These leaders became involved in a variety of issues and won posts on county commissions, rural electric boards, grain cooperative boards, and Governor Janklow's new water district boards. John Sieh was present at the final banquet. He credited George Piper with inspiring these new community activists. "The reason George Piper was a successful leader," said Sieh, "was because George Piper encouraged others to take leadership responsibilities. George may have been the founder and the first leader, but he understood what it took for the group to grow stronger. That is why United Family Farmers was able to stop Oahe. That is why we won."[37]

Epilogue

In the years following termination of the Oahe project, bitter disappointment persisted in the James River valley. A prolonged dry spell during the late 1980s helped uphold the regret and frustration felt by Oahe diehards. Those who had opposed Oahe were doggedly informed about the disservice they had done.

Oahe proponents forgot to figure that there was never a guarantee that irrigators would receive Missouri River water. Whenever drought caused reservoir inflows to dwindle, river users from throughout the vast Missouri River basin disagreed over who should receive preferential treatment. Lower-basin states and navigation interests relied on their superior political power and supportive reservoir management by the Army Corps of Engineers to block requests by upper-basin states to protect water levels in Missouri River impoundments. By the 1980s, South Dakota's reservoir recreation industry was a thriving enterprise that drew anglers from across the Midwest. During the drought, recreation interests on Oahe reservoir were seriously injured because water was released to float downriver barges. Habitat for walleye and salmon was severely diminished. Some biologists feared the reservoir fishery came close to a disaster. There is little reason to believe that irrigation interests would have fared any better than recreation. It is also likely that recreation and irrigation would have competed for the scraps left over after navigation and downstream interests got what they needed. If the Oahe irrigation project had been built as planned and withdrawals had been made to water-thirsty lands near Aberdeen, reservoir levels would have dropped even farther than they did. The threat to the reservoir's fishery might have become deadly.

The 1990s delivered altogether different conditions that should have sparked reconsideration by Oahe proponents. No one disputed the importance of the irrigation project's sophisticated and expensive drainage plan. Without artificial drainage, irrigated and nonirrigated lands in the project area would have been ruined. The vital role of the James River in the drainage plan was well documented. The river's modified tributaries and drainageways in the project area would have served a similar, though supportive, role.

Weather events in 1993, 1994, 1995, and 1997 would have translated into trouble had the Oahe project been built. Never before in modern history had the James River been subjected to such flooding as it was during those years. The century's high-flow record on the river, set in 1995, was shattered just two years later. Precipitation in the region came in unprecedented amounts. Spring floods along the river stretched into summer, then fall, and even into winter. Imagine a center pivot stranded in standing water. . . . Imagine a center pivot in frozen water. . . . Not only were some of Oahe's proposed irrigation lands inundated, but the engineering works that would have been implemented on streams and the river would have been overwhelmed by the high flows. The Oahe project's subsurface drainage infrastructure would have filled with water or backed up and would have been unable to function. Inevitably, costly repairs and replacement would have been necessary. Who would have paid? The burden would have fallen on irrigators and taxpayers in the Oahe sub-district. The finances of many farmers were already stretched thin by flood losses. Who could have anticipated such disparate and equally destructive circumstances—extreme drought and severe flooding—during one ten-year time frame?

Couple these problems with valid concerns—had Oahe been built—regarding the suitability of Oahe soils for irrigation. Couple them with the region's brief and unpredictable growing season. Couple them with ongoing problems regarding adequate prices for surplus crops. Couple them with concerns about James River water quality and the destruction of wildlife habitat. What about irrigation acreage limitations imposed on farm families in the lake plain? What about the need to mitigate? An abundance of unwilling sellers littered the ownership roster of lands proposed for mitigation. What about the impact of large canals on shallow aquifers and small streams, had Oahe been built? What about the unrelenting financial obligations that would have been imposed on irrigators? What would have happened to the project's costly infrastructure at the conclusion of its life cycle? What about the need there would have been to use more farm chemicals on irrigated lands? What about the condemnation necessary to build canals and reservoirs? What about farmers and ranchers driven from their homes? What about the salted-up lands that haunted other Bureau of Reclamation projects? Would that have been the destiny of Oahe, too?

In his biography *A Farmer Takes a Stand*, Ken Holum described Oahe opponents as "short-sighted and selfish individuals [who] succeeded in destroying the [Oahe] project." He downplayed their success by proclaiming that it is "harder to build than to destroy" and that he was "one of the builders."

Was it easier for George Piper to oppose Oahe or for Ken Holum to promote it? Piper and other United Family Farmers were regularly maligned in the state's major newspapers. They faced countless obstacles erected by local, state, and national politicians. They confronted a powerful federal agency that had grown accustomed to running roughshod over those who disagreed with it. They were scorned by the business establishment and by every chamber of commerce in South Dakota. During their early years, especially, they stood seemingly alone in a pervasively pro-Oahe culture.

Oahe supporters often referred to themselves as being "pro-development." They dismissed Oahe opponents as "aginners"—people who oppose everything. Being *against* everything *is* a problem. So it is with those who are *for* everything. Ken Holum and many others, including some who fought Oahe, worked hard to bring amenities such as electricity and telephones to rural South Dakotans. Those were commendable campaigns. But comparisons with the value of the Oahe project and the value of rural electric and rural telephone service, commonly made by Oahe proponents, were inappropriate.

An irony of the Oahe controversy is that Holum's so-called destroyers did build something worthwhile. The same people who helped kill the Oahe irrigation project were instrumental in creating the WEB rural water system. And WEB, it is now clear, serves northeastern South Dakota as indispensably as the rural telephone and electricity systems Ken Holum worked so hard to develop.

Notes

1. The Deceivers

1. James Malin, *The Grassland of North America: Prolegomena to Its History* (Gloucester MA: P. Smith, 1967).

2. Walter Prescott Webb, *The Great Plains* (1931; reprint, Lincoln: University of Nebraska Press, 1981), 369.

3. Fred Coffin, *First Report of the Commissioner of Irrigation* (1890).

4. Coffin, *First Report*, 12.

5. Wallace Stegner, *Beyond the Hundredth Meridian: John Wesley Powell and the Second Opening of the West* (New York: Viking Penguin, 1992), 333.

6. Donald Worster, *Nature's Economy* (Cambridge: Cambridge University Press, 1985), pp. 219–53. Worster's chapter 12 carries the title, "Dust Follows the Plow."

7. *Aberdeen Daily News*, 5 April 1893.

2. The Big Dry

1. Herbert Schell, *History of South Dakota* (Lincoln: University of Nebraska Press, 1975), 292.

2. Robert Hipple, interview by author, tape recording, Pierre SD, 10 August 1988. Montgomery Collection, Northern State University, Aberdeen SD (hereafter, Montgomery Coll.).

3. Henry Hart, *The Dark Missouri* (Madison: University of Wisconsin Press, 1957), 116.

4. Hart, *Dark Missouri*, 113–14.

5. *Omaha World Herald*, June 1943. During April, too, the paper ran many stories about the Missouri River and flooding.

6. Quote from the *Omaha World Herald*, 17 June 1943.

7. Rufus Terral, *The Missouri Valley* (New Haven CT: Yale University Press, 1947), 189.

8. Hipple interview, August 1988.

9. Terral, *Missouri Valley*, 222.

10. Albert Williams, *The Water and the Power* (New York: Duell, Sloan and Pierce, 1951), p. 241.

11. Williams, *Water and Power*, p. 242.

3. The Big Dam

1. Ted Albright, interview by author, tape recording, Hughes County SD, 7 December 1988, Montgomery Coll.

2. The Big Bend is a stretch of the Missouri River, now backed up behind Big Bend dam (Lake Sharpe), situated between Pierre SD and Chamberlain SD.

3. Donald Miller, "The History of the Movement for Hydro-Electric Development on the Missouri River in South Dakota," master's thesis, University of South Dakota, 1930. Another source is the *Sioux Falls Argus Leader*, 24 November 1959.

4. "The Biggest Dam Job in the World," *Farm Journal*, October 1950.

5. Martha Sutherland Coon, *Oahe Dam Master of the Missouri* (Irvington-on-Hudson NY: Harvey House, 1969), 27.

6. *Mobridge [SD] Tribune*, 5 December 1946.

7. *Pierre Daily Capital Journal*, 28 October 1952.

8. Roy Houck, *South Dakota Stockgrower*, 15 December 1952.

9. Frank Ferguson, "Oahe-James Irrigation Project," speech given to the Natural Resource Conservation Conference, sponsored by the Izaak Walton League, Sioux City IA, 18 October 1952.

10. M. Q. Sharpe, speech delivered to a meeting of the Missouri Basin Interagency Committee, 1 December 1952, Omaha NE.

11. U.S. Army Corps of Engineers, Omaha NE, documents/records in the Acquisitions Office.

12. Dale Lewis, *Roy Hauck, Buffalo Man* (Fort Pierre SD: Roy Hauck, 1992), 106.

13. Art and Helen Metzinger, interview by author, tape recording, Hughes County SD, 10 March 1989, Montgomery Coll.

14. Metzingers interview.

15. Metzingers interview.

16. Metzingers interview.

17. Metzingers interview.

18. U.S. Senate. Sub-committee of the Public Works Committee, "Land Acquisition Policies and Evaluation of Recreation Benefits," 86th Cong., 2nd sess., 16–17 May

1960. Also a letter written by Mrs. Metzinger, read into the record by Senator Francis Case.

19. Metzingers interview.

20. Michael Lawson, *Dammed Indians: The Pick-Sloan Plan and the Missouri River Sioux* (Norman: University of Oklahoma Press, 1994), 63.

21. Lawson, preface to *Dammed Indians*.

22. Peter Carrels, "Indian Land Dispute Opens Old Wounds," *High Country News*, 11 September 1989.

23. Arthur Morgan, *Dams and Other Disasters* (Boston: Poster Sargent, 1971), 47–50.

24. Morgan, *Dams and Other Disasters*, 56.

25. Morgan, *Dams and Other Disasters*, 56.

26. *Aberdeen American News*, 16 February 1957.

27. Greater South Dakota Association, 24 October 1958, membership bulletin.

28. President John F. Kennedy, "Excerpts of Remarks Made at Oahe Project and Missouri River Basin Power Transmission System," Pierre SD, 17 August, 1962. The excerpts were issued as a news release by the Office of the White House Press Secretary on 17 August 1962.

29. "Land of the Big Muddy," *Time*, 1 September 1952, 36.

30. U.S. Army Corps of Engineers, letter to Peter Carrels, 1 January 1994. Also U.S. Fish and Wildlife Service, 7 June 1982, "Post-Authorization Mitigation Report, Fish and Wildlife Mitigation, Lake Oahe and Lake Sharpe."

31. *Aberdeen American News*, 12 January 1959.

32. *Aberdeen American News*, 15 February 1959.

33. Meeting minutes, 1 June 1960. The minutes of this organizational meeting can be found in the Montgomery Collection.

34. Hipple interview, August 1988, and a further interview, tape recording, Pierre SD, 21 April 1989, Montgomery Coll.

35. *Aberdeen American News*, 6 November 1960.

36. South Dakota State College, Cooperative Extension Service, "Water . . . in South Dakota, for South Dakota" brochure, 1960.

37. "Water in South Dakota" brochure.

38. *Huron Daily Plainsman*, 13 November 1960.

4. The Big Dream

1. U.S. Department of the Interior, Bureau of Reclamation, Region 6, "Report on Oahe Unit," June 1960.

2. "Report on Oahe Unit," 112.

3. "Report on Oahe Unit," 168.

4. George Schuller, interview by author, tape recording, Claremont SD, 17 August 1988, Montgomery Coll.

5. Schuller interview.

6. Schuller interview.

7. William Safire, *Safire's Political Dictionary* (New York: Random House, 1978) 353.

8. Marc Reisner, *Cadillac Desert* (New York: Penguin, 1987) 154.

9. Missouri Basin Survey Commission, "Land and Water," 12 January 1953, 284–86.

5. The Dean of Oahe

1. Ken Holum, interview by author, tape recording, Washington DC, 13 April 1989, Montgomery Coll.

2. U.S. Bureau of Reclamation, "Report on Financial Position, Missouri River Basin Project," December 1963.

3. Ken Marsh, interview by author, tape recording, Sully County SD, 2 September 1988, Montgomery Coll.

4. Oahe Conservancy Sub-district, board of directors meeting minutes, 25 August 1961.

5. *Groton Independent*, 7 November 1963.

6. *Redfield Press*, 13, 20, 27 August 1964. Also see the meeting minutes "Detailed minutes of the Hearing on Petitions Presented Requesting Organization of an Irrigation District within Spink County," 7, 14, and 28 August 1964.

7. Brown County Commission, meeting minutes, 12 June 1964, 24 July 1964, 24 August 1964, and 24 September 1964.

8. James Lewis, letter to Oahe Conservancy Sub-district board of directors, 14 December 1964.

9. Lewis letter to Oahe sub-district directors, 14 December 1964.

10. *Aberdeen American News*, 30 January 1966.

11. *Aberdeen American News*, 6 January 1965.

12. C. W. Renz, letter to Lloyd Wilson, 16 February 1965.

13. Nelson Hunstad, letter to Governor Nils Boe, 8 January 1965.

14. *Huron Daily Plainsman*, 6 January 1965.

15. *Huron Daily Plainsman*, 6 January 1965.

16. United Family Farmers, "Guide to Master Contract," undated booklet.

17. *Aberdeen American News*, 24 January 1966.

18. U.S. House Sub-Committee on Irrigation and Reclamation, *Hearing on H.R. 27 and H.R. 1163*, Huron SD 90th Cong., 1st sess., 27 October 1967.

19. U.S. House sub-committee, *Hearing on H.R. 27 and H.R. 1163*, Washington DC, 90th Cong., 2nd sess., 24 May 1967.

20. U.S. Senate Committee on Interior and Insular Affairs, *Hearing on the Oahe Unit*, Washington DC, 90th Cong., 1st sess., 13 September 1967.

21. U.S. Senate, *Hearing on the Oahe Unit*, 1st sess., 13 September.

22. U.S. Senate, *Hearing on the Oahe Unit*, 1st sess., 13 September.

23. U.S. House Sub-committee on Irrigation and Reclamation, *Hearing on H.R. 27 and H.R. 1163*, Redfield SD, 90th Cong., 1st sess., 28 October 1967.

24. U.S. House sub-committee, *Hearing on H.R. 27 and H.R. 1163*, Redfield SD, 28 October.

25. U.S. House sub-committee, *Hearing on H.R. 27 and H.R. 1163*, Redfield SD, 28 October.

26. U.S. House sub-committee, *Hearing on H.R. 27 and H.R. 1163*, Redfield SD, 28 October.

27. U.S. House sub-committee, *Hearing on H.R. 27 and H.R. 1163*, Redfield SD, 28 October.

28. Russell Berry, interview by author, tape recording, Brookings SD, 23 November 1988, Montgomery Coll.

29. U.S. House of Representatives, Congressional Record, 16 July 1968, page H 6715.

30. Rollyn Samp, interview by author, tape recording, Sioux Falls SD, 23 June 1996, Montgomery Coll. Samp served as an aide to Governor Frank Farrar.

31. *Sioux Falls Argus Leader*, 23 October 1970.

32. Senator George McGovern, Congressman James Abourezk, and Congressman Frank Denholm, letter to Fred Holscher, 1 February 1972.

33. *Aberdeen American News*, 3 September 1972.

6. The Dissidents

1. Virgil Gilbert, interview by author, tape recording, Huron SD, 23 February 1989, Montgomery Coll.

2. George Stapleton, "Blue Envelope" communication to Jim Hart, April, 1975.

3. Bud Maher, letter to Senator George McGovern, 27 January 1975.

4. George Piper, interview by author, tape recording, Beadle County SD, 9 September 1988, Montgomery Coll.

5. Art Moran, interview by author, tape recording, Huron SD, 14 September 1988, Montgomery Coll.

6. Moran interview.

7. Holum interview.

8. *Huron Daily Plainsman*, n.p., n.d., Montgomery Coll.

9. WPA Writers Program (Vermillion: University of South Dakota, 1941). Also Virginia Driving Hawk Sneve, *The Dakota's Heritage* (Sioux Falls SD: Brevet Press, 1973). Also Ernest F. Berringer, U.S. Board on Geographic Names, letter to author, 18 November 1982.

10. Edmund Bray and Martha Coleman Bray, *Joseph Nicollet on the Plains and Prairies* (St. Paul: Minnesota Historical Society Press, 1976) 174.

11. W. S. Reeves, "Report of the Drainage and Flood Control Investigation in the James River Valley through South Dakota" (December 1922).

12. *Huron Daily Plainsman*, 2 August 1957.

13. *Huron Daily Plainsman*, 2 August 1957.

14. "Report on Oahe Unit," June 1960.

15. U.S. Bureau of Reclamation, public hearing on Draft Environmental Statement, Initial Stage of the Oahe Unit, 29 November 1972, Aberdeen SD.

16. Public hearing, Initial Stage of the Oahe Unit, 29 November 1972.

17. Reisner, *Cadillac Desert*, 442. It should be noted that Reisner incorrectly associated Ben Schatz with the Oahe Project.

18. *Minneapolis Tribune*, 19 November 1972.

19. Piper interview, 9 September.

20. Piper interview, 9 September.

21. Piper interview, 9 September.

22. John Elsing, interview by author, tape recording, Spink County SD, 22 September 1988, Montgomery Coll.

23. Elsing interview.

24. Elsing interview.

25. Albright interview.

26. *Minneapolis Tribune*, 22 July 1973.

27. *Minneapolis Tribune*, 22 July 1973.

28. *Minneapolis Tribune*, 22 July 1973.

29. Tim Schreiner, interview by author, tape recording, Aberdeen SD, 9 January 1989, Montgomery Coll.

30. Schreiner interview.

31. Piper interview, 9 September.

7. The Defender of Oahe

1. George McGovern, interview by author, tape recording, Washington DC, 12 April 1989, Montgomery Coll.

2. Reisner, *Cadillac Desert*, 237.

3. Senator George McGovern, letter to Jim Lewis, 5 September 1973.

4. McGovern letter to Lewis.

5. *Huron Daily Plainsman*, 14 September 1972.

6. George Piper/United Family Farmers, news release, 28 September 1973.

7. John Elsing, letter to Esther Eide, George Piper, and Roger Steinberg, 24 September 1973.

8. Proceedings of the conference, including a transcript of remarks, appear in the Congressional Record, Vol. 120, 4 March 1974, no. 26.

9. Ken Holum, letter to Senator George McGovern, 15 January 1974.

10. Holum interview.

11. Ned Hundstad, interview by author, tape recording, Aberdeen SD, 7 October 1988, Montgomery Coll.

12. John Sieh, interview by author, tape recording, Brown County SD, 9 August 1988, Montgomery Coll.

13. Senator George McGovern, letter to Governor Richard Kneip, 20 August 1974.

14. Governor Richard Kneip, letter to Senator George McGovern, 4 September 1974.

15. KKAA Radio broadcast, Aberdeen SD, 16 May 1974.

16. Senator George McGovern, letter to Virgil Gilbert, 9 April 1974.

17. Senator George McGovern, identical letters sent to Henry Schmitt, publisher of the *Aberdeen American News*, and Robert Raschke, 15 November 1974.

18. Martin Weeks, interview by author, tape recording, Vermillion SD, 7 February 1989, Montgomery Coll.

19. George Cunningham, letter to Ken Holum, 11 July 1974.

20. George Piper, interview by author, tape recording, Beadle County SD, 15 September 1988, Montgomery Coll.

21. Sieh interview.

22. Sieh interview.

23. *Aberdeen American News*, 30 October 1974.

8. Judgment Denied

1. John Davidson, letter to George Piper, 11 September 1973.

2. *Calvert Cliffs' Coordinating Committee v. United States A. E. Com'n*, 449 F. 2nd 1109 (1971).

3. John Davidson, interview by author, tape recording, Vermillion SD, 4 April 1991, Montgomery Coll.

4. Davidson interview.

5. Davidson interview.

6. Davidson interview.

7. Davidson interview.

8. Davidson interview.

9. It should be noted that in March 1975, Preston Funkhouser told a meeting of the Oahe Conservancy Sub-district board that the pumps and motors for the facility were designed specifically for raising reservoir water into irrigation canals and might not be adaptable to other pumping uses. See *Huron Daily Plainsman*, 4 March 1975.

10. Weeks interview.

11. Andrew Walch, telephone interview by author, 28 January 1994.

12. A. E. Bielefeld, letter to William Clayton, U.S. attorney, 30 August 1976.

13. Weeks interview.

14. S. T. Harding, J. R. Iakisch, and C. E. Jacob, "Report on Drainability of Land in the Oahe Unit of the Missouri River Basin Project," 31 December 1954, released by U.S. Bureau of Reclamation.

15. Davidson interview.

16. Ray Winger, deposition, *United Family Farmers, Inc. v. Kleppe*. See Oahe Conservancy Sub-district, "Soils and Drainage Hearing," 7 March 1977, Redfield SD. A copy of Winger's deposition was submitted as part of the hearing record.

17. Ralph Toren, letter to Martin Weeks, 5 April 1974.

18. *United Family Farmers, Inc. v. Kleppe*, 418 FSupp. 591 (1976).

19. Walch interview.

20. A. E. Bielefeld, letter to Peter Taft, assistant attorney general, Land and Natural Resources Division, Department of Justice, 20 August 1976.

9. The Shifting Debate

1. Charles Kearns, "Why Oahe?" Kearns Machinery Company, Sioux Falls SD, 1975.

2. South Dakota Department of Environmental Protection, "Oahe Unit and Initial Oahe Unit Position Paper," January 1974.

3. *Watertown Public Opinion*, 26 February 1975.

4. *Watertown Public Opinion*, 26 February 1975.

5. *Watertown Public Opinion*, 26 February 1975.

6. *Watertown Public Opinion*, 26 February 1975.

7. Ed Glasgow, memorandum to Friends of Oahe board of directors, 12 March 1975.

8. Senator George McGovern and Senator James Abourezk, letter to Fred Holscher, 19 March 1975.

9. Senator George McGovern, letter to Robert Raschke, 24 April 1975.

10. Newspaper ad, United Family Farmers, n.p., n.d.

11. Roy Runge, 28 June 1975. A recording of remarks at the Medicine Knoll rally was

made by Cottonwood Productions of Wakonda, sc. This tape is in the Montgomery Collection.

12. Senator James Abourezk, speech to United Family Farmers, 28 June 1975, at Medicine Knoll sd rally. Abourezk's remarks were recorded on the Cottonwood Productions tape now in the Montgomery Collection.

13. Abourezk speech at Medicine Knoll.

14. Jerald M. McNeary, Friends of Oahe attorney, letter to National Endowment for the Humanities, 3 May 1976.

15. George Piper, letter to Norm Nelson, 22 August 1975.

16. Curt Hohn, letter to Senator James Abourezk, 31 July 1975.

17. Hohn letter to Abourezk, 31 July 1975.

18. Senator James Abourezk, letters to Governor Richard Kneip and to the South Dakota legislature, 22 September 1975. Also Senator James Abourezk news release, 3 October 1975, and Senator Abourezk constituent newsletter, October 1975.

19. Ken Holum, letter to Senator James Abourezk, 28 September 1975.

20. Governor Richard Kneip, letter to Mike McHugh, 22 December 1975.

21. Ken Stofferahn, interview by author, tape recording, Pierre sd, 17 February 1994, Montgomery Coll.

22. *Aberdeen American News*, 12 February 1976.

23. Schreiner interview.

10. The Young Defector

1. Curt Hohn, interview by author, tape recording, 11 October 1988, Aberdeen sd, Montgomery Coll.

2. Hohn interview, 11 October.

3. Hohn interview, 11 October.

4. Hohn interview, 11 October.

5. Hohn interview, 11 October.

6. *Aberdeen American News*, 2 April 1976.

7. *Huron Daily Plainsman*, 6 April 1976.

8. George Cunningham, letter to Mike McHugh, president, Friends of Oahe, 13 April 1976.

9. *Saturday Evening Post*, 13 August 1938.

10. Bud Maher, interview by author, tape recording, 15 October 1988, Huron sd, Montgomery Coll.

11. *Huron Daily Plainsman*, 19 September 1976.

11. The Public's Crucial Decision

1. Senator George McGovern, letter to Fred Holscher, 14 October 1975.

2. *Webster [SD] Reporter and Farmer*, 28 April 1976.

3. *Groton [SD] Independent*, 13 October 1976.

4. *Mobridge [SD] Tribune*, 14 October 1976.

5. Robert Hipple later acknowledged the quotation. Hipple interview, April 1989.

6. *Redfield [SD] Press*, 14 October 1976.

7. *Webster [SD] Reporter and Farmer*, 6 October 1976.

8. Jay Davis, interview by author, tape recording, 18 December 1989, Aberdeen SD, Montgomery Coll.

9. *Potter County [SD] News*, 21 October 1976.

10. *Webster [SD] Farmer and Reporter*, 20 October 1976.

11. *Aberdeen American News*, 21 October 1976.

12. Virgil Ellwood, interview by author, Aberdeen SD, 21 March 1996.

13. Senator George McGovern, "Letter from Washington," 27 September 1976.

14. John Bieber, speech, State Water Conference, 30 October 1976. An audio copy of the speech is part of the Montgomery Collection.

15. McGovern interview.

16. *Watertown [SD] Public Opinion*, 19 August 1975.

12. The Daring New Majority

1. Senator George McGovern, letter to Bureau of Reclamation Commissioner Gilbert Stamm, 6 November 1976.

2. Senator George McGovern, letter to Martin Weeks, 5 February 1975.

3. Robert McPhail, faxogram to the commissioner, Bureau of Reclamation, 7 December 1976.

4. Minutes, Oahe Conservancy Sub-district board meeting, 6 January 1977.

5. Sub-district minutes, 6 January 1977.

6. Bud Yackley, letter to *Onida Watchman*, 16 December 1976.

7. Curt Hohn, interview by author, tape recording, Aberdeen SD, 6 November 1988, Montgomery Coll.

8. G. G. Stamm, letter to Senator George McGovern, 21 December 1976.

9. *Aberdeen American News*, 29 May 1977.

10. *Aberdeen American News*, 14 January 1977.

11. *Minneapolis Tribune*, 6 March 1977.

12. Kay Cool, interview by author, tape recording, Pierre SD, 6 December 1988, Montgomery Coll.

13. *Aberdeen American News*, 4 July 1976.

14. *Aberdeen American News*, 4 July 1976.

15. U.S. Bureau of Reclamation, Missouri-Oahe Projects Office, "Report on Oahe," June 1960, p. 37.

16. The significance of the Stratford slough was demonstrated in 1992 when the Nature Conservancy, a national conservation organization interested in preserving ecologically valuable tracts of land, acquired land within the Stratford slough area.

17. South Dakota Department of Game, Fish and Parks, "Upper James River Scenic and Recreational Nomination," 28 October 1976.

18. Jack Merwin, interview by author, tape recording, Pierre SD, 31 August 1988, Montgomery Coll.

19. Kay Cool, remarks during a public meeting on the James River nomination, Aberdeen SD, 30 September 1976. See South Dakota Game, Fish, and Parks, "Upper James River."

20. Oahe Conservancy Sub-district board of directors meeting minutes, 16 February 1977.

21. *Aberdeen American News*, 18 February 1977.

22. *Aberdeen American News*, 8 February 1977.

23. Wells Lamont's first glove-manufacturing facility was located above a furniture store in downtown Aberdeen. W. O. Wells, an Aberdeen buggy-whip and hosiery jobber, and Maurice Lamont were partners. The Lamonts sold their interest in the company in 1967.

24. Frances (Peg) Lamont, interview by author, 18 May 1997.

25. *Aberdeen American News*, 8 February 1977.

26. *Huron Daily Plainsman*, 19 April 1977.

13. The District of Columbia

1. Guy Martin, interview by author, tape recording, Washington DC, 12 April 1989, Montgomery Coll.

2. Brent Blackwelder originally helped found the Environmental Policy Institute. The organization was later renamed the Environmental Policy Center.

3. Bob Lane, telephone interview by author, tape recording, 27 September 1996, Montgomery Coll.

4. The schedule, topic, and locations for the hearings were as follows:

    1. 3 February 1977, Land Acquisition, Blunt SD

    2. 16 February 1977, James River, Aberdeen SD

    3. 7 March 1977, Soils and Drainage, Redfield SD

    4. 17 March 1977, Benefits and Costs, Redfield SD

    5. 31 March 1977, Impacts, Canalside Irrigation, and Contracts, Miller SD

    6. 14 April 1977, Wildlife, Aberdeen SD

    7. 28 April 1997, Alternatives to Oahe, Gettysburg SD.

5. Preston Funkhouser, testimony at the Land Acquisition Hearing, sponsored by the Oahe Sub-district, 3 February 1977.

6. Helen Metzinger, interview by author, tape recording, Hughes County SD, 10 March 1989, Montgomery Coll.

7. *Sioux Falls Argus Leader*, 24 January 1977.

8. Roy Runge, testimony, Land Acquisition Hearing, sponsored by Oahe Conservancy Sub-district, 3 February 1977.

9. Roy Runge, interview by author, tape recording, Hughes County SD, 30 August 1988, Montgomery Coll.

10. Marylou and Earl Briggs, interview by author, tape recording, Hughes County SD, 5 December 1988, Montgomery Coll.

11. Hohn interview, 6 November 1988.

12. Mrs. Margaret Pope, telephone interview by author, 15 February 1989.

13. John Sieh, Oahe sub-district Land Acquisition Hearing, transcript, 3 February 1977. Sieh read: "The Committee (of Congress) believes that the Bureau of Reclamation's policy of withholding appraisal reports is indefensible and in violation of the policies stated [in federal law]."

14. Tom May, Oahe sub-district Land Acquisition Hearing, 3 February 1977.

15. Marylou Briggs, interview by author, tape recording, Hughes County SD, 5 December 1988, Montgomery Coll.

16. *Aberdeen American News*, 20 February 1977.

17. *Sioux City [IA] Journal*, 22 February 1977.

18. William Peters, testimony, Oahe Sub-district Soils and Drainage Hearing, 7 March 1977.

19. John Sieh, Soils and Drainage Hearing, 7 March 1977.

20. Allen Talbott, Soils and Drainage Hearing, 7 March 1977.

21. Environmental Protection Agency, letter to Bureau of Reclamation, 19 February 1976.

22. "Are the Soils Irrigable?" *Farmer*, 20 March 1976.

23. S. T. Harding, J. R. Iakisch, and C. E. Jacob, "Report on Drainability of Land in the Oahe Unit of the Missouri River Basin Project," 31 December 1954, released by the U.S. Bureau of Reclamation.

24. L. N. McClellan, letter to commissioner, 28 January 1955.

25. Ray Braun, interview by author, tape recording, Spink County SD, 19 October 1988, Montgomery Coll.

26. Braun interview.

27. Elsing interview.

28. Dr. Larry Fine, interview by author, tape recording, Brookings sd, 21 November 1988, Montgomery Coll.

29. R. C. Maierhofer, address to session titled "Drainage of Reclamation Lands," Billings mt, 24 January 1963.

30. *Aberdeen American News*, 18 March 1977.

31. Robert J. Barbera, Phil Carver, and Robert K. Davis, "The Oahe Unit: An Economic Re-Evaluation;" Johns Hopkins University, 1974.

32. Bob Lane, telephone interview by author, tape recording, 27 September 1996, Montgomery Coll.

33. Lane interview.

34. Lane interview.

35. Rolf Wallenstrom, telephone interview by author, tape recording, 8 May 1997, Montgomery Coll.

36. *Pierre Daily Capital Journal*, 21 March 1977.

14. A Flurry of Desperate Deeds

1. Phyllis Huss, interview by author, 2 February 1997. Others listed on the suit were Frank Dixon and Robert Orr, businessmen from Aberdeen; C. H. (Jumbo) Peterson, former mayor of Huron; Carol Reed, a landowner from the West Brown Irrigation District; and Keith Kettering, a landowner from the Spink County Irrigation District.

2. *Huron Daily Plainsman*, 8 April 1977.

3. U.S. Department of Interior, "U.S. Department of Interior Water Projects Review; Oahe Unit: South Dakota," April 1977.

4. Holum interview.

5. Martin interview, 12 April.

6. Martin interview, 12 April.

7. Cecil Andrus, memo to director, Office of Management and Budget, 13 April 1977.

8. President Carter, "Statement on Water Projects," news release, 18 April 1977.

9. The complete list of the projects on President Carter's list
(project name/location/agency/FY1978 request/total—both figures in millions):
Applegate Lake/Oregon/coe/$7.4/$74.0
Atchafalaya River & Bayous/Louisiana/coe/$5.1/$10.1
Bayou Bodcau/Louisiana/coe/$2.4/$10.0
Cache Basin/Arkansas/coe/$2.0/$88.5
Grove Lake/Kansas/coe/$1.0/$83.9
Hillsdale Lake/Kansas/coe/$14.0/$38.6
LaFarge Lake/Wisconsin/coe/$2.0/$36.9

Lukfata Lake/Oklahoma/COE/$0.2/$36.9

Meramec Park Lake/Missouri/COE/$10.0/$88.7

Richard Russell/Georgia–South Carolina/COE/$21.0/$254.9

Tallahala Creek/Mississippi/COE/$5.0/$52.0

Yatesville/Kentucky/COE/$7.2/$42.7

Columbia Dam/Tennessee/TVA/$20.0/$110.4

Auburn Dam/California/BOR/$39.7/$898.6

Fruitland Mesa/Colorado/BOR/$7.7/$82.5

Narrows Unit/Colorado/BOR/$9.7/$139.2

Oahe Unit/South Dakota/ BOR/$17.0/$414.4

Savery-Pot-Hook/Colorado, Wyoming/BOR/$6.0/$71.3

Key: COE: Corps of Engineers; BOR: Bureau of Reclamation; TVA: Tennessee Valley Authority.

10. Charles Kearns, interview by author, tape recording, Sioux Falls SD, 22 November 1988, Montgomery Coll.

11. *Pierre Capital Journal*, 1 July 1977.

12. Senator James Abourezk, letter to members of the Senate, 24 June 1977.

13. Hohn interview, 6 November 1988.

14. Hohn interview, 6 November 1988.

15. *Huron Daily Plainsman*, 17 August 1977.

16. Cecil Andrus, letter to Douglas Haeder, 9 November 1977.

17. WEB is an acronym for Walworth, Edmunds, and Brown Counties, the counties orginally represented in the coalition to improve domestic water supplies in north-central South Dakota. The next phase of planning added Campbell, Spink, and Day Counties to the proposed service area.

15. The Sub-district Is Defended

1. A portion of the *Pierre Times* editorial quoted in the epigraph to this chapter was printed in the *Aberdeen American News* of 12 October 1977. Resurrection after deauthorization was possible only if Congress pursued and approved reauthorization. This scenario was unlikely in the case of any federal project. Oahe's controversial history would make its chances for reauthorization even more remote.

2. *Huron Daily Plainsman*, editorial reproduced in the *Aberdeen American News*, 29 January 1978.

3. *Pierre Capital Journal*, 24 January 1978.

4. *Pierre Capital Journal*, 24 January 1978.

5. *Sioux Falls Argus Leader*, 30 January 1978.

6. Keith Higginson, letter to John Sieh, 16 May 1977.

7. Keith Higginson, telephone interview by author, tape recording, 14 May 1997, Montgomery Coll.

8. Martin interview, 12 April.

9. Keith Higginson, telephone interview by author, tape recording, 14 May 1997, Montgomery Coll.

10. R. Keith Higginson, letter to John Sieh, 28 July 1977.

11. Guy Martin, memorandum to Keith Higginson, 14 September 1977.

12. Daniel P. Beard, deputy assistant secretary, Department of Interior; remarks before conference of the South Dakota Natural Resources Council, Huron SD, 29 October 1977.

13. *Aberdeen American News*, 19 October 1978.

14. Bud Seaton, interview by author, tape recording, Brown County SD, 1 November 1989, Montgomery Coll.

15. *Aberdeen American News*, 15 October 1978.

16. *Aberdeen American News*, 15 October 1978.

17. *Aberdeen American News*, 29 October 1978.

18. *Aberdeen American News*, 29 October 1978.

19. The *Sioux Falls Argus Leader* editorial was reprinted in *Aberdeen American News*, 8 January 1978.

20. The results of the 1978 election:

John Sieh, 2,183 votes/James Sperry, 1,323 votes

Bill Piper, 1,820 votes/Melvin Eckmann, 1,645 votes

Ken Marsh, 704 votes/Ed Niece, 372 votes

Steve Thorson, 20,044 votes/Curt Johnson, 11,546 votes

21. Gerald Andrews, telephone interview by author, 12 May 1996.

16. Not Quite Deauthorization

1. Hohn interview, 6 November 1988.

2. Guy Martin, telephone interview by author, 3 October 1997.

3. Martin interview, 12 April.

4. Keth Higginson, memorandum to Bureau of Reclamation regional office in Billings MT, 17 February 1979. The memo describes the directives of Guy Martin.

5. Martin interview, 12 April.

6. *Aberdeen American News*, 13 April 1980.

7. *Aberdeen American News*, 13 April 1980.

8. *Aberdeen American News*, 22 April 1980.

9. *Aberdeen American News*, 20 June 1980.

10. Tom Fischbach, interview by author, Warner SD, 22 March 1998.

11. *Aberdeen American News*, 23 June 1980.

12. McGovern interview.

13. The county commissions that endorsed deauthorization were Edmunds, Faulk, Clark, Spink, and Campbell. The county commissions that endorsed congressional hearings be held on deauthorization were Brown, Day, and Walworth.

14. Hohn interview, 6 November 1988.

15. William Janklow, interview by author, tape recording, Brandon SD, 14 December 1988, Montgomery Coll.

16. Martin interview, 12 April.

17. Governor Janklow was granted a permit to sell Missouri River water to ETSI, but a lawsuit launched by Missouri River lower-basin states and railroads blocked the project. Governor Janklow claimed Berkley Bedell helped coordinate the opposition to ETSI.

18. U.S. Senate, Sub-committee on Water and Power, *Hearing on S.B. 1553*, Pierre SD. 97th Cong., 1st sess., 12 September 1981.

19. U.S. Senate sub-committee, *Hearing on S.B. 1553*, Pierre SD, 12 September. Included on the list of project features the sub-district wanted eliminated from the Oahe authorization were Byron dam and reservoir; Byron pumping plant; James, East Main, West Main, Redfield, Cresbard, and Faulkton canals; Cresbard dam and reservoir; James River siphon; Blunt dam and reservoir; and irrigation areas and related works proposed for the areas of the east and west lake plain.

20. Owen Ambur, interview by author, tape recording, Washington DC, 13 April 1989, Montgomery Coll.

21. Janklow interview. Janklow described what Watt had told him.

22. Janklow interview.

23. Tom Daschle, interview by author, tape recording, Aberdeen SD, 15 December 1989, Montgomery Coll.

24. Daschle interview.

25. Janklow interview.

26. Janklow interview.

27. Daschle interview.

28. CENDAK and the Garrison extension were not referred to by these names in the bill. CENDAK was included in the bill under language that authorized feasibility studies regarding "alternate uses of facilities constructed for use in conjunction with the Oahe unit." The Garrison extension plan was referenced as a future use of the Garrison project. It would also receive feasibility study money. Also to receive study money was a plan to reformulate the Pollock-Herreid Irrigation Project.

29. Hohn interview, 6 November 1988.

30. S.B. 1553.

31. Senator James Abdnor, letter to George Piper, 22 February 1982.

32. Janklow interview.

33. Ron Frankenstein, interview by author, tape recording, Spink County SD, 22 February 1989, Montgomery Coll.

34. Hohn interview, 6 November 1988.

35. Hohn interview, 6 November 1988.

36. Dave Weiman, interview by author, tape recording, Washington DC, 14 April 1989, Montgomery Coll.

37. John Sieh, United Family Farmers annual banquet, 7 March 1992.

Index

Missouri Slope Irrigation District, 37,
48–49, 51, 167
Missouri Valley Authority: proposed, 16
Mitchell SD, 77–78, 154
Mobridge SD, 21–22, 174–75
Mocassin Creek, 142
Moody, Gideon, 3–5
Moran, Art, 62–63
Morris, the rainmaker, 1, 34
Mundt, Karl, 22, 54–55, 57–58, 78
Murphy, Jerimiah, 111, 181

Naessig, Leonard: in 1976 and 1980 Oahe
Conservancy Sub-district board elec-
tions, 121, 124, 130–31, 194; on Oahe
Conservancy Sub-district board, 135;
and S.B. 1553, 197
National Audubon Society, 63, 67
National Bank of South Dakota, 181
National Committee on the Humanities,
107
National Endowment for the Humanities,
107
National Environmental Policy Act
(NEPA): and Bureau of Reclamation,
62, 90–91; Environmental Impact
Statement (EIS) provisions and, 62;
and Oahe Unit EIS, 63, 67, 90; re-
quirements of, 90; United Family
Farmers lawsuit and, 91–92, 98. *See
also* Bureau of Reclamation; Wright,
J. Skelley; Oahe Unit
National Irrigation Congress, 5
Newell, Frederick, 5, 6
Newell SD, 6
Newlands, Francis, 5
Newlands Reclamation Act, 5
Nichol, Fred, 94, 97, 99

Nicollet, Joseph, 65, 142
Nixon, Richard, 57–58, 62, 81, 83, 163
Nixon administration, 57–58, 81

Oahe, xi, 18
Oahe: A Question of Values, 107–8, 182
Oahe Conservancy Sub-district (and
board of directors): 79, 81–83, 103,
134, 191; early legislation to create,
29, 32–33; election to form, 35; early
organization and boundaries of, 29,
33–34, 167; first board of directors of,
47; later elections for directors:
(1974), 83, 85–88; (1976), 118–27,
129–31, 135; (1978), 180–82, 184–87;
(1980), 193–94, 197; (1982), 200–
201; master contract authority election
of, 53–54; and one man–one vote
lawsuit, 166, 171–72, 176; promotes
Oahe Unit deauthorization, 176; public hearings on Oahe Unit, 137, 149–
54, 156–60; and Ken Holum, 58; requests Oahe Unit moratorium, 162;
termination of, 202. *See also* Hohn,
Curt; Funkhouser, Preston; Sieh,
John; United Family Farmers
Oahe dam: as part of Pick-Sloan plan, 17;
closure ceremony, 29; and condemnation of land, 23–28; dimensions of,
30; ecological impacts of, 21, 31;
groundbreaking for, 21; initial funding
for, 20–21; opposition to, 21–23; proposed downsized version of, 23; origin of name, 18; role in Oahe
irrigation project, 36–37. *See also*
Army Corps of Engineers; Hipple,
Robert; Houck, Roy; Oahe reservoir
Oahe Dryland Farmers, 49